Essential Personalit

Essential Personality

Donald C Pennington

First published in Great Britain in 2003 by
Arnold, a member of the Hodder Headline Group
338 Euston Road, London NW1 3BH

http://www.arnoldpublishers.com

Co-published in the United States of America by
Oxford University Press Inc.,
198 Madison Avenue, New York, NY 10016

British Library Cataloguing in Publication Data
A catalogue record for this book is available from the British Library

Library of Congress Cataloging-in-Publication Data
A catalog record for this book is available from the Library of Congress

ISBN 0 340 761180 (pb)

1 2 3 4 5 6 7 8 9 10

2007 2006 2005 2004 2003

Typeset in 10 on 12 Sabon for Dorchester Typesetting, Dorchester, Dorset
Printed and bound in Great Britain by MPG Books Ltd, Bodmin, Cornwall.

What do you think about this book? Or any other Arnold title?
Please send your comments to feedback.arnold@hodder.co.uk

For Kyla, Tom, Jed and Toby

Contents

Acknowledgements

The purpose of this book is to provide an accessible, short and relatively comprehensive introduction to theories and studies of personality psychology. I have taught personality psychology at undergraduate level for the best part of 20 years. Teaching and supporting students to learn has helped me understand much better the issues, range of theories and value of empirical evidence in personality psychology. So thanks to all those students for helping me to comprehend better this area of psychology.

I have enjoyed writing this book, especially since most of it was written at a table in the bay window of a house overlooking the harbour in Porthleven, Cornwall. At times my daughter, Kyla, and sons, Tom, Jed and Toby, were with me and took me off to the pub in the evening. So thanks to Kyla, Tom, Jed and Toby.

My thanks also to Kathleen Williams, Helen Lee, Joginder Lully and Veena Parekh who did such an excellent job of typing various chapters of this book.

Finally, my thanks to Claire Thompson for all the work involved in tidying up the book prior to sending it to the publisher.

1

Introduction to Personality

- What is personality?
- Biological and environmental perspectives
- Debates in personality psychology
- Science and theory in personality psychology
- Cross-cultural perspectives on personality
- About this book
- Summary
- Further reading

1.1 WHAT IS PERSONALITY?

Imagine that you are watching a television programme about film stars and that awards are being given for the best male and female film star personalities of the year. What do you understand by the use of the word 'personality' in this context. Is it to do with a role the film star played in an Oscar-winning film? Or is it to do with work they do off-stage, such as helping various charities or raising money to feed starving people in developing countries? The context of the television programme would no doubt answer the above questions. Nevertheless, in this context we tend to think that the word 'personality' refers to some larger-than-life characteristics of the film stars.

Imagine another, quite different situation, where your best friend has introduced you to someone you have not met before. You spend half an hour talking to this person. Afterwards you say to your best friend something along the lines that you feel you 'hit it off' well with this new person and that this was probably because you thought you have similar personality characteristics.

Finally, imagine that you are reading a popular magazine and there is a special feature on personality. The feature contains a short personality questionnaire, which you complete. You score your answers to the questions and find that you come out as thoughtful, emotional and extrovert. This does not accord with how you believe yourself to be, so you reject the questionnaire as a load of rubbish.

The above imaginary scenarios have a number of things in common, and ones that are of interest to personality psychologists. First, the word 'personality' is very general, and one that may be used in many, diverse and different ways. Second, our everyday use of the word does usually tend to focus on specific aspects of personality – particularly characteristics such as extrovert, thoughtful, conscientious, intelligent and many more that I am sure you can think of. Third, personality in some way and as used in everyday language attempts to capture the essence or key important characteristics when applied to a specific person. Fourth, nearly everybody is interested in, even fascinated with, other people and wishes to find shorthand ways to describe their personality. This is also true in relation to ourselves: each of us is interested in understanding ourselves better and having a clearer picture of how others see us and what personality characteristics others think we possess. Fifth and finally, personality is an area of psychology that is of central importance and has been since the development of psychology as a scientific discipline over a hundred years ago.

In this book I will consider a range of approaches to the psychological study and measurement of personality that have been and still are important in personality psychology. In introducing personality psychology this chapter seeks to introduce you to the ways in which psychologists have approached the conceptualisation of personality, the debates that exist and that it is important to understand, and what it means to adopt a scientific approach to the study of personality.

1.1.1 Defining personality

Getting you to think about how we use the word 'personality' in everyday life has probably led you, correctly, to regard the idea of a definition of personality as rather difficult to achieve. Certainly, any definition, to be of use to psychologists, will have to be at a general, abstract level to encompass such a high degree of diversity. Let us consider a number of definitions offered by highly influential personality psychologists.

- Personality is that which predicts what a person will do in a given situation … it is concerned with *all* the behaviour of the individual, both overt and under the skin (Raymond Cattell).
- Personality is the more or less stable and enduring organisation of a person's character, temperament, intellect and physique, which determines his unique adjustment to his (or her) environment (Hans Eysenck).
- Personality is the dynamic organisation within the individual of those psychophysical systems that determine his unique adjustments to his (or her) environment (Gordon Allport).

These three definitions have five aspects in common and have been taken from an article that appeared over 40 years ago (Sanford, 1963). First, there is an emphasis on the idea that each person has a unique personality. Even identical twins, who have exactly the same genetic make-up, have different personalities – although they probably also have more in common than unrelated people (Plomin, 1994). Second, there is an assumption that accurate knowledge of a person's personality will allow prediction of their future behaviour to be made. Third, personality is concerned with the whole person in terms of behaviour, thought and feelings. Fourth, the personality of an individual helps them, to a greater or lesser extent, to adjust to their environment. Different people may adjust well and be successful in their work and personal lives. Others may adjust less well and experience mental problems, such as anxiety and stress, as a result. Finally, personality is said to be 'dynamic', by which is meant that whilst stable and enduring it is also subject to change over the life of a person. For example, research has shown that as people get older they become more conservative and less socialist in their political outlook (Eysenck and Eysenck, 1985).

1.1.2 Approaches to personality

One of the problems of producing a useful definition of psychology is that different psychologists adopt quite different approaches in their attempts to understand and research human personality. There are four main approaches, each of which is covered by one or more chapters in this book. These are: the psychoanalytic approach, the dispositional approach; the behavioural and cognitive approach; the humanistic approach.

The **psychoanalytic approach**, developed by Sigmund Freud (see Chapter 3), is based on the key assumptions that much of mental life takes place at an unconscious level and that unconscious motives explain human behaviour. The psychoanalytic approach generally characterises people as having internal, unconscious conflicts, the most important of which result from early childhood, and may require considerable mental energy to deal with. In extreme cases these internal, mental conflicts may dominate the individual and prevent him or her adjusting to life well enough to sustain an intimate relationship or develop a successful career. The psychoanalytic approach assumes that people attempt to free themselves of these conflicts and, in consequence, reduce the tension and anxiety that may be felt.

The **dispositional approach** is based on the idea that individuals have relatively stable characteristics or traits that are shown in how they behave in a range of different situations. Within the dispositional approach (see Chapter 6) each person is assumed to be unique, and to possess a unique configuration of personality characteristics and traits. One of the most popular and heavily researched theories of dispositions highlights the 'big five' factors of personality (Costa and McCrae, 1985). The big five dispositional factors are neuroticism, extroversion, openness, agreeableness and conscientiousness. Each person is regarded as possessing each of these dispositions, but in varying degrees, thus making each person unique.

The **behavioural and cognitive approach** (see Chapter 7) is concerned with understanding personality in terms of how a person acquires and learns a set of behaviours. The approach has its foundations in the learning theories of Ivan Pavlov and B.F. Skinner. These are based on the idea that behaviour is either reinforced or punished. When reinforced, behaviour is likely to be repeated on future occasions; when punished, it is not likely to be repeated. The behavioural approach takes an environmental perspective, which will be considered later in this chapter. At one extreme, learning theorists claim only the environmental experiences of a person are an important consideration. However, cognitive learning theorists argue that mental processes and thought

Table 1.1 Four approaches to personality psychology, key assumptions and an example of each

Approach	Key assumptions	Example
Psychoanalytic approach	Mental life at an unconscious level. Unconscious motives explain human behaviour. Unconscious conflicts affect how a person adjusts to life.	Unpleasant and traumatic childhood experiences may be 'buried' in the unconscious but may affect negatively how an adult relates to people.
Dispositional approach	Individuals possess relatively enduring and stable traits that affect how they behave in different situations.	The 'big five' factors of personality: neuroticism, extroversion, openness, agreeableness and conscientiousness.
Behavioural and cognitive approach	Based on learning theory and the idea that the reinforcement and punishment of behaviour establishes a unique set of behaviours then called personality.	Rewards in the environment given to a child will establish a set of behaviours that follow the the person into adulthood.
Humanistic approach	Conscious, subjective experience of the world is important. Each person's subjective experience is unique. People thrive for fulfilment in life and to understand themselves better.	Success in a person's work career may give them a sense of fulfilment, happiness, reward and satisfaction with their life.

have to be taken into account to explain personality (Bandura, 1989; Rotter, 1966).

The **humanistic approach** places greater emphasis and importance on a person's conscious, subjective experience of the world. Humanistic psychologists such as Carl Rogers and Abraham Maslow (see Chapter 8) regard each person's subjective experience as unique, meaningful and part of the defining characteristic of what it is to be human. Humanistic psychologists also regard each person as attempting to understand themselves, and to realise as fully as possible their potentials and aspirations in life. A summary of these four approaches and their different assumptions is given in Table 1.1.

1.2 BIOLOGICAL AND ENVIRONMENTAL PERSPECTIVES

These four main approaches to personality each sit within two overarching perspectives. The **biological perspective** is to do with understanding the extent to which personality – whether traits, unconscious motives or how you experience the world – is determined by genetics or what you biologically inherit from your parents. The **environmental perspective**, by contrast, attempts to understand personality and its development from the point of view of environmental forces and the experiences of the individual from the time he or she was born.

These two overarching perspectives, because they occupy quite different positions with respect to the origins of personality, result in the nature–nurture debate in psychology.

1.2.1 The biological perspective

The Human Genome Project may throw light on how genes affect behaviour and psychological characteristics. However, personality psychologists have a long-standing interest in discovering the extent to which biology determines personality. One of the most commonly used research methods has been that of twin studies (see Chapter 2). Identical twins have exactly the same genetic make-up, whilst fraternal twins share just 50 per cent of genes, the same as ordinary brothers and sisters. A large-scale study by Loehlin and Nichols (1976) gave 514 pairs of monozygotic (identical) twins and 336 pairs of dizygotic (fraternal) twins a large number of personality questionnaires to complete. Generally, it was found that monozygotic twins were more alike on numerous personality characteristics than fraternal twins. This evidence has been used to support the view that many aspects of personality are biologically determined.

Other psychological research has looked at more general and complex aspects of personality, called **temperaments**, which include sociability, emotionality and general activity level (Endler, 1989). Endler (1989) has argued and attempted to demonstrate that these aspects of temperament are present in early infancy and follow the individual through the teenage years into adulthood. This has been supported by other recent research (for example, Buss and Plomin, 1984; Royce and Powell, 1983), which has shown that sociability, emotionality and activity level are present at birth, stable across time and influence many aspects of a person's behaviour.

Sociability, for example, has been conceptualised into three broad categories – difficult, easy, and slow to warm up. Evidence that a child categorised as 'difficult' or 'easy' was likely to show the same temperament 30 years later came from a longitudinal study (see Chapter 2) conducted by Caspi *et al.* (1988). Buss *et al.* (1973) produced evidence that monozygotic twins were more alike with respect to sociability than dizygotic twins.

In relation to the four approaches mentioned earlier, the psychoanalytic has a strong biological basis as does the dispositional approach. In contrast, the behavioural and humanistic approaches adopt a more environmental perspective.

1.2.2 The environmental perspective

The **environmental perspective** considers the influence of key forces and experiences in the environment that impinge on and influence the individual. Environmental influences can produce both similarities and differences between people. Differences because each and every person experiences and is brought up in a unique environment. For example, your home, parents and extended family, set of friends and educational experience are unique to you. However, each person is brought up and experiences a particular culture, family, social class and set of friends. These are likely to produce similarities between people brought up in the same culture or sharing similar family or social class experiences. We will look at cross-cultural aspects of personality later in this chapter.

An example of how similar family experiences may affect different individuals in different families can be seen in the highly influential work of Bowlby (1969; 1988) on the attachment a child makes to his or her parents, especially the mother. Ainsworth *et al.* (1978) identified two broad types of attachment – secure and insecure. Insecure attachments have been shown to be more prevalent where, for example, a family experiences poverty, where there is child abuse and where the mother is seriously depressed (Cicchetti and Barnet, 1991). Hence, the similar negative social experiences of different children in different families may have common effects. Insecure attachment in early childhood has been claimed to affect how an adult engages in interpersonal relationships, especially intimate relationships (Carlson and Sroufe, 1995).

In summary, environmental experiences have been shown to influence strongly complex and general aspects of personality described under the general heading of 'temperament'.

1.3 DEBATES IN PERSONALITY PSYCHOLOGY

We have already seen that the biological and environmental perspectives seem to occupy opposing and conflicting positions with respect to explaining the origins of personality. We will look at this next in the context of the **nature–nurture debate**. There are a number of other important debates that the psychological study of personality needs to consider, and we will look briefly at these here.

1.3.1 The nature–nurture debate

Few psychologists would subscribe or put forward a position that either only biology or only environmental influences can explain human personality. In many respects to enter into the nature–nurture debate with an either/or approach or attempt at a resolution is meaningless. Each person is born into the world with a given genetic make-up, each person then experiences a unique set of environmental conditions and forces. The nature–nurture debate in contemporary psychology is much more about understanding the relative contribution of both biology and environmental forces to the human personality. At the same time the four different approaches to personality – psychoanalytic, dispositional, behavioural and cognitive, and humanistic – do

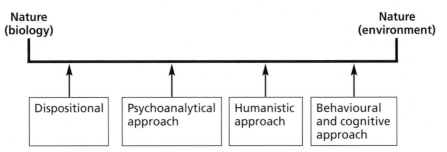

Figure 1.1 The relative positions of the four main approaches to personality psychology on the nature–nuture continuum

occupy different positions on what we may think of as a continuum between nature (biology) and nurture (environment). This is shown in Figure 1.1

The interaction of nature and nurture may usefully be thought of in terms of the concept of a **reaction range**, as suggested by Gottesman (1963). This concept suggests that biology may set the limits, or range, for the person with respect to a characteristic, ability or other quality. The extent to which the limit or range is reached or attained depends on environmental experiences. For example, a person may be born with the potential to be good at mathematics or athletics. However, unless the person engages in mathematic study at school and university or plays a particular sport, his or her potential may not be realised. In another way, if a culture or social grouping does not value and promote mathematics then a person with a biologically given high potential may well not realise this very much.

When reading through the chapters in this book dealing with the different approaches try to consider just how important biology (nurture) and environment (nature) are for a particular theory.

1.3.2 Freewill versus determinism

A long-standing debate within personality psychology is to do with whether or not people have freewill and are free to choose how to behave and how to think, and whether they are free to change their personality. On the other side of the debate is the deterministic position whereby all our actions, thoughts and personality are determined and hence predictable. The fact that human behaviour is notoriously difficult to predict provides some kind of argument against an extreme determinism position. At the same time people do, at times, behave in predictable ways in many situations. This was demonstrated in a dramatic way in the classic study conducted by Zimbardo *et al.* (1982) where prison conditions were simulated. Zimbardo and colleagues randomly allocated volunteers to the role of prisoner or guard in a simulated prison; to their horror the roles took over the individuals and the study had to be stopped after only a few days. Guards became authoritarian and punishing, while the prisoners took on a passive and submissive role. Zimbardo *et al.*'s study vividly demonstrates the limits of freewill! Hence, whilst people may have a degree of freewill over their personality and how they behave, the Zimbardo *et al.* study produces evidence against an extreme position of total freewill.

Like the nature–nurture debate, the freewill–determinism debate can also be conceptualised on a continuum with the four approaches to personality occupying different positions with respect to the extent to which there is or is not freedom to choose. This is shown in Figure 1.2.

It is important to understand that adopting a position claiming that people have complete freewill is inconsistent with a scientific approach to

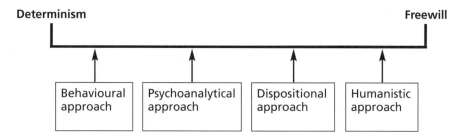

Figure 1.2 Relative positions of the four main approaches to personality psychology in the freewill–determinism debate; note that an approach that has a strong biological (nature) position will also have a strong deterministic position

personality. This is because science is primarily concerned with producing laws to explain human behaviour. Hence, the humanistic approach is the least scientific approach in personality psychology. Adopting a strong deterministic position may be seen as opposed to the idea of personal responsibility and self-control that is needed for any society to work. It is probably fair to say that most psychologists acknowledge both freewill and determinism in any theory of personality.

1.3.3 Idiographic or nomothetic?

Theoretical and research strategies towards personality psychology can be seen as either idiographic or nomothetic (Allport, 1955). The **nomothetic approach** is one in which scientific procedures are adopted in an attempt to establish universal laws of human behaviour and thought. Hence, the nomothetic approach seeks to obtain precise, valid and reliable measures of personality (see Chapter 2) in an attempt to establish what is common and lawful between or across people. The nomothetic approach makes extensive use of statistical procedures to detect patterns of behaviour of large groups of people. With the dispositional, or trait, approach to personality (see Chapter 6), for example, common traits are sought to describe all people. The trait of extroversion, which we came across earlier as one of the 'big five' personality traits, is assumed to be a dimension upon which all people can be located. Some people are seen as highly extrovert, some as average and others as not extrovert at all.

The **idiographic approach**, in contrast, focuses on the individual, and attempts to understand and describe the unique personality of any one person. The idiographic approach does not seek to establish universal laws about human personality and behaviour. Instead, it gives a detailed characterisation of a single person and often uses case studies and qualitative methods of research (see Chapter 2).

It would probably be true to say that most personality psychologists recognise the value of both the nomothetic and the idiographic approaches. Some psychologists, such as Sigmund Freud (see Chapter 3) and Gordon Allport (see Chapter 6), used both approaches in their attempts to understand human personality. Sigmund Freud, for example, made famous the use of case studies to highlight many of his theoretical ideas and concepts. At the same time, Freud regarded himself as working in the scientific tradition by seeking to establish common, unconscious conflicts that existed in all people, whatever their culture. Humanistic psychologists work almost exclusively in the idiographic tradition, whilst behavioural psychologists use the nomothetic approach almost exclusively. The dispositional approach largely uses the nomothetic tradition, but some psychologists working in the dispositional approach use and see value in the idiograph tradition.

1.3.4 Conscious and unconscious

Another debate within personality psychology is to do with the extent to which conscious and unconscious mental processes influence how we think, feel and behave. Unconscious mental processes are, by their very nature, hidden from direct awareness and are usually regarded as not able to become conscious. Freudian psychoanalytic theory firmly regards the unconscious as the driving force for all conscious experience, feelings and behaviour. The trouble with this claim, as we shall see in Chapter 3, is that it is not possible directly to examine or investigate the unconscious from a scientific viewpoint. Since the unconscious is hidden from the individual it is also hidden, and hence not amenable, to scientific enquiry.

At the other extreme is the viewpoint that only conscious experience, thought and feeling, is of interest to the personality psychologist. This is best exemplified in the humanistic approach, but may also be seen as a view adopted by the behavioural and cognitive approach. Self-awareness, self-understanding, and belief in the ability of a person to change his or her personality depends heavily on consciousness. Valuing subjective experience, as do humanistic psychologists, relies upon being available to report to others (and yourself) on what you are thinking and feeling at any one time.

Whilst Freud thought unconscious motives were the driving force for thought, feeling and behaviour he did not deny the existence of consciousness. For Freud, the conscious was necessary but not the most important mental system in humans.

Finally, many psychologists regard the defining feature of humanity to be to do with consciousness and reflection. Conscious and free choice to think and behave in certain ways can be seen to distinguish human beings from other animals.

1.3.5 The person and the situation

Focusing on the individual in an attempt to understand and explain personality rests on the assumption that personality characteristics or dispositions will result in a person behaving in a consistent way across a range of institutions. An example may help clarify what is meant by this assumption of what is called **cross-situational consistency** (Mischel, 1968). Imagine your best friend has a highly extrovert – personality, that is, he or she likes to be with other people, is outgoing, sociable and the 'life and soul of the party'. The dispositional approach to personality assumes that someone categorised as extrovert will show cross-situational consistency – that is, they will exhibit extrovert behaviour across a wide range of social situations, such as at a party, in the coffee shop with a small group of friends, in classroom discussion, when at home with family, etc., etc. But what evidence is there to support this assumption?

Mischel (1968) reviewed research using self-report personality tests to predict the actual behaviour of a person and found that personality variables, such as extroversion, predicted behaviour rather poorly. The reason for this, Mischel claimed, was that personality psychologists did not take into account the situation in which the person was behaving. Consider our example of the extrovert friend given above. Suppose he or she was in a small group conducting a seance (trying to contact the spirits of people from the 'other side'). In this situation the person might be very quiet, subdued and even scared – the situation may cause him or her to behave not like an extrovert but like an introvert. As we shall see in Chapter 9, personality research is investigating and trying to understand how situations influence personality and hence behaviour (Mischel and Shoda, 1998).

Mischel (1991) conceptualises the important influences on behaviour in a situation as those elements that are psychologically meaningful for the person. Mischel proposed that *both* person variables and the psychologically meaningful aspects of the situation had to be taken into account to predict and explain behaviour. This person-situation interaction is illustrated in Figure 1.3.

Figure 1.3 For Mischel, the interaction of the person and the situation predicts behaviour; focusing on the person only does not allow behaviour to be predicted

1.4 SCIENCE AND THEORY IN PERSONALITY PSYCHOLOGY

Earlier in this chapter we considered a number of definitions of personality in the context of psychologists adopting a scientific approach to understanding and explaining personality. In this section we consider what is involved in using scientific methods to investigate and theorise about personality. Chapter 2 looks at a range of research methods used by psychologists to study personality. It is worth briefly considering personality from a non-scientific perspective. One way is reflected by the idea that we all operate, in some sense, as psychologists in our everyday lives. We all hold ideas of what other people and ourselves are like, and commonly use traits or dispositions to describe people. We all have what may be called **implicit personality theories** (Kemp, 1988). Such theories are called implicit because they are not usually communicated to other people, and are private views held by individuals (Furnham, 1988). It may be that each person holds a slightly different implicit personality theory about people. People develop implicit personality theories as a result of experience, socialisation, culture and media influences. As such they are not scientific and not based on good evidence, hence they may often be incorrect and unreliable.

1.4.1 Scientific theory and its functions

Science may be characterised as producing a theory or theories that in turn, generate hypotheses, which are then tested through the use of rigorous methods of research. Rigorous methods of research (see Chapter 2) – for example, experiments – produce data or information that is used to support or reject the hypothesis derived from a theory. If the data or information produced from the research supports the hypothesis then support is given to the theory too. However, if the data does not support the predictions of the hypothesis then the hypothesis may be rejected and this might, ultimately, result in the theory being rejected. Usually a theory is only rejected when there is another theory to take its place. If there is not an alternative theory, or the existing theory has received a good deal of support in the past, it will be retained. This may be so even though on this occasion a hypothesis or prediction derived from the theory has not been supported by evidence from the research conducted. A concrete example may help clarify the above.

Suppose you have developed a theory stating that extroverts like being with other people and are very sociable because they have good social skills. What predictions or hypotheses could be derived from this theory? One hypothesis could be that extroverts are more likely to start conversations with strangers than people who are not extroverts. Another hypothesis could be that extroverts make more positive statements to other people than non-extroverts. See if you can think of another two hypotheses to derive from our theory. So we have a theory and a number of hypotheses or predictions. The next step in the scientific procedure is to collect evidence, through the use of a scientifically accepted method, to see whether or not the hypothesis is supported by the data or evidence. To test the hypothesis about extroverts starting conversations with strangers we could devise an experiment in which extroverts and non-extroverts are put in a room with people they do not know. Video recordings of the social interaction that takes place could be made. These recordings could then be analysed to collection information about who speaks first and to whom. This experiment could be run a number of times with different extroverts and non-extroverts to see if a consistent pattern emerged with many people. If the video recordings show extroverts initiating or starting conversations with strangers our hypothesis is supported and this lends support to our theory. If not, our hypothesis can be rejected and support is not given to the theory. This is depicted in Figure 1.4.

Notice that care has been taken to say that a theory may be supported or not supported by the evidence relating to a hypothesis. Care has also been taken to avoid saying a theory has been proved to be true. This is because Karl Popper, an influential philosopher of science, states that a theory can never be proved true since future research may produce evidence that refutes the theory. Hence, for any theory to be a scientific theory it must be capable, in principle, of being refuted. Science then, according to Popper (1963), progresses through research that falsifies rather than confirms theories. In practice, what happens is that theories are retained as long as empirical

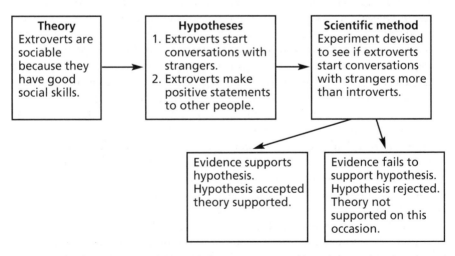

Figure 1.4 How science proceeds through theory, generation of hypotheses and testing of hypotheses through the use of scientific methods

support or support from data gained from scientific methods is forthcoming. A theory that continually fails to enjoy supporting evidence should be rejected. A theory which does not produce testable hypotheses or predictions cannot be regarded as a scientific theory in the first place.

You might ask the question 'Where does a scientific theory come from in the first place?' Two explanations have been offered. First, theories come about through what is called *induction*. This means that theories are developed, through a process of induction, from facts and actual observations. The problem with this explanation is how a scientist would know when enough facts or observations have been gathered to permit a theory to be developed. The more favoured explanation is that theories are developed as a result of *deduction* (Hempel, 1966). This means that people largely use their own imagination mixed with common sense to deduce a theory. Deriving hypotheses and testing predictions using scientific methods will determine whether the theory is rejected or supported. If the latter, the theory is retained until a better one is developed.

1.4.2 Personality theory and science

In Chapters 3 to 8, which deal with the four main approaches (psychoanalytic, dispositional, behavioural and cognitive, and humanistic) we have already considered, you will find numerous theories of personality within each approach. Two approaches – the dispositional, and behavioural and cognitive – most closely conform to the description of science given above. Both approaches have developed a number of different theories; however, both make extensive use of rigorous scientific procedures to produce data and evidence to test the theories.

The psychoanalytic approach, particularly that of Sigmund Freud, is not regarded as operating within a scientific tradition or framework. There are a number of reasons for this. First, critics argue that many of the theories and concepts are not testable since specific predictions or hypotheses cannot be derived from the theory and then examined by using accepted scientific methods. For example, the unconscious by definition is not observable or possible to gain knowledge of directly. Because of this any hypotheses or predictions cannot be examined scientifically, making the theory of unconscious mental processes neither refutable nor subject to confirmation. Second, the different theories within the psychoanalytic approach are not usually subjected to scientific testing. In fact, the proponents of the theories do not use scientific methods themselves to test them. Third, the psychoanalytic approach has its strength in the explanatory power it has for understanding human behaviour. Psychoanalysts, such as Freud, thought this was more valuable and important than spending time on scientifically testing the theories.

The humanistic approach can also be regarded as operating outside a scientific framework. Indeed, many humanistic psychologists regard the use of science to investigate human thought and behaviour as inappropriate and misguided. Because humanistic psychologists are primarily concerned with subjective experience it is not surprising that they are uninterested in, or even opposed to, the use of scientific procedures, such as laboratory experiments, to investigate people.

To understand why some approaches to and many theories of personality endure in personality psychology we need to appreciate how theories are to be evaluated, and their purpose in psychology.

1.4.3 Evaluation of theory

Clearly one important dimension on which to evaluate a theory in personality psychology is whether or not it is scientific. We have already seen what this entails, and, in psychology, whether or not a theory can be classed as scientific is often used to reject or accept the theory in the first place. However, we have seen that theories endure in personality psychology that are not regarded as scientific – sometimes even by the psychologists that produced them in the first place. This must mean that criteria other than whether or not a theory is scientific may be equally important in deciding the value of a theory. Three main criteria are often used in this context.

First, is the extent to which a theory is **comprehensive**. The comprehensiveness of a theory is to do with the range of human thought and behaviour it attempts to explain. In many respects, the more comprehensive a theory the better. Psychoanalytic and humanistic theories tend to be comprehensive, and attempt to explain and understand the whole person. In contrast, some dispositional and learning theories deal only with certain aspects of the individual and are less comprehensive. Some philosophers of science regard science as progressing through theories becoming more comprehensive overtime. Kuhn's view (1970) of psychology generally is that it is in a pre-scientific stage and that whilst it aspires to be a science it cannot be seen to be so because of the existence of so many different conflicting or competing theories. This is well evidenced in personality psychology, where numerous approaches and theories exist with little prospect of them developing into a more unified or single theory.

Second, there is the idea that a theory should be simple or parsimonious. Theories that are simple, do not have numerous and complex concepts, and are concise are considered to be more desirable and better. Freudian psychoanalytic theory, as you will see in Chapter 3, is certainly not parsimonious – although whether it is unnecessarily complex is open to debate. In contrast, behavioural theories or learning theories, as considered in

Chapter 7, are relatively parsimonious. This is because, for example, the operant conditioning learning theory of B.F. Skinner reduces the explanation of human behaviour to stimulus–response sequences, and the role of reinforcement and punishment.

Third, the extent to which a theory is useful or has applied value is an important criteria to evaluate theories against. A theory can be said to have applied value if it helps people to live better, more satisfying and fulfilled lives, or if it helps people to adjust better to the problems and difficulties life throws at them (Kelly, 1955). Applied value may be to do with effective therapies being developed from a theory to help treat people with psychological problems or disorders. Applied value may also be to do with providing greater fulfilment in life for those who are already well adjusted and function well in society. Most, if not all, of the theories you will encounter in this book have applied value to a greater or lesser extent. Often scientific methods are used to establish whether or not a therapy or psychological treatment programme is effective and helps people.

Other criteria than these three main ones, which are often used to assess the value of a theory in personality psychology, include coherence, acceptability and intuitive appeal. The coherence of a theory is to do with how well the different ideas and concepts hold together to produce an internally coherent theory and the absence of inconsistencies. Acceptability and intuitive appeal are related. A theory has to be acceptable in a general way and this may be related to the times and social context prevailing when the theory is developed. For example, it is doubtful if any psychologist would find a theory of personality based on the idea of aliens from another planet controlling the minds of human beings! Finally, intuitive appeal may provide some explanation of why some people prefer one theory to another, regardless of how scientific or well supported the theory is. As you read through the various approaches and theories you will probably prefer one to the others. You may wish to think about why this may be the case.

1.5 CROSS-CULTURAL PERSPECTIVES ON PERSONALITY

The vast majority of theory and research on personality you will read about in this book has been developed and conducted by psychologists from western society; this means from the United States of America and western European countries (especially Great Britain, Germany and France). Personality psychologists assume, and often claim, that theories and concepts apply to all people round the world, regardless of the cultural context in which they grow up and live. Is this a fair and correct assumption to make and in what important ways may cultures be seen to differ? We will look at the second part of this question first.

A major distinction in the literature on cross-cultural psychology (for example, Smith and Harris Bond, 1998; Triandis, 1997) is made between cultures that emphasise the independence and autonomy of the individual, and cultures that emphasise the interdependence of individuals around a community or society. Hofstede (1980) conducted research across over 40 countries and suggested a major dimension called individualism–collectivism to distinguish between cultures. This is a psychological distinction about different cultures and is to be regarded as a continuum or dimension rather than an either/or categorisation. By the word **individualism** is meant a culture that places greater value on individual autonomy and achievement than interdependence on other people in a group or society. By the word **collectivism** is meant a culture that places greater value on groups (such as families, communities or nations) than individual autonomy and achievement. Typically western societies such as Canada, Australia, the United States of America and Great Britain are positioned towards the individualism end of this dimension. By contrast, collectivism is particularly strong in many countries in Asia, Africa and the Pacific Islands (Triandis, 1997). Some countries have been found to occupy more of a middle position on this continuum – for example, Turkey, Norway and Israel. This is shown in Figure 1.5.

With this dimension of individualism–collectivism in mind, the question is how this may affect personality. Markus and Kitayama (1991) suggest that individualistic cultures exhibit a strong belief in the independence of the self from other people. Hence, personality characteristics, traits or dispositions (see Chapter 6) are of key importance in describing, judging and understanding other people and oneself. In contrast, collectivist cultures place greater emphasis on the connectedness or interdependence of people. As a result traits and dispositions are less important to describe people, and people are defined more in terms of how they relate to and depend on other people.

In the rest of this book we will consider cross-cultural differences in relation to the theory or approach that is under consideration. Also, the individualism–collectivism continuum or dimension will be referred to in relation to cross-cultural differences with a particular theory of personality.

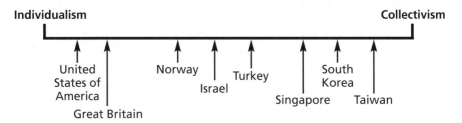

Figure 1.5 Relative position on the individualism–collectivism continuum of various countries around the world (adapted from Hofstede, 1980)

1.6 ABOUT THIS BOOK

This book provides an introduction to the major theories and approaches to personality that are regarded as important and influential within psychology. Chapters 3 to 8 deal with the major theories of personality – psychoanalytic, dispositions, learning theories and humanistic psychology. Each of these chapters considers applications of the theories and an evaluation. For many of the important psychologists in personality psychology, a brief biographical sketch is also provided. The psychoanalytic approach has numerous different theories and concepts related to individual psychoanalysts. This has meant that three chapters are given to providing a picture of this approach. Chapter 3 deals exclusively with Sigmund Freud's psychoanalytic theory. Chapter 4 considers post-Freudian theoretical developments as made in the work of Carl Jung, Alfred Adler, Anna Freud (Sigmund Freud's daughter) and Erik Erikson. Chapter 5 details more recent theoretical developments in psychoanalysis, known as the **object relations approach**; here we look at the theories of Melanie Klein and Heinz Kohut, and the present-day influences of these theorists.

Chapter 9 provides an overview of other approaches to personality – for example, personology, narratives and psychobiography – that are emerging as new and exciting developments within personality psychology. Chapter 2 follows on from the present chapter by considering how psychologists actually go about researching, studying and assessing personality; that is, the research methods used to investigate and collect information about personality.

1.7 SUMMARY

- There are four main and broad approaches to personality; these are the psychoanalytic approach, the dispositional approach, the behavioural and cognitive approach, and the humanistic approach. Each approach is characterised by a number of different theories and concepts.
- The biological and environmental perspectives can be related to each of the four approaches. The biological perspective is concerned with how inheritance and genetics may influence and/or determine personality. The environmental perspective regards the experiences and environmental forces operating on an individual as the major influences on personality.
- There are a number of debates in personality psychology. These are the nature–nurture debate, freewill versus determinism, idiographic versus nomothetic approaches, conscious and unconscious, and the person–situation debate.

- A scientific approach to the study of personality involves theory, hypothesis and the testing of hypotheses by using rigorous and established scientific methods. Hypotheses are derived from a theory. If evidence supports a hypothesis support is gained for the theory. If evidence fails to support a hypothesis the hypothesis may be rejected and the theory questioned. Theories of personality may be evaluated according to such criteria as scientific, comprehensiveness, simplicity, applied value, acceptance and intuitive appeal.
- The extent to which a theory applies to all people is a question considered by cross-cultural examination. One major dimension for distinguishing between cultures is the individualism–collectivism continuum. Where a culture is placed in this dimension may affect aspects of personality.

1.8 FURTHER READING

Mischel, W. (1999) *Introduction to Personality*. (6th edn) Fort Worth, TX: Harcourt Brace. Chapter 1 provides a more detailed treatment of some of the issues and topics raised in this chapter. Chapter 18 gives a full discussion of the person–situation debate in personality psychology.

Smith, P.B. and Harris Bond, M. (1998) *Social Psychology Across Cultures* (2nd edn). London: Prentice Hall. Looks in some detail at the collectivism–individualism dimension, and considers a number of cross-cultural aspects of personality.

2
The Study and Assessment of Personality

- Introduction
- Approaches to the study of personality
- Methods of studying personality
- Issues in personality assessment
- Problems of measurement
- Ethical considerations
- Summary
- Further reading

2.1 INTRODUCTION

Suppose that you have been given a research project to design and conduct on personality. Specifically, you have been assigned to work with a group of three other people on a project looking at how the personality characteristic of being, to put it in everyday language, a 'control freak' may affect interpersonal relationships. You assume that needing to be in control (a more psychological way of expressing the idea of 'control freak') can be seen as a continuum. At one end would be the extreme position of a person trying to control everything and everyone in his or her life. At the other end would be the opposite extreme position of a person not wanting or attempting to control anything in his or her life. How might the group go about investigating the effect of the personality characteristic of need to control on interpersonal relationships? You discuss this with other members of the group and find that each of the four of you has quite different ideas about how to conduct the research. You wish to use a questionnaire method to measure need for control and satisfaction with interpersonal relationships. Another member of the group wants to conduct a number of in-depth case studies of individuals at different points on the continuum. The third member of the group wants to conduct a laboratory experiment in which specific aspects of interaction between two people are measured in relation to people scoring high or low on need for control. The fourth member of the group wants to observe people in real-life settings. How might you resolve this difference and agree on one research method for the project?

This is not an easy question to answer since each of the four methods of studying personality has merits and weaknesses. In the end you might find the fairest way to get group agreement would be to write down each method on a piece of paper, put the four pieces of paper in a hat and select one at random!

In this chapter we will look at a range of methods used by psychologists to study and assess personality. We will also consider the problems encountered when attempting to measure personality, and ethical guidelines that need to be adhered to when researching personality.

2.2 APPROACHES TO THE STUDY OF PERSONALITY

Designing any research study in psychology may be seen as a decision-making process. One of the first decisions that needs to be made is whether you are going to adopt a quantitative or qualitative approach to the study of personality.

A **quantitative approach** is characterised by collecting data that can, if required, be turned into numbers or numerical data of some sort. This numerical data can then be subjected to both descriptive and inferential statistics (see, for example, Coolican (1999) for a thorough treatment). Briefly, descriptive statistics will provide a summary of all the numerical data you have collected. Perhaps the most commonly used descriptive statistic is the mean or average. Inferential statistics will tell you, among other things, whether a difference between two sets of data is meaningful and one that should be taken notice of. For example, suppose it was found that people who have poor interpersonal relationships scored high on a need for control questionnaire, and people with good interpersonal relationships scored low on the same questionnaire. Inferential statistics would tell you if the difference in scores is one that is significant or, in layman's terms, one to take notice of and conduct more research on. In general, quantitative approaches require measures of personality and other aspects of behaviour and thought that produce numerical data. The most common methods of study into personality that fall into this category are laboratory experiments and questionnaires.

A **qualitative approach** typically produces data in the form of spoken or written language, such as that resulting from case studies where a small number of people are given in-depth interviews. Interviews may be tape recorded and the interview subsequently transcribed to produce a full account of what has been said and, often, how things were expressed. Such data is clearly not readily or easily amenable to statistical analysis. Indeed, qualitative approaches used in interviews and case studies are not designed to produce numerical data. Analysis of qualitative data is usually done by selecting themes or recurring issues that emerge from an in-depth interview and from interviews with a number of people. A detailed account of a range of qualitative approaches, which is beyond the scope of this chapter, is given in Breakwell *et al.* (2000). In the next section of this chapter we will consider some commonly used approaches: interviews and case studies.

In relation to the four main approaches to personality psychology considered in Chapter 1, the dispositional, and behaviour and cognitive approaches typically use the quantitative approach. This is not exclusively the case as you will see in Chapter 6 when the work of Gordon Allport is considered. Allport used a mixture of both quantitative and qualitative methods to investigate personality. In contrast, the psychoanalytic and humanistic approaches use, almost exclusively, qualitative methods of research. In fact, it is unusual for either of these two approaches to use quantitative methods such as the laboratory experiment.

Both the quantitative and qualitative approaches have strengths and shortcomings. Quantitative methods are regarded by many as more scientific since research, for example, using a laboratory experiment is capable of replication by another group of researchers. Replication is important since psychologists want to know whether or not conducting the same research at a different time, in a different place, will produce the same results. By contrast, qualitative methods are often difficult, if not impossible, to replicate. For example, how an interviewer proceeds will depend as much, if not more, on the person being interviewed as the researcher.

Quantitative methods have their strength in statistical analysis; however, critics argue that reducing people to a set of numbers loses much of the richness about people, whilst the qualitative approach does capture the richness and uniqueness of a person. In many ways it is possible to liken the

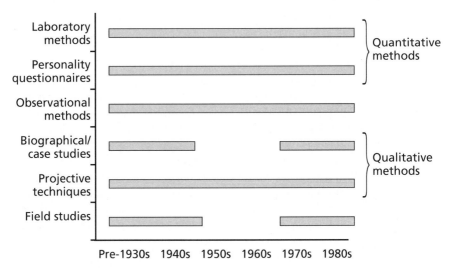

Figure 2.1 Historical trends in the use of different research methods in personality psychology (adapted from Craik, 1986)

qualitative methods to the ideographic approach that was discussed in Chapter 1. Also quantitative methods are more typical of the nomothetic approach.

Craik (1986) analysed historical trends in the use of various research methods in personality psychology. As can be seen from Figure 2.1, the use of the laboratory experiment and personality questionnaires (both quantitative methods) has been predominant. However, qualitative methods such as projective techniques (see later in this chapter) and biographical/case study methods have also enjoyed usage over the past 50 to 60 years.

2.3 METHODS OF STUDYING PERSONALITY

In this section a range of methods of studying personality are briefly considered. More detailed treatments of these methods are to be found in textbooks specialising in research methods in psychology (see, for example, Coolican, 1999).

The methods considered here are the main ones used in personality research; however, they do not represent all methods used. What these methods all have in common is that they produce empirical evidence – whether quantitative or qualitative – which ultimately allows for a theory of personality (and its predictions, where appropriate) to be evaluated.

2.3.1 Laboratory experiments

The laboratory experiment is the method *par excellence*, representing a scientific approach to the study of personality. The laboratory experiment allows research to progress from theory to hypothesis/prediction to testing the prediction under highly controlled conditions. The laboratory experiment allows for cause and effect relationships between variables to be studied. To highlight the key aspects of the experiment consider the example of need for control and effect on interpersonal relationships given at the start of this chapter. Remember that one member of the group wanted to conduct a laboratory experiment. This could be done as described below. The hypothesis or prediction can be stated as follows:

- people with a high need for control will demonstrate poor interpersonal relationships
- people with a low need for control will demonstrate good interpersonal relationships.

To get people with high and low need for control a questionnaire could be developed and issued to one hundred people. Then the research could select the ten people who score highest on need for control and the ten people who score lowest, for inclusion in the experiment. High and low need for control is called the **independent variable**, which is the variable that has been manipulated by the experimenter.

The experimenter then has to devise a task for these people to carry out in the laboratory. For example, this could require each of the 20 participants (high and low need for control) to talk to a stranger for ten minutes about a given topic. Each of the conversations would be video recorded and the recordings analysed by the researcher. Measures could be taken of the amount of time the participant spends looking at the stranger in the region of the eyes (eye contact) and the general orientation of the body of the participant to the stranger (orientated towards the person or away from the person). These are measures taken by the researcher and called the **dependent variables**. Those who look at the stranger in the region of the eyes a great deal, and orient their body towards the stranger may be seen as showing good interpersonal skills. Hence, if the measures of the dependent variable show participants who score high on need for control as engaging in low levels of looking and a body orientation away from the stranger then our first hypothesis, given above, would be supported.

Another type of variable, called a **confounding variable**, may question or cast into doubt the validity of these findings. For example, suppose all the high need for control participants are males and all the low need for control participants females. Since females are generally regarded as having better interpersonal skills than males, the findings of the experiment cannot be attributed to personality any more than they could to the sex of the participant. It is, therefore, important that the researcher controls as many potentially confounding variables as possible. In this case, having five males and five females in each of the two groups of ten participants will avoid a confounding variable.

The major strength of the laboratory experiment is the high degree of control that can be obtained over variables and the potential to establish cause–effect relationships. The major shortcoming is that the experiment is artificial and the findings may not generalise to everyday life. This means that the laboratory experiment lacks what is called **ecological validity**.

2.3.2 Self-report questionnaire

By far the most common way of measuring personality, especially in the dispositional approach, is by the use of self-report questionnaires. Personality psychologists have devised, according to strict criteria, literally thousands of questionnaires to measure a vast range of dispositions or personality traits. Self-report questionnaires rely on a person making an honest response to a question asked, or to choosing between alternatives. Self-report questionnaires come in a number of formats, and we will consider two of these. First, some questionnaires use a simple yes/no or either/or format. The 16 PF questionnaire developed by Cattel (see Chapter 6) attempts to measure 16 personality factors such as extraversion/introversion by asking people to state a preference from two alternatives. For example, two questions that appear in the 16 PF are as follows.

- I trust strangers. Sometimes or practically always.
- I would rather work as: an engineer or a social science teacher.

The use of an either/or format has the advantage that it forces people to answer in one way or another. There is not a 'do not know' category available. Another example of a forced-choice questionnaire is Rotter's Internal–External Locus of Control scale. Here you are asked to select one from two statements that most reflects how you are, as in the following example.

- Statement (a) It is silly to think one can really change another's basic attitudes.
- Statement (b) When I am right I can convince others.

Second are personality questionnaires where you are asked to express how you think or feel about an issue on a five-point or seven-point scale (other scales can be used such as a three-point scale – agree, do not know, disagree). These scales are generally called Likert scales, an example of which is shown in Figure 2.2.

I keep my home neat and tidy.

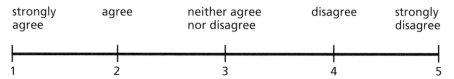

Figure 2.2 An example of a Likert scale

The use of a Likert-type scale enables numerical data to be produced. Both of the above response formats have the attraction of being quick and easy to administer. Self-report questionnaires are used extensively in personality research.

2.3.3 Interviews

Whilst interviews are usually categorised under the qualitative approach this does not have to be the case. An interview is usually conducted on a one-to-one basis between the researcher and the interviewee. As such interviews can broadly be seen as falling into one of three types: structured, semi-structured and unstructured. Structured interviews are where the researcher has prepared a list of questions to ask in advance of the interview. Often the researcher sticks only to those questions prepared in advance; this may limit the amount of information obtained from the interviewee. A structured approach to interviewing assumes that the psychologist knows exactly what he or she is interested in and does not want to explore other issues or matters that the interviewee may wish to raise. At the other end of the spectrum is the unstructured interview. Here the researcher may have a general topic to present to the interviewee, but has not formulated any specific questions in advance. Essentially, the psychologist allows the interviewee to determine what is covered and where the interview goes. In contrast to the structured approach, the unstructured interview is very much led by the person being interviewed to reflect that person's views, concerns etc. with respect to the general topic. The semi-structured interview offers, in many ways, a halfway position between the structured and unstructured interviews. The semi-structured interview offers the best of both worlds since it allows the psychologist to prepare certain questions in advance, and also permits the interviewee to say what he or she wants to on the topic.

The structured interview can produce quantitative and qualitative data depending on how the questions are set up in advance. The unstructured interview produces qualitative data. The semi-structured interview can produce both quantitative and qualitative data should the researcher desire such a combination. No one interview technique is better than another; the choice of which to use will depend on what the researcher wants to investigate and the type of data to be produced.

2.3.4 Correlational research

Suppose you were interested in the relationship between the personality variable need for control, from our example at the start of this chapter, and intelligence. In **correlational research** psychologists seek to establish whether or not a relationship exists between two variables. To investigate the relationship between these two variables you could ask, say, ten people to complete a personality questionnaire on need for control and the same ten people to complete an intelligence test. Assuming a high score in each case indicates high need for control and high level of intelligence, the data shown in Table 2.1 might be produced.

Table 2.1 Hypothetical data produced by ten people completing two questionnaires

Person	Need for control score	Intelligence test score
1	55	120
2	20	90
3	60	125
4	30	100
5	40	105
6	15	85
7	50	115
8	30	95
9	65	130
10	45	110

If you look at this data you will notice that a high need for control is related to a high score on the intelligence test and a low need for control is related to a low score on the intelligence test. You might then infer that as need for control increases so does intelligence level. This would represent a positive correlation.

A correlation has two important features that are different to each other: the direction of the correlation and the strength of the correlation. Broadly speaking the direction of a correlation can be positive, negative or no direction (represented by zero). A perfect positive correlation has a value of 1.0 and a perfect negative correlation a value of −1.0. A negative correlation is where one variable increases whilst the other variable decreases. For example, as a person grows older their speed of response slows down – that is, as age increases response speed decreases.

Data produced from measuring two variables is often depicted on a scattergram, as shown in Figure 2.3. Each dot on the scattergram represents the two measures of the two variables for a single person. The scattergram shows the direction of correlation.

The second important feature of a correlation is its strength. A strong

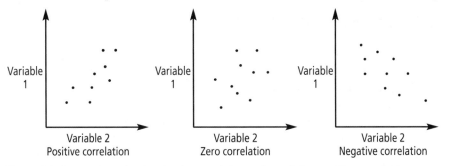

Figure 2.3 Scattergrams showing the three basic types of correlation: positive, zero and negative correlation

correlation will produce a figure tending towards $+1$ or -1. A weak correlation will produce a figure tending towards zero. Strong correlations indicate a strong relationship (positive or negative) between two variables. Whilst a correlation gives you an indication of the relationship between two variables it cannot tell you about cause and effect. For example, in our imaginary data we saw that high need for control positively correlated with high level of intelligence. This cannot be taken to mean that high need for control causes high intelligence or vice versa. Attempting to establish a cause–effect relationship is more the province of the laboratory experiment.

2.3.5 Twin studies

The naturally occurring phenomena of identical (monozygotic) and fraternal (dizygotic) twins has been used by personality researchers to investigate the extent to which personality characteristics may be biological or genetically determined. Identical twins share exactly the same genetic make-up and if both share the same environment (are brought up in the same home together) then, it is argued, similar personality characteristics can be seen to have a genetic base. Fraternal or dizygotic twins share 50 per cent of genes. Hence, if these twins share the same environment, the genetic influence on personality, if there was any, would be expected to be less than for monozygotic twins. Generally, twin studies use correlational techniques whereby the personality measure of a trait for one twin is correlated with that of the other twin. Rushton *et al.* (1986), for example, compared monozygotic and dizygotic twins in relation to five personality traits. As can be seen from Table 2.2, for each personality trait monozygotic twins shared a higher positive correlation than dizygotic twins. Indicating these personality traits may have a genetic base.

Critics may argue that since identical twins share the same environment and often identify strongly with each other and, for example, are often dressed alike so that people cannot tell one from the other, then the greater similarity of personality traits may be due to environmental influences. One way round this is to compare personality characteristics of monozygotic twins

Table 2.2 Correlations on five personality traits for monozygotic and dizygotic twins (adapted from Rushton *et al.* 1986)

Personality trait	Monozygotic twins	Dizygotic twins
Altruism	0.53	0.25
Empathy	0.54	0.20
Nurturance	0.49	0.14
Aggressiveness	0.40	0.04
Assertiveness	0.52	0.20

Table 2.3 Correlations for three personality traits on monozygotic (MZ) twins reared together and reared apart (adapted from Rowe, 1987)

Personality trait	Twins (MZ) reared apart	Twins (MZ) reared together
Extroversion	0.61	0.51
Neuroticism	0.53	0.50
Intelligence	0.72	0.86

reared together and apart with dizygotic twins reared together and apart. Rowe (1987) did this for the personality traits of extroversion, neuroticism and intelligence. As can be seen from Table 2.3, identical twins reared apart or together are quite similar. This indicates the influence of genetics when the environments are different.

Caution is often needed when interpreting findings from studies using identical twins reared apart. The assumption is that each twin experiences a different environment. However, this may not be the case since it is exceptional for identical twins to be separated in the first place, and often whilst living in different homes, they may be in the same street and therefore spend much time together.

2.3.6 Case studies

Perhaps more than any other psychologist, Sigmund Freud is known for developing the use of case studies. In broad terms the case study is an in-depth analysis of a single person (or occasionally a small group of people). The psychologist goes into great detail about the individual, recording many historical aspects and information about present-day matters. Often a semi-structured or unstructured interview approach is used, and what the person says is tape recorded and transcribed at a later time. A case study usually takes place over a period of time, and sometimes over a number of years. Both qualitative and quantitative data can be obtained from a case study. For example, in a case study of a person who has an obsessive-compulsive disorder, the number of times a person washes each day may be recorded. Usually, however, production of qualitative data is the prime objective of a case study. Case studies are often used with people who show atypical or abnormal behaviour. In these instances it is important that only qualified psychologists conduct a case study. Wrongly conducted case studies may cause somebody with mental distress to become worse and more disturbed.

Freud used case studies, as we shall see in Chapter 3, to highlight his concepts and theories. Freud kept no records of what took place with his patients at the time, and usually made his case study notes later the same day, in the evening. Gordon Allport, working in the dispositional approach, regarded case studies as essential to understanding the person. Humanistic psychologists, such as Carl Rogers, also make extensive use of case studies.

The advantages of case studies as a method of personality research are that they provide in-depth insight into a person, and produce insights in ways not achievable by the experimental method. Case studies may also be useful in generating ideas about the nature of people, which can then be investigated with more quantitative methods such as questionnaires or experiments. However, case studies have serious shortcomings. The main one is that what is found out about one person from a case study cannot easily be applied or generalised to other people. The case study is specific to an individual. Another shortcoming is that the researcher's own views may influence how the case study is interpreted. For example, the parts of the case Freud recalled in the evenings may only have been those that supported his theories. In short, it is difficult to make case studies scientific or objective. Case studies may make a valuable contribution to personality research when used with other, more objective, methods such as experiments or correlational research. They do provide rich sources of information not obtainable by other methods.

2.3.7 Single-person research

In recent years single-person research has become popular, and represents a combination of experimental and case study methods. With single-person research the psychologist will manipulate independent variables and take measures of the dependent variable. In essence this method mirrors the experiment but is conducted on a single person over a period of time. An example may help clarify this. Hall *et al.* (1968) reported a single-person experiment concerned with attempting to reduce the disruptive behaviour of a young teenager in the classroom and increasing the amount of time the teenager spent studying. The experiment with the teenager took place over 30 sessions divided into four phases. In the first phase observations were made of time spent studying in the classroom – this gave a baseline. As you can see from Figure 2.4, this was around 25 per cent of the time. In the next phase the teenager was paid extra attention by the teacher. In the third phase the teacher went back to giving normal amounts of attention, and in the fourth phase extra attention was once again given. As can be seen from Figure 2.4, the teenager spent much more time studying when given extra attention, and reverted to low levels of study when not given attention.

Single-person research is particularly appropriate when trying to change the behaviour of an individual and where the researcher wishes to find out the effects of different treatments on the person. Quantitative data is readily produced using this method, and qualitative data can also be gained from interviewing the person.

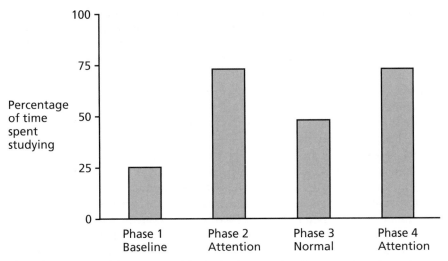

Figure 2.4 Amount of time spent studying in the classroom by a teenager when given extra and normal amounts of attention by the teacher (adapted from Hall *et al.* 1968)

2.3.8 Observational techniques

Observation and accurate recording of behaviour is a fundamental requirement of scientific research and underlies the confidence we can have in both quantitative and qualitative data produced from experiments, interviews, case studies and single-person studies. Observations must be reliable to be of any value in psychology (we will look more closely at the issues of reliability and validity later in this chapter). Observations may be systematic and unsystematic, they can also take place in laboratory settings and field or naturalistic settings.

Systematic observation requires a great deal of preparation on the part of the researcher before actually making the observations. Decisions have to be taken about what behaviour exactly, out of all behaviours, to observe and record. Over what period of time are observations going to be made, and for what length of time? Where video recording can be made in the laboratory or other setting, then observation and recording of behaviours of interest can be taken a number of times from the same recording – this helps increase the reliability of the measures or data recorded. Analysing a video recording means that different aspects of behaviour can be monitored and recorded on different viewings. Observing behaviour in the absence of video recording does not give the researcher a second chance if something is missed. It is not possible to rewind in real life!

Consider the study we looked at in the previous section where the psychologist was interested in the amount of time a teenager spent studying in the classroom. Before conducting the study and observing the teenager in the classroom, agreement would need to be reached over which behaviours were evidence of studying. What might you choose to observe? Behaviours that you might think of as representing studying include reading a textbook, taking notes from the board, answering questions asked of the class by the teacher. See if you can think of any more. In this study not only would different studying behaviours have to be observed, so too would a recording of the length of time the teenager spent in each behaviour. Using this example, it can be seen that systematic observation requires a lot of thought and planning before it actually takes place.

Unsystematic observation does not mean unscientific or disorganised. It may be that the researcher is not quite sure which behaviours are important to observe, in which case the psychologist will observe all that takes place and decide afterwards what are the important behaviours. Unsystematic observation is often used in the early days of a research project, and provides ideas for how to go about making systematic observations.

Naturalistic observation takes place in everyday, real-life settings rather than the artificial setting of the laboratory. As the term implies, observation takes place in a natural setting. Both systematic and unsystematic observation approaches may be used. However, naturalistic observation does not readily permit video recording, and may raise ethical issues if attempted. Hence, to get the best out of naturalistic observation the psychologist should have a clear idea of what behaviours are to be observed. This means detailed planning in advance for systematic observation. Naturally occurring behaviour may only occur once; the researcher cannot properly recreate the event in the laboratory. Naturalistic observations may be discreet or more intrusive; if those being observed are aware of the observation this may affect how they behave. This is not what the researcher wants since he or she is attempting to observe behaviour as it occurs naturally. Other drawbacks of naturalistic observations are that the findings may not be generalisable to other situations, and that the observer may unwittingly allow his or her preconceived ideas to influence what is observed, recorded and what a behaviour actually represents.

2.3.9 Projective techniques

An alternative to self-report questionnaires and interviews that is widely used by researchers in the psychoanalytic approach is that of **projective techniques** or tests. Projective techniques assess personality indirectly by presenting a person with an ambiguous figure or picture and asking them to provide an interpretation or give meaning to what is shown. The basic idea is that the interpretation or meaning given by a person will represent their feelings, attitudes, desires and motives. In short, the person projects his or her thoughts and feelings on to the ambiguous picture to give it meaning. Psychoanalysts take this further and claim that the projections reflect unconscious thoughts, desires and feelings rather than ones that are conscious to the person. As you can probably see already there are a number of dangers and shortcomings with the use of projective techniques. We will return to these after considering two examples of projective tests.

Perhaps the most well-known and widely used projective test is the **Rorschach inkblot test** (developed by Rorschach in 1921, with scoring systems developed, for example, by Exner, 1986; and Klopfer and Davidson, 1962). The Rorschach inkblot test consists of ten inkblots mounted on cards similar to those shown in Figure 2.5. (You can make your own inkblots by folding a sheet of paper in two, opening it up and putting ink on one side. Close the paper and open it to get your inkblot.)

Figure 2.5 Ank inblot similar to the ones used in the Rorschach inkblot test

The test is normally conducted one to one, with a highly trained person showing inkblots to another person. The psychoanalyst asks the person what they see in the inkblot, and encourages the person to elaborate on what they see. Scoring the responses is quite a complex process, and one system (Exner, 1986) scores a response according to five basic categories. These are as follows:

1. location – which part of the inkblot is used
2. determinant – the qualities of what is seen, such as shape, movement etc.
3. popularity/originality – is it what is commonly seen by other people or highly unusual
4. content – what the content of the object is etc.; i.e. what is actually seen
5. form level – how obviously what is seen fits the part of the inkblot used.

Interpretation of the projections made by a person seeing these inkblots requires extensive training, with the psychoanalyst looking for recurrent themes in the associations made to the ambiguous figures.

Another commonly used projective test is the Thematic Apperception Test

Figure 2.6 An ambiguous picture of people similar to those used in the Thematic Apperception Test

(TAT) developed by Murray (1962). The TAT consists of 20 pictures that show one or more persons in an ambiguous situation. Figure 2.6 gives an example of a picture similar to the ones used in the actual TAT.

The task of the person shown each picture is to make up a story that fits around the picture. The psychoanalyst then analyses each story, looking for common themes, much the same as with the Rorschach inkblot test.

The major strength of projective techniques is that they do not make it obvious to the respondent what the test is about. This is more likely to elicit honest and unbiased responses. There are two major shortcomings, however. First, there is no easy way of ensuring that the associations made to an ambiguous figure or picture actually reflect unconscious thoughts and feelings. Second, how the responses are interpreted may differ from psychoanalyst to psychoanalyst, or psychologist to psychologist, and reflect a particular theoretical perspective. Given this, there is no objective way of sorting out differences of interpretation. These two major shortcomings have limited the use of projective tests to the psychoanalytic approach.

2.3.10 Evaluation of different methods

The range of methods we have considered offer the personality psychologist many different ways of approaching a research question or project. The most scientific methods, such as the laboratory experiment, offer a high degree of control and confidence in measures taken. This, however, is at the expense of ecological validity or generalisability to everyday life. More qualitative methods such as case studies and interviews have higher ecological validity but are limited in generalisability to other people. Self-report questionnaires offer a quick and easy approach to personality measurement, but do bring with them problems, which we will look at later in this chapter. Some of the problems of self-report measures are not found with projective techniques, but as we have seen above, projective techniques have serious shortcomings.

Table 2.4 Summary of the key strengths and weaknesses of different research methods in personality psychology

Research methods	Key strengths	Key weaknesses
Laboratory experiments	High degree of control over independent and other variables. Establishes cause–effect relationships.	Artificial environment – lack of ecological validity. Not all aspects of personality can be studied in the laboratory.
Self-report questionnaires	Quick and easy to administer. Many based on sound statistical principles.	Problems of reliability and validity. People may not fill them in honestly.
Interviews	Can gain both quantitative and qualitative data. Allow a more in-depth analysis of a person. Conducted in everyday settings.	People may not be willing to talk about certain topics. Structured interviews may limit what is found out; unstructured interviews difficult to compare.
Correlational research	Provide information about whether or not a relationship exists between two variables.	Cannot provide information or evidence for cause–effect relationships.
Case studies	Provide in-depth information about a person in their everyday life.	Difficult to generalise findings to other people. May produce too much information to analyse adequately.
Single-person studies	Brings experimental approach to study of individual over time.	Difficult to generalise findings to other people
Projective techniques	Respondent does not know what tests are about, so likely to respond honestly.	Indirect measure so difficult to be sure response relates to the interpretation made.

The picture that emerges then, is that the researcher has to decide which methods suit his or her research best, and be aware that any method has both strengths and shortcomings (see Table 2.4). Whilst scientific criteria dominate the choice of methods to use, different approaches to personality adopt different methods.

2.4 ISSUES IN PERSONALITY ASSESSMENT

How do psychologists assess how good a particular test of measurement of personality is? To have confidence in any personality assessment, whether by self-response questionnaire or projective technique, we need to know how reliable and valid the test is. As we will see, reliability is easier to establish than validity.

2.4.1 Reliability

The definitions of personality that were discussed at the start of Chapter 1 all emphasise the idea that personality is relatively stable over time. In consequence, we should expect a test of personality to produce a similar measure at different points in time. If the test does this, then it may be called reliable; if not then it is not reliable and is of little value. For example, a self-report questionnaire to measure the personality trait of extroversion should produce similar measures for the same person over the period of a year. If the person fills in a personality questionnaire three times over the period of a year we would expect a reliable test to produce similar measures of extroversion. There are caveats to this, of course, such as the person experiencing a dramatic lifestyle change in this period. This type of reliability is called **test–retest reliability**.

Another type of reliability associated with self-report personality questionnaires is called **internal consistency**. A test may be regarded as internally consistent if each of the items in the test measures the same aspect of personality. Hence, if a test of extroversion has 15 items and all measure extroversion, then it is internally consistent. If a test has poor internal consistency then many of the items or questions will not be to do with, for example, extroversion. Poor internal consistency makes a test unreliable and of limited use.

A different type of reliability is to do with how well two or more researchers show agreement when making detailed observations and recordings of behaviour. If two or more researchers show high agreement over how each categorises or records behaviour then inter-rater reliability is high.

If agreement is poor between two or more researchers, then inter-rater reliability is low. Confidence in how behaviour is coded and recorded can only be gained from high inter-rater reliability.

2.4.2 Validity

Validity is about whether the personality test or measure is actually measuring what it claims to be measuring. Personality tests, self-response and projective, are designed to measure certain aspects or features of personality. A valid test measures what it claims to measure. Establishing the validity of personality assessment is more difficult than establishing the reliability of a test. There are three main types of validity: content validity, criterion validity and construct validity.

Content validity is to do with how well the items or questions in a personality questionnaire appear to represent what the test is supposed to measure. There is an element of subjectivity in determining content validity, which requires a degree of agreement about what a particular personality trait, such as extroversion, is about. If there is a disagreement about the personality trait then it will be difficult to get high content validity.

Criterion validity is achieved if the measures from a personality test can be related to some behavioural criterion that psychologists are able to agree on. One way to achieve this is in relation to the extent to which the score on a personality test can predict behaviour or performance in the future. Another way of establishing criterion validity is to correlate test scores with another accepted and established test that also measures the same personality characteristic. The trouble here is that if the new test correlates very highly with the established test then one wonders why a new test is being produced in the first place!

Construct validity is related to the theoretical ideas behind the personality trait or characteristic under consideration. Any personality trait can be regarded as a hypothetical construct – that is, a concept that does not exist in a physical sense but is suggested as a way of organising how we view personality. With construct validity an assessment is made about whether the test or items on the questionnaire reflect the personality construct. This may, in the end, be a subjective judgement where agreement can only be reached when two or more psychologists are working from the same theoretical perspective.

To summarise, a good personality assessment or measure of personality is one that can be shown to be both reliable and valid. Only tests that meet these criteria are of use in psychological research, since unreliable and invalid tests are not likely to be measuring in a consistent way what they claim to be measuring. The various types of reliability and validity are summarised in Table 2.5.

Table 2.5 Summary of main types of reliability and validity used in personality assessment

Reliability	Description
Test–retest reliability	The same or similar test of personality produces a similar score at different times.
Internal consistency	The extent to which items in the test actually measure the personality characteristic.
Inter-rater reliability	The extent to which two or more raters agree on how behaviour is observed and recorded.
Validity	**Description**
Content validity	How well the items or questions in the test represent the personality trait that it is supposed to measure.
Criterion validity	Extent to which test scores can predict behaviour *or* the extent to which a new test correlates with an established test of personality.
Construct validity	How well the test measures the hypothetical construct of personality.

2.5 PROBLEMS OF MEASUREMENT

The use of personality questionnaires and tests bring with it a number of problems to do with how the respondent provides responses. We will consider three such problems here: social desirability, response sets and mood.

When completing a personality questionnaire people are often conscious, rightly or wrongly, that they feel they are being judged in some way. For example, if a personality questionnaire is measuring friendliness or self-esteem then the person completing the questionnaire may want to be seen in a more favourable light than may in fact be the case. This is called **social desirability**. So instead of answering the questionnaire in an open and honest way, the respondent attempts to answer in ways that he or she thinks present a more socially desirable personality. A number of techniques have been developed to establish the extent to which a person is answering in a social desirable way. For example, one way is to use a forced-choice approach to questions. Here two equally attractive or unattractive options have to be selected from. Another technique is to measure social desirability in the questionnaire by embedding a number of special questions.

Social desirability is an example of a general problem in personality measurement called **response sets**. Response sets are patterns of responding to a questionnaire that are consistent to a person. For example, in a questionnaire using a five-point scale with the middle point labelled 'neither agree nor disagree' a person might respond by ticking this middle point for every single question. With yes/no type questions a response set might be, for example, where a person ticks 'yes' every time, indicating that the questionnaire is not being taken seriously. Response sets threaten the validity of the measures produced from people responding to a questionnaire. Careful design of a personality measure can go a long way to avoiding response sets.

The mood of a person may also affect how the questions on a personality test are responded to. Someone in a good mood on one occasion may answer questions quite differently to how they might answer when in a bad mood on a different occasion. If the researcher is aware that a person is in an unusually emotional state or in a mood not characteristic, then great caution should be taken when interpreting the responses of a personality questionnaire.

Even with these problems of measurement for personality questionnaires, and the need to establish reliability and validity, the use of questionnaires is widespread and popular in personality research.

2.6 ETHICAL CONSIDERATIONS

The British Psychological Society (BPS) and the American Psychological Association (APA) as well as the national psychological organisations of other countries publish clear guidelines on the ethical principles that must be adopted when conducting research using people. Below are summarised the key ethical principles, and you are referred to an appropriate body such as the BPS for full details (through the Internet, see www.bps.org.uk). Here we briefly consider the issues of consent, deception, debriefing, right to withdraw, confidentiality, protection from harm, and observational studies.

When conducting any type of research it is desirable and you are obliged to obtain consent before somebody participates in an experiment, completes a questionnaire, etc. This should be **informal consent**, where participants are given full details about the research and what is going to happen before taking part in the actual study. When research involves children, the consent of parents or legal guardians must be obtained.

Deception should not be used in research studies. However, much research does involve deception to a greater or lesser extent since, if the participants were told all about the purpose of the study they may behave in ways to please the researcher rather than how they would behave naturally. Deception should be avoided wherever possible, and if deception has to be used, then participants must be fully debriefed after taking part.

Debriefing is where each participant is informed about all aspects of the study immediately after taking part. If deception has been used this should be stated and the reasons for using deception given. Participants in a study should leave in a positive and content state of mind.

Before taking part in a study each participant should be made aware that he or she has a right to withdraw at any point should they wish to do so. The study that the participant takes part in should not cause any physical or psychological harm. Sometimes a study, inadvertently, causes somebody to get upset or stressed. It is the task of the psychologist to debrief in such a way that the person leaves in the same state of mind they were in before taking part. This may not always be possible, but every effort should be made to achieve this.

Before taking part in the study and when debriefing, participants should be assured that any data or measures resulting from their participation will be held in strictest confidence. Permission must be granted from the participant if the researcher wishes to make the data of a person public so that the person could be identified.

With observational research in naturalistic settings, consideration must be given to whether the privacy of a person is being invaded. Naturalistic observation often does not seek permission in advance to observe people in public places. One of the strengths of naturalistic observation is that the data produced has high ecological validity, but this may only be the case when people are aware that they are being observed as part of a psychological study. Where possible permission should be sought in advance, and debriefing given after observations have been made. Observations that do not take place in public places must have the prior consent of the people to be observed before the study can go ahead.

It is of vital importance that all research in psychology, personality research, as well as other types of research using people, conforms to the high standards and ethical principles laid down by the professional body of psychology in any particular country. Research that is not ethical should not be conducted. You may think that this will limit what can be researched, but imagination and careful thought usually finds a way forward.

2.7 SUMMARY

- A quantitative approach to the study of personality is characterised by data collection that allows statistical analysis to take place. Typically such data comes from experiments and/or self-report personality questionnaires. A qualitative approach typically produces detailed written information derived from interviews and case studies. The dispositional and behavioural approaches to personality typically adopt quantitative approaches, and the psychoanalytic and humanistic adopt qualitative approaches.

- Personality psychologists employ a range of methods to study personality; these include laboratory experiments, self-report questionnaires, interviews, correlational research, twin studies, case studies and projective techniques. Observation and accurate recording are of fundamental importance in all methods of studying personality. Systematic observation requires detailed preparation and is important to establish so that confidence in the data produced is high. There are three main types of reliability: test–retest reliability, the internal consistency of a personality test, and inter-rater reliability. Validity is concerned with the extent to which a personality test actually measures what it claims to be measuring. There are a number of different types of validity, including content validity, criterion validity and construct validity.

- Personality questionnaires suffer from a number of measurement problems. These include social desirability, response sets and the mood of the person at the time of completing the questionnaire. Response sets are patterns of responding to a questionnaire that may not reflect the true personality of the person.

- All research conducted in personality psychology must conform to ethical guidelines issued by, for example, the British Psychological Society. The main ethical considerations are to do with consent, deception, debriefing, right to withdraw, confidentiality and protection from harm. Wherever research is conducted on children, parental assent must first be obtained. Research that does not conform to ethical guidelines should not be conducted.

2.8 FURTHER READING

Coolican, H. (1999) *Research Methods and Statistics in Psychology.* (3rd end). London: Hodder. Popular, accessible and well-regarded introductory textbook to research methods, descriptive and influential statistics used in psychology. Has a useful section on report writing.

Breakwell, G.M., Hammond, S. and Fife-Shaw, C. (eds) (2000) *Research Methods in Psychology* (2nd edn). London: Sage. Excellent text with chapters written by specialists in their fields. Range of very useful chapters on qualitative methods.

British Psychological Society (BPS) (1998) *Code of Conduct, Ethical Principles and Guidelines.* Leicester: British Psychological Society. Provides a comprehensive set of guidelines for a code of conduct for psychologists and psychological research. Available from the BPS, St Andrews House, 48 Princess Road, Leicester LE1 7DR; or visit the BPS website at www.bps.org.uk/about/rules.cfm.

3 Freud and Psychoanalysis

3.1 DOES FREUD STILL MATTER?

A little over a century ago Freud published *The Interpretation of Dreams*; this book drew the attention of western society to Freud. In looking back over the twentieth century, *The Interpretation of Dreams* was seen as one of the ten most important and influential books. One hundred years on and you are about to read a major chapter in this book on Freud and his theories. You may ask whether this chapter has been included solely for historical interest or whether Freud is still relevant today. The answer to both questions is yes, but some consideration of why Freud is still regarded as important to personality psychology in the twenty-first century is warranted.

Psychologists and philosophers alike (for example, Billig, 1999; Badcock, 1994) regard Freud as having revolutionised and dramatically changed the way we think about ourselves. Much of this is now commonly accepted and has entered everyday language – such phrases as 'don't be so defensive', 'you are very anal', and 'don't project your fears on to me' exemplify this. However, the huge change that gradually took place in the late 1890s through to the early 1900s is difficult to imagine now. Try to put yourself into the Victorian mind. Galileo had claimed, in the 1600s, that the earth was not at the centre of the universe, as previously thought. Darwin, in the late 1800s, produced his theory of evolution stating that the origin of and change to a species occurred through random mutation and survival of the fittest. The theory of evolution was and still is seen as a major challenge to established religions. Then Freud, at the turn of the nineteenth century, produced theories stating that human beings were basically irrational and driven by their sex instinct. This potentially conflicts with our view that science, religion and society are based on rational behaviour and order. The revolution caused by Freud in how we see ourselves was that the irrational rather than the rational is the driving force behind what we say and do. If that was not bad enough to the Victorian mind, Freud further stated that, in addition, irrational thoughts are not directly accessible because they are unconscious. To a greater or lesser extent, the ideas of irrationality and unconscious thoughts have been accepted as part of what it means to be human.

Freud also changed the way in which we think about and treat mental disorder or atypical behaviour. In the mid- to late 1800s the dominant mode of thought about mental disorder was that it was due to organic dysfunction, i.e. a physical disorder of the brain. Focusing on anxiety disorders Freud changed this to regarding many mental disorders as psychological in origin (usually dating back to a person's childhood) and treatable using psychological techniques. We commonly accept psychotherapy as a valid and important way of treating people, and the types of therapies now available are extremely varied and numerous.

Freud matters today both because of the enormous influence he has had over psychology and psychiatry, and because many of his ideas and concepts are as relevant today as they were a hundred years ago. In this chapter we will explore Freud's ideas and theories, and consider evidence for some of the claims he made.

3.2 BIOGRAPHICAL SKETCH

Pictures of Freud, whether photographs or drawings, are few in number; basically because Freud did not like posing for photographs. Almost all pictures commonly reproduced in textbooks, show Freud formally dressed and with a stern look on his face. What was Freud like as a person? Numerous biographies have been written (Jones, 1953; 1955; 1957; Gay, 1988; Breger, 2000, for example), and the impression that comes across is of a man who was incredibly hard-working, formal and patriarchal, and somewhat on the obsessive side. For example, Freud was addicted to smoking cigars, had tried giving up on a number of occasions but was unsuccessful, and developed cancer of the jaw in the 1920s probably as a result of this addiction. Some of the personality features associated with Freud are representative of an anal personality (see Section 3.8 of this chapter). A visit to the Freud museum in Hampstead, London, is well worthwhile and gives some sense of the man.

Sigmund Freud was born in 1856 in Freiberg, Moravia (which is a small town in Czechoslovakia); his father, Jacob, was a Jewish wool merchant and his mother, Amalia, was the second wife of Jacob. Amalia was aged 20 and Jacob 46 at the time of Freud's birth. Jacob and Amelia had another seven children, with Freud always being the favourite of his mother. Freud had a very close relationship with his mother but was more distant from his brothers and sisters, as well as his father. When he was aged three, Freud and his family left Freiberg, moved briefly to Leipzig, then to Vienna. Vienna remained Freud's home for nearly 80 years. He left Austria with his daughter Anna in 1938 because of the Nazi persecution of Jews there. He moved to London and a house in Hampstead where he died a year later. Anna managed to bring a large amount of his possessions out of Vienna to London, including his couch, books and numerous small statues given to him by friends and colleagues. Anna continued to live in the house in Hampstead until her death in 1982. Subsequently the house was turned into the Freud Museum and is now open to the public.

Sigmund Freud studied medicine at the University of Vienna Medical School in 1873 and qualified in 1881. Rather than practise medicine, he turned to psychological research. He became interested in psychology, and obtained a grant to visit Paris and study under the famous French neurologist Jean-Martin Charcot. This was a turning point in Freud's career since he learned hypnosis for the treatment of hysteria (a disorder at that time common in women and often shown through paralysis of parts of the body) from Charcot. Following his four-month visit to Paris he returned to Vienna and worked with Joseph Breuer using hypnosis to treat hysterical or neurotic disorders. This resulted in a joint publication, *Studies in Hysteria*, in 1895; this book contained the famous case study of Anna O, whom Breuer was treating. Freud broke relationships with Breuer, abandoned hypnosis as a form of treatment and went on to develop psychoanalysis both as a theory and a therapy.

Freud married Martha Bemays in 1886 and this marriage produced six children, with Anna being the youngest. In 1896 Freud's father died, and this seemed to precipitate a crisis in his life that led to an intense period of self-analysis over the next few years. Many of the dreams reported and analysed in his book *The Interpretation of Dreams* are his own, though he does not usually acknowledge this.

In 1905 Freud published another book, *Three Essays on the Theory of Sexuality*, which received widespread rejection (partly because of the assertion about childhood sexuality, and its importance in child development and consequences for the adult). This book placed the human sexual instinct, or Eros, in a position of central importance in mental functioning. Freud published a great number of books throughout his life and was a prodigious letter writer. In 1920 he published another controversial book, *Beyond the Pleasure Principle,* in which he introduced the death instinct, or Thanatos, to explain human aggression and the senseless loss of life in the First World War of 1914–18. Freud's later writings, such as *Civilization and its Discontents* and *The Future of an Illusion* published in the late 1920s and early 1930s, looked at the relationship between individuals and the society in which they live, and the function of religion for the individual respectively. Freud was an atheist and attempted to explain religion and the need people have for religion purely in psychoanalytic terms.

Freud became famous throughout the world and was a controversial figure because of his theories and ideas. Freud had many ardent followers but also many who rejected his ideas and developed their own theories (for example, Junes, Adler and Erikson – see Chapter 4).

Freud developed cancer of the jaw in the early 1920s and, until his death in 1939, suffered greatly from this worsening condition. In all he had some 33 operations and wore a prosthesis in his mouth to fill in the area that had been taken away. At times Freud was in great pain over these 19 years, increasingly so towards the end of his life. Sigmund Freud died at 7 Maresfield Gardens, Hampstead, London, in September 1939.

3.3 INSTINCTS

For Freud, **instincts** are fundamental causes of behaviour and operate at a level beyond our awareness in the unconscious. Freud used the German word *Trieb,* which is commonly translated as instinct but concerns the ideas of a drive, impulse or motivating force operating at an unconscious level in each of us. Freud drew on the ideas of Charles Darwin and the evolution of the sexual instinct in both humans and other animals. Freud speculated on how the over-riding role of instincts, resulting in instinctive behaviour in the animal kingdom (especially in relation to sex), may affect human beings. In this sense, we can characterise Freud as a biologist of the mind.

3.3.1 The nature of instincts

Freud described instincts as having four aspects: a source, an aim, an object and an impetus. The **source** of an instinct is a physiological need (hunger, warmth, comfort, sex, for example). For example, in the adult, sexual instincts *should* according to Freud have their source in the genital zone of the body. The **aim** of the instinct is to satisfy the physiological need and hence reduce the tension or discomfort (hunger, thirst) caused. A distinction may be made between the ultimate aim being achieved and an intermediate aim. The former is where gratification of the need is met; the latter where a substitute or partial gratification is achieved. For example, pornographic material might fulfil an intermediate aim of the sex instinct but is unlikely to fulfil the ultimate aim.

The **object** of an instinct is the means by which the need is satisfied or reduced. For different people different objects may act to satisfy the same need. (For example, think about the huge variety of what can be eaten to satisfy hunger needs.) Finally, the **impetus** of an instinct represents the force or strength with which the instinct is consciously felt by a person. For example, you may feel mildly hungry or thirsty through to ravenously hungry or parched. The same idea applies to the sex instinct.

For Freud the source and aim of an instinct remain constant throughout a person's life. Note though that the strength with which a person may feel a psychological need may be biologically determined. This means a person may be born with a strong or weak sexual instinct or drive. The object and impetus of an instinct vary with changes in the self and the environment. For example, if you are starving hungry and all there is to eat is a hamburger this is most likely what you will eat! Your values and attitudes towards the production of food by farmers may lead you to eat only organic produce. In another way stimuli in the environment may increase or decrease the impetus of an instinct. For example, watching an extremely violent video may increase the impetus of the aggressive instinct.

Instincts, then, are biologically determined but vary according to the individual, his or her development and environmental factors. Table 3.1 summarises these four aspects of instincts.

Table 3.1 The four aspects of instincts suggested by Freud

Aspect	Description	Example
Source	Physiological or bodily need	Hunger, thirst
Aim	To satisfy the need and reduce tension caused	Reduce hunger or thirst
Object	The means by which the need is satisfied or reduced	Eating hamburgers
Impetus	The force of strength with which the instinct or need is felt	Mildly hungry to ravenously hungry

3.3.2 The sex instinct

The aim of the sexual instinct or **libido**, according to Freud, is to bring about pleasure through the reduction of sexual needs. This was the fundamental idea put forward in *Three Essays on the Theory of Sexuality* (Freud, 1905). Freud challenged the prevailing view that sexuality was absent in childhood and only becomes present in puberty. Freud also challenged the view that the aim is sexual union through sexual intercourse. In principle, sexual gratification may be achieved through a wide variety of means, some of which may include what we normally regard as sexual perversions. For example, somebody with a fetish may achieve gratification through engagement in that fetish. Scopophilia is a perversion in which a person is fixated at looking at the genitals of another person and receives sexual gratification as a result. Instead of being a stage towards sexual union, looking at the genitals of another becomes an end in itself.

More broadly, Freud talked about **erogenous zones** of the body; those Freud focused on were the mouth, anal and genital areas, and are of key importance because of a child's psychosexual development (see Section 3.7). However, Freud regarded the newborn infant as polymorphously sexually perverse, which means that any area of the body may become an erogenous zone. In normal development, it is the month, anus and genital areas that provide the greatest levels of pleasure/displeasure through feeding, expulsion of faeces and self-stimulation of the genitals (what Freud called childhood masturbation).

Freud's idea of the sex instinct is broader than that of pure sexual thoughts, feelings and behaviour. For both the child and the adult it is to do with pleasure and gratification more widely associated with a general, life-preserving instinct. Life-preserving instincts include hunger, thirst, comfort and sex, although notice that eating (or drinking) may serve to meet specific aims of both the hunger and sex instinct. Freud is often regarded as having been obsessed with sex; whilst this is one perception, it is an unfair characterisation. What Freud recognised was the importance of pleasure generally, and sexual feelings more specifically, in our lives.

Freud regarded all types of love (whether romantic, filial, friendship, love of humanity generally) as deriving from the sexual instinct. Romantic love is regarded as the normal object of the sexual instinct, whereas other types of love are where the normal object (romantic love) has been inhibited or deflected from the normal aim. The first love object of the child, usually the mother, is used as a model or **prototype**, albeit at an unconscious level, for the individual's choice of a romantic partner in adult life.

Self-love, or **narcissism**, is the normal state of the very young child. As the child develops, Freud characterised the process as giving up love of the self for love of other people. However, adolescents become preoccupied with their appearance, identity, etc. and this can be seen as a return of narcissism during this period of development.

3.3.3 The death instinct

Up until 1920 Freud held firm to his assertion that the life instinct, Eros or the libido, was the prime and sole determinant of human thought and behaviour. However, his publication of *Beyond the Pleasure Principle* set Thanatos, or the death instinct, alongside Eros, or the sexual instinct, and put each on an equal footing of importance.

Using the death instinct, Freud claimed that the object (aspect of an instinct) of 'all life is death'; the aim of the death instinct is to return life to its original state from whence it came. Many people rejected Freud's ideas; others used the death instinct as the starting point for their theorising (see, for example, the section on Melanie Klein, in Chapter 5). For Freud, this marked a radical development of his theories with the result that life and death instincts are competing and present in each of us. It is difficult to know what caused this change in Freud's thinking. Some biographers (Jones, 1953; Gay 1988), in part, attribute it to the horrors and senseless loss of life that took part in Europe during the First World War. It seems that Freud was at a loss to explain these events within a framework where only life-preserving instincts were present. The introduction of the death instinct with its consequential aggression and destructiveness of humans offered an acceptable explanation to Freud. It also offered an explanation that preserved the biological and unconscious foundations of human behaviour.

The introduction of the death instinct also allows a better understanding and explanation of **sadism** and **masochism**. Sadism is where a person obtains pleasure, often sexual, from inflicting or causing pain to another person. At the extreme it is a perversion; this happens when sexual pleasure comes solely from inflicting pain on another person. Masochism is where the individual experiences pleasure, often sexual, from inflicting pain and humiliation on the self. Both sadism and masochism show the sexual instinct and death instinct operating together.

3.3.4 Instincts and anxiety

We have seen that instincts (life or death) create in the individual, at an unconscious level, needs. These needs are based on bodily or physiological needs and, for Freud, become represented at a psychological level. At the psychological level an instinctual need becomes a wish. A wish that goes

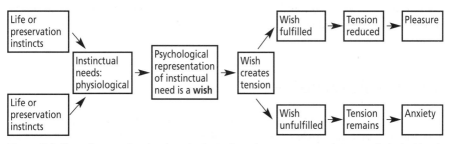

Figure 3.1 Flow diagram showing how instinctual needs are represented at a psychological level and may result in anxiety for the individual if not fulfilled

unfulfilled creates tension in an individual, if the wish is fulfilled the tension is released or reduced. It is this tension release that, for Freud, is pleasurable. Pleasure, then, is the absence of tension caused by the fulfilment of an instinct-created wish. On the other hand if the wish remains unfulfilled or even only partially fulfilled the tension remains and this results in **anxiety**. This is shown diagrammatically in Figure 3.1.

Anxiety is of central importance in Freudian theory and, as we shall see in what follows, explains the reason for having defence mechanisms (Section 3.6) and demonstrates the operation and function of the different personality structures – id, ego and superego (see Section 3.5).

3.4 LEVELS OF AWARENESS

We saw earlier in this chapter that Freud changed the way people thought about themselves by suggesting that human thought and behaviour may, at bottom, be based on irrational processes and that these processes are not normally accessible to conscious thought. The unconscious in Freudian theory (and therapy for that matter) is one of the fundamental aspects of human personality. In what follows we shall consider what Freud meant by the terms unconscious, preconscious and conscious in relation to mental processes. Before that, it might prove useful to give a historical context to the unconscious.

Freud did not invent or discover the unconscious, nor could he lay claim to being the first person to talk about unconscious mental processes (Ellenberger, 1970; Whyte, 1978). The basic idea that the human mind is made up of a part that is not normally accessible to conscious thought can be traced back over 3000 years to the Greeks. However, the importance of a distinction between conscious and unconscious thought became important as a result of the work of the philosopher Descartes in the seventeenth century. Descartes' famous phase, 'I think therefore I am' (*cogito ergo sum*), squarely places conscious thought as a defining feature of what it is to be human. As a result of this, awareness and conscious thought define what it is to be rational (and hence civilised and distinct from other animals). In contrast, the unconscious is seen as irrational and more akin to how animals other than humans behave.

The discovery of hypnosis, or animal magnetism as it was then called, by Mesmer in the eighteenth century was further evidence of a human unconscious. In the nineteenth century spiritualism was very popular across Europe and offered further support for the idea that people have a part of their mind that is unconscious.

Freud's great and original achievement was to bring together the ideas of biological instincts, the unconscious and child development into one integrated theory.

3.4.1 Unconscious, preconscious and conscious

For Freud the **unconscious** represented the greatest part of the mind, and contains instincts and drives that determine our conscious thoughts and behaviour. However, we are not aware of this. The unconscious also contains early childhood memories, often of traumatic events, which have been deliberately 'forgotten' or **repressed** (see Section 3.6).

How can you know you have an unconscious if you are not aware of it? This is a very fundamental question that has led many psychologists to reject Freudian theory. For Freud, evidence of the unconscious and what it may contain was obtained indirectly through, for example, slips of the tongue (so-called accidental behaviour) and through Freud's famous therapeutic technique of **free association** (see Section 3.10.1). Freud, then, inferred the contents of the unconscious from what people said and did. For example, suppose you broke a china ornament that was on a table top; you claim that the breakage was accidental. However, Freud did not believe in accidents for most of human behaviour. Freud might claim that the breaking of the china ornament was unconsciously motivated, and would ask about the significance of the ornament. You might, in answer to questioning, reveal that the ornament was a gift from your girlfriend or boyfriend and that you had recently had a row or argument. Freud might then interpret the breaking of the ornament as unconsciously deliberate because you were annoyed with the other person and wished to exact revenge because of the recent row.

The problem with this approach, as you can probably see, is that many interpretations for the breaking of the ornament are possible. How then do you decide which one is correct? Freud got round this by saying that human behaviour was *overdetermined*. By this he meant that more than one explanation exists for any one example of our behaviour. Most psychologists regard this, not surprisingly, as unsatisfactory since no objective assessment can be made. More generally, the very nature of unconscious thoughts and motives is not open to scientific investigation. At best an unconscious part of the mind can only be inferred and not directly observed. However, within Freudian theory the unconscious is central and its existence not questioned by Freud or other psychoanalytic psychologists.

Freud used the term **preconscious** to refer to thoughts and memories that we are not presently consciously thinking about but can readily bring to awareness. For example, until this moment you are probably not thinking about your home address; but now you can bring it to conscious thought. Many memories and thoughts, usually based upon our experiences, are lodged in the preconscious. Recall or recognition memory makes us aware of them. Such memories are those studied by experimental cognitive psychologists. However, some memories or thoughts in the preconscious result from unconscious; here memories are, according to Freud, censored or distorted or changed before being allowed into the preconscious. It is these such memories or thoughts that would interest Freud since analysis of them would yield indications about the unconscious.

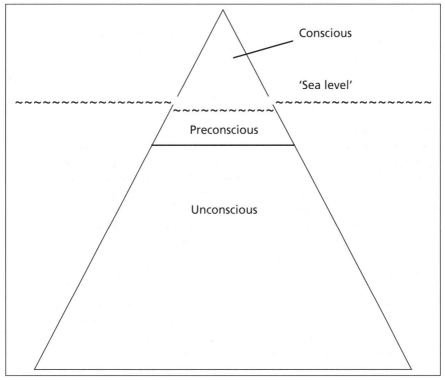

Figure 3.2 The mind as an iceberg: the triangle represents the iceberg and shows the unconscious as composing the largest part of the mind, and conscious the smallest

The conscious part of the mind, the here and now as it were, represents what we are actually aware of at any one time. The conscious part of the mind is aware of current sensations and perceptions but plays only a small, of vital, role in our mental processes. Freud likened the mind to an iceberg, and this is represented in Figure 3.2.

This figure shows that the greatest part of the mind is hidden, like an iceberg where the greater part is hidden to our view because it is submerged under water. The conscious part of the mind is the small part of the iceberg that can be seen above water.

3.5 PERSONALITY STRUCTURES: THE ID, EGO AND SUPEREGO

Freud continually developed and expanded his theories following the publication in 1895 of *Studies in Hysteria* with Joseph Breuer. It was not until 1923, with the publication of *The Ego and the Id*, that he created a structural model of the mind that also drew relationships between unconscious and conscious processes. The three structures, which he called the id, ego and superego, are not to be seen as physically existing in the brain but represent hypothetical constructs.

3.5.1 The id

The **id** is the original and oldest part of the personality. Freud regarded the newborn infant as consisting mentally of pure id. Because the id is the original system for an individual it contains the inherited psychological representation of the instincts. Hence, as shown in Figure 3.1 you can see that the id contains instinctual wishes, deriving from both life and death instincts. The id is the source of all mental energy and was characterised by Freud as a 'cauldron full of seething excitations' (Freud, 1933).

The id has no sense of reality, no comprehension of the passage of time, and does not operate in any logical or rational way. According to Freud (1933:74):

> The id of course knows no judgements of value: no good and evil, no morality. It even seems that the energy of these instinctual impulses is in a state different from the other regions of the mind, far more mobile and capable of discharge.

The id operates according to only one principle: to achieve immediate gratification or satisfaction of its wishes. This Freud called the **pleasure**

principle since the release of tension resulting from the fulfilment of a wish is felt as a pleasurable experience (see Figure 3.1). The id wants whatever brings satisfaction to a wish; anything that frustrates or blocks this is bad and raises tension levels.

The id, then, is the primary system of personality, has instinctual wishes demanding fulfilment and has no knowledge of reality. In effect, the id says 'I want, I want, I want and I want now!' The id knows no restraints or means of delaying gratification. As such, we can see the id as irrational and more akin to how animals other than humans operate. The id is an entirely unconscious part of our personality.

3.5.2 The ego

The individual would not be able to survive very long if the only part of its personality was the id, hence Freud proposed that the **ego** developed out of the id. The ego is responsible for the survival and continuation of the individual. To do this the ego must be in contact with reality to know and assess how the irrational and instinctual demand of the id can be met. Hence the id operates according to the **reality principle**. The ego is able to distinguish what is in the mind and what exists in reality in the external world. Since opportunities to gratify the demands of the id are not readily available in the external world the ego develops mechanisms to delay gratification of the id. These delaying tactics Freud called **defence mechanisms**, and we shall look at these in more detail in Section 3.6.

A developmental task for the young child is to develop a primitive ego to cope with and delay the demands of the id. A person, as an adult, possessing a strong ego (to be distinguished from the idea of egocentricity or a person being very self-centred) is able to control and manage the demands of the id.

For Freud the ego, as the executive of the personality, operates at all three levels of awareness – unconscious, preconscious and conscious.

3.5.3 The superego

The **superego** (or the 'above I', which is the literal translation from German) develops after the ego and is guided by moralistic and idealistic principles. The superego contains the values and ideals of the family and culture into which a person grows and develops. Like the id, the superego has no contact or understanding of reality and strives to ensure the person is always operating to the highest moral standards and perfection. The superego may be seen as containing two sub-systems within it: the **ego-ideal** and a person's **conscience**.

The ego-ideal is a hypothetical construct of what a person *should* be like. It is the ideal self that we may dream about or aspire to. But since the superego has no contact with or idea of reality the ego-ideal is unusually unrealistic and not achievable. Perhaps the strongest influences on the ego-ideal for Freud are the child's parents; this relates to the Oedipus complex (see Section 3.7.3). A person's conscience is the superego's way of rewarding and punishing; if you do something wrong (morally or fail to live up to your ego-ideal) punishment will follow by your conscience making you feel guilty.

The superego operates largely at an unconscious level but also at the preconscious and conscious levels of awareness. Since the superego is not in touch with reality it is again the ego that has to control and manage the demands of the superego. A person with a strong superego and a weak ego will be dominated by perpetual feelings of guilt due to never being good enough or able to achieve the perfection of the ego-ideal.

3.5.4 Interactions

The ego can be seen as the executive or manager of the personality. As such the ego has to manage the opposing demands of the id and the superego whilst all the time being in touch with reality. The id and superego make opposing demands since many of the instinctual needs of the id (for example, sexual gratification) would not be permitted by the superego's ego-ideal. If

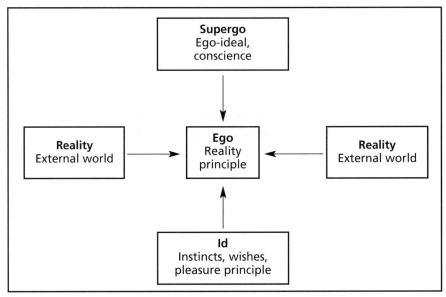

Figure 3.3 Representation of the opposing demands of the id and supergo on the ego; the ego must control these and take reality into account before making a response

instinctual needs are immediately gratified then the conscience will punish the person by making him or her feel guilty. Figure 3.3 represents the demands placed upon the ego, from this it can be seen that the ego is perpetually coping with competing demands and this is one reason why Freud's theory of personality is often referred to as a **conflict model** of personality.

From Figure 3.3 we can also see the likely effects of one of these structures of personality being dominant or strong within an individual. For example, a person with a weak ego will be overwhelmed by both id and superego demands. This is likely to result in inconsistent or unpredictable behaviour since at one point in time the ego will give in to the id and at another point the ego will give in to the superego. Alternatively, a person with an especially powerful and demanding superego (for Freud this would result from over-harsh parents) will experience high levels of guilt and a sense of failure because he or she can never live up to their ego-ideal.

A strong ego will be in command, as it is best able, of the opposing forces of the id and ego. Indeed Freud saw one of the primary and most important tasks of psychotherapy as helping a person develop a strong ego.

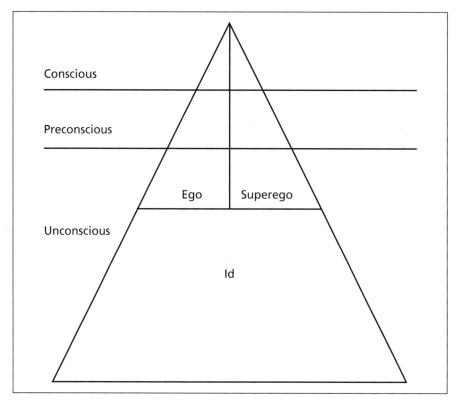

Figure 3.4 The levels of awareness (unconscious, preconscious and conscious) related to the three structures of personality (id, ego and superego)

In the previous section we looked at the three levels of awareness proposed by Freud – unconscious, preconscious and conscious. In this section we have seen that the id is entirely unconscious, and the ego and superego operate at all three levels of awareness. Figure 3.4 shows how the three levels of awareness relate to the three structures of personality.

3.6 REPRESSION AND OTHER DEFENCE MECHANISMS

In considering how the ego copes with the competing and unreasonable, and often irrational, demands of the id and the superego it was stated that one strategy was to delay or attempt to delay gratification of the id and the demands of the ego-ideal. Freud developed the concept of **defence mechanisms** in 1926, three years after the publication of *The Id and the Ego*. It was his daughter Anna who developed, refined and recategorised the functioning and types of defence mechanism (see Chapter 4). For Freud defence mechanisms, especially that of **repression**, came to play a greater and greater central role in his theories. Defence mechanisms are operated by the ego at a largely unconscious level. Broadly speaking, the defence mechanisms at the ego's disposal fall into three types: those that deny (repression being the prime example), those that falsify reality and those that distort reality. This is shown in Figure 3.5. In what follows we shall look at repression in some detail because of its central and fundamental importance in Freudian theory. We will then look briefly at other types of defence mechanism including

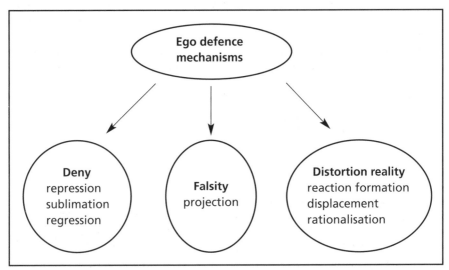

Figure 3.5 Three categories of defence mechanism are employed by the ego to delay id demands

reaction formation, displacement, projection, rationalisation, identification and sublimation.

3.6.1 Repression

The defence mechanism of **repression** is central and basic to Freudian theory. The ego represses id demands by not allowing them to be conscious. This is different from suppression, which may be characterised as the ego's conscious attempt to banish thoughts from conscious into the preconscious. Repression may be seen as unconscious, motivated forgetting. Look back to Figure 3.1. Here we see that an unfulfilled wish (the lower path) leaves tension and anxiety in the person. Anxiety levels may rise and rise as a result of the wish not being gratified or fulfilled. The ego employs defence mechanisms such as repression in order to reduce anxiety levels. By keeping a wish or need repressed in the unconscious, the ego avoids the displeasure of anxiety. Figure 3.6 modifies the lower path shown in Figure 3.1. However, repressing the wish does not mean it will go away. For Freud many of the important repressions occur in early childhood, especially at the time of the Oedipus complex (see Section 3.7.3) in a child's psychosexual development. Such wishes may never be fulfilled or gratified, may remain repressed and follow the person into adulthood. The ego has to expend mental energy to maintain repressions, this is energy that may prevent the ego responding properly to reality. If, at the extreme, all the ego's energy is taken up with maintaining repressions then the individual will be incapacitated and not able to deal with day-to-day living activities. In many ways repression is the cornerstone of Freudian theory.

Freud distinguished between two types of repression: primal repression and repression proper. Primal repression refers to the initial or first repression of

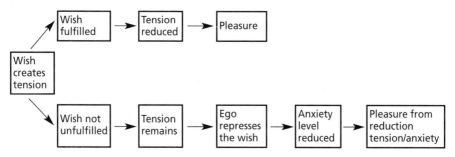

Figure 3.6 Modification of the lower path shown in Figure 3.1 where the ego employs the defence mechanism of repression to reduce tension and anxiety level (note that the reduction in anxiety is rewarding or pleasurable, thus reinforcing the repression to remain in place)

wishes and ideas that takes place in the first five to seven years of a child's life. Many of these result from the oral, anal and phallic stages of development, and the Oedipal complex (see Section 3.7.3). The consequence of primal repression is that the wish or need is fixated, or frozen, for the individual. This means that no further change can be made to what has been repressed. In effect, primal repressions stay with an individual for life and little can be done about them. Repression proper is where thoughts or wishes associated with primal repressions may enter the preconscious and potentially be brought to conscious awareness. However, the ego exerts repression proper to ensure that they do not reach consciousness. One of the tasks, then, of psychoanalytic therapy is to try to bring these types of repression to a person's consciousness. This allows two things: first, to help the person come to terms with his or her repressions and, second, to provide insight into the primal repressions. Repression proper is, in a sense, the psychoanalyst's entry into what has been repressed by the ego into the unconscious. For Freud repressions cannot be removed, but awareness of them may permit strengthening of the ego so that the ego can adjust and come to terms with them.

3.6.2 Repressive coping style

Freud's concept of repression has entered everyday language and we commonly refer to somebody as repressing an idea or having a repressive personality. According to recent research (Myers, 2000) between 10 and 20 per cent of the population may exhibit a repressive style of coping with life. A person with a repressive coping style is characterised as generally avoiding anxiety by avoiding negative experiences that may produce or raise levels of anxiety. In effect this means that such people avoid emotions. This is quite similar to the Freudian characterisation of repression. Weinberger (1990) developed a fourfold classification of coping styles, shown in Table 3.2. Repressors are people falling into the low anxiety and high defensiveness category. Weinberger (1990) details repressors as people who do not acknowledge their emotions and do their best to convince themselves that they do not experience negative emotions. Thus, for example, a repressive coping style in response to a bereavement of someone close would be to deny feelings of loss and grief. This may mean that the person does not deal properly with the bereavement, with the result that more mental energy is directed towards denial.

However, a repressive coping style can be seen in a person's behaviour. For example, Derakshan and Eysenck (1997) showed that repressors were more likely to exhibit higher facial anxiety, higher speech anxiety (stuttering), and less eye contact than non-repressors. Whilst a repressive coping style has

Table 3.2 The four categories according to level of anxiety and defensiveness; the repressive coping style is characterised by low anxiety and high defensiveness (after Weinberger, 1990)

		Level of anxiety	
		Low	High
Level of defensiveness	Low	Low anxiety Low defensiveness	High anxiety Low defensiveness
	High	**Repressive coping style** Low anxiety High defensiveness	High anxiety High defensiveness

shown people to be psychologically healthy, Myers (2000) has reviewed over 20 years of research and found that physical health may be at risk. For example, some evidence shows people with a repressive coping style to have high blood cholesterol and suffer more from cardiovascular disease (Myers, 2000).

This research on the repressive coping style does seem to provide support for Freud's concept of repression. Note, though, that whilst research claims psychological health for such people, Freud would not agree. Freud would probably claim that a repressive coping style was unhealthy in itself.

3.6.3 Other defence mechanisms

We have spent some time considering repression in detail because of its central importance in Freudian theory. The ego employs, according to Freud, many other defence mechanisms to cope with the demands placed upon it. Table 3.3 lists the most important, and offers a short description and an example of each. It is worth considering sublimation in a little more detail since all the other defence mechanisms only achieve partial success, whilst sublimation may be seen as a successful defence mechanism of the ego.

Sublimation is the redirection of threatening unconscious impulses, which may derive from id wishes, into socially acceptable behaviour. Hence, the more the ego uses sublimation the more successful it is likely to be at coping with all the demands placed upon it. An example may help to clarify this idea. Take aggressive id impulses resulting from the death or destructive instinct. One way to sublimate such impulses is to engage in an aggressive activity – this may be boxing or rugby where there is high-level physical contact. Another way would be to develop language and written skills where aggression is represented – for example, through writing horror stories or

Table 3.3 Examples of defence mechanisms used unconsciously by the ego

Defence mechanism	Description	Example
Reaction formation	Behaving in ways directly opposite to unconscious impulses, feelings.	Behaving in a friendly way to someone you dislike.
Displacement	Transferring impulses and feelings to an originally neural or innocent target.	Scapegoating where a social group is wrongly blamed, e.g. the Jews.
Projection	Attributing one's own unacceptable impulse or to another person.	Saying somebody else is frightened of the dark when, actually, you are.
Rationalisation	Also known as intellectualisation. Remove the emotional content of an idea or event by logical analysis.	Coping with the death of someone close to you by intellectual analysis.
Identification	Behaving in a similar way to someone you regard as a role model.	Son imitating father in the garden with toy wheelbarrow.
Sublimation	Redirection of threatening impulses to something socially acceptable.	Use of aggressive impulses in a sport such as boxing.

crime novels. Freud regarded the sublimation of the sex instinct into work as one of the major achievements of individuals, resulting in modern, civilised societies.

Sublimation as a defence mechanism of the ego is successful because the id is allowed expression of instinctual needs and wishes. Also the ego does not have to tie up mental energy in maintaining repressions or using other defence mechanisms.

All the defence mechanisms shown in Table 3.3 help a strong ego to keep anxiety levels low and cope with the competing demands of the id, superego and reality. However, sublimation apart, overuse of defence mechanisms by a person will tie up too much mental energy and prevent the person coping with the daily demands of life.

3.7 PSYCHOSEXUAL DEVELOPMENT AND PERSONALITY TYPES

One of Freud's lasting contributions to the psychology of child and lifespan development was to highlight and emphasise the importance of early childhood (up to five to seven years of age) to the adult personality. Whilst many developmental psychologists fundamentally disagree with Freud's claims about psychosexual development, what is not now at issue is that early experiences are of critical importance. Because of the life instincts, particularly the sexual instinct, Freud focused on the erogenous zones of the mouth, anus and genitals as strong sources of instinctual needs and wishes in the child. Not only do these parts of the body change, according to Freud, in terms of being sources of pleasure/displeasure for the infant, they also represent **prototypes**. For Freud, prototypes in relation to the oral, anal and phallic stages of psychosexual development represent the original mode of adjustment to situations that will confront the adult throughout his or her life. Freud saw the trauma of birth for the baby as the prototype of all anxiety feelings later in life. Extreme anxiety causes feelings of being totally out of control, and this is how Freud thought of the baby at birth when flooded with stimuli from the external world.

The oral, anal and phallic psychosexual stages also have personality types for the adult associated with each.

3.7.1 The oral stage

The **oral stage** starts immediately after birth because the mouth is the first area, or erogenous zone, of the body to be associated with pleasure for the baby. Clearly this has to operate at an unconscious level and, for Freud, in the absence of any kind of ego. Hence, feelings of hunger derive directly from the id and because an ego, even in a primitive form, does not exist the baby requires immediate gratification to reduce feelings of anxiety. The breast (or bottle) becomes the first object of sexual desire for the baby since feeding through sucking the nipple reduces hunger and is thus experienced as pleasurable. For Freud this represents the first and earliest emotional tie to the external world, and remains in memory as the first love object for the baby. The mother consequently becomes the prototype of all love relationships in the teenager and adult. The experience of feeding at the breast (or bottle), if largely pleasurable, will result in an expectation in the adult of loving relationships being smooth. On the other hand if feeding at the breast is frustrating and associated with displeasure the adult might expect loving relationships to be difficult to sustain.

In the early days of breast feeding the baby typically falls asleep, satiated, at the breast. For Freud this meant that the baby does not care for the love object once gratified. If this is not outgrown the adult may love somebody only as long as he or she can exploit them for pleasure and reward. Such a person is unlikely to be able to sustain a loving relationship.

Abraham (1927) characterised the oral stage as being composed of first the oral passive and then the oral aggressive sub-stages. The oral passive stage occurs during the first few months of life and is characterised by the baby being oral dependent, gaining pleasure from sucking at the breast. The oral aggressive stage starts as the baby begins teething. Here the baby comes to realise that the breast is not part of the self and not always available when the baby wishes it to be. Frustration at this and at wishes (hunger) not being fulfilled leads to oral gratification being achieved at times through aggressive acts such as biting or grabbing the breast.

3.7.2 The anal stage

The **anal stage** typically occurs during the second year of a baby's life as it gains control of the anal muscles during potty training. As the baby gains control of the anal muscles it learns that it is able to retain or excrete faeces voluntarily. For Freud the young child is seen as gaining pleasure from excretion, but also gaining pleasure from retaining faeces since the membranes of the anus become stimulated. How a child is potty trained and the response of the child to such training is seen to have significant consequences in later life. This is because the parents, when trying to potty train the child, are external authority figures. Potty training during the anal stage of development is the prototype for how the teenager and adult will respond to authority figures in the future.

Abraham (1927) regarded this stage as also falling into two sub-stages: the anal expulsive and anal retentive. In the first stage, the anal expulsive, the young child is seen as not caring for the parents and enjoying expulsion – hence not responding to potty training. In the anal retentive stage the child regards its faeces as a possession to be parted with out of love for the parents. Performing on the potty for the parents then means that defecation is a 'gift' from the child to the parents. The prototype here is giving something of oneself to another whom you love.

Towards the end of the anal stage retention pleasure outweighs elimination pleasure and the child is able to defecate as appropriate.

3.7.3 The phallic stage and Oedipus complex

The **phallic stage** occurs between the ages of three to six years. It is unfortunate that Freud named the stage in relation to the male penis rather than a name that would cover both sexes. At this stage the erogenous zone that achieves primacy shifts from the anus to the genital areas. Specifically the penis in boys and the clitoris in girls. During this stage boys and girls discover that playing with their genitals is pleasurable. Because the superego is yet to develop (it develops as a result of the Oedipus complex, according to Freud) children in this stage are not inhibited from playing with their genitals in front of other people. Adults may find this embarrassing but young children seem to find this good fun! Freud called this childhood masturbation. The most important aspect of the phallic stage is the **Oedipus complex.**

The Oedipus complex, as applied to both males and females, is one of Freud's most controversial ideas, and one that most people find hard to understand and accept.

In the young male the Oedipus complex, or more correctly conflict, arises because the boy develops sexual desires for his mother. Basically, he wants to possess his mother (not have sexual intercourse). However, the boy thinks that his father will discover these thoughts and if this happens fears losing the thing he most loves. In the phallic stage this is the boy's penis. Hence, as a result of his sexual desires for his mother, and fear of discovery by the father the boy develops castration anxiety. This is the Oedipal conflict. To make matters worse for the young boy, Freud claims that he is aware that a girl has no penis. The boy thinks the girl has been castrated and this may happen to him as well!

To cope with the Oedipal conflict the boy represses his desires for his mother and, as a reaction formation, identifies with his father. The consequence of this is that the boy takes on the gender role of the male, and adopts values and an ego ideal that becomes the superego. Note that the resolution of the Oedipal conflict is to *repress* desires, not get rid of them altogether.

For the young female matters are more complicated. The young girl desires the father, but realises that she does not have a penis. This leads to the development of penis envy and the wish to be a boy. The young girl resolves this by repressing the desire for the father and substitutes the wish for a penis for a wish to have a baby. Unconsciously, the girl desires a baby by her father since this would satisfy her repressed wish for a penis. Additionally, the girl blames her mother for having no penis and becomes hostile to her because of this. However, all this is repressed and the girl identifies with her mother. Thus the girl takes on the female gender role.

The Oedipus (or Electra complex as it is sometimes called) is less than satisfactory for the girl and critics of Freud have regarded this as patriarchal and sexist (Mitchell, 1974). Perhaps Freud used the term phallic stage because it was based for both boys and girls on the penis – castration anxiety in boys and penis envy in girls. Table 3.4 summarises the Oedipus complex.

Table 3.4 The unfolding of the Oedipus (and Electra) complex for the young boy and young girl during the phallic stage of psychosexual development

Male Oedipus complex	Female Oedipus (Electra) complex
• Sexual desire for the mother, fear of hostility from the father discovers these desires.	• Sexual desire for the father, realisation she does not have a penis.
• Leads to anxiety that boy will lose his penis as punishment from the father. Castration anxiety.	• Leads to penis envy, baby seen as a substitue for a penis. Wants baby by father.
• Represses desire for mother, castration anxiety reduced as a consequence.	• Represses desire for father and wish to have a baby by the father.
• Identifies with the father and takes on male gender role.	• Identifies with the mother and takes on female gender role.
• Superego develops to replace Oedipus complex.	• Weak superego develops to replace the Oedipus (Electra) complex.

3.7.4 Latency period and genital stage

Following the phallic stage the child enters a latency period through to the onset of puberty. During this period Freud assumed that the ego repressed the sexual instinct. This is reinforced by the suppression of sexual matters by parents and teachers. With puberty and the onset of maturation processes through male and female hormones comes the genital stage. Here sexual desires are reawakened and sexual energy is normally directed to the opposite sex. For Freud the aim of the sexual instinct changes from auto-eroticism (stimulation of the erogenous zones) to that of reproduction.

Freud is quite prescriptive in that he regarded the normal outlet for the sexual instinct and desires to be somebody of the opposite sex and achieved through genital sexual intercourse. Clearly all people do not develop like this, with some becoming gay or lesbian, others engaging in anal intercourse or oral sex. Freud does attempt to explain such 'perversions' in his later writings.

The psychosexual stages of development we have considered are summarised in Table 3.5.

3.7.5 Personality types

Transition through each of these stages of development is not always, nor perhaps usually, smooth for the child. At each stage **fixation** may occur. This happens when the libido or sexual instinct fixates on a particular erogenous zone. Hence the common saying that a person has an 'oral fixation' or 'anal

Table 3.5 Summary of Freud's psychosexual stages of development

Psychosexual stage	Age	Erogenous zone	Description
Oral	birth to 1 year	Mouth	Child gains pleasure through the mouth. Mother is first love object. Two sub-stages of oral passive and oral aggressive.
Anal	18 months to 2½ years	Anus	Pleasure from controlling bowels, satisfaction from both retention and elimination. Two sub-stages of anal explusive and anal retentive.
Phallic	3 to 6 years	Genitals	Penis for the boy, clitoris for the girl, give pleasure from self-stimulation (masturbation). Oedipus conflict for boy results in castration anxiety and, for girl, penis envy. Resolved by identification with same-sex parent.
Latent	6 years to puberty	None	Repression of sexual desires and needs. Child spends time learning values of family and culture.
Genital	Puberty to adulthood	Genitals	Heterosexual sex is the norm. Genitals primary in sexual desire, object is opposite-sex person and reproduction.

fixation'. When this happens in the anal stage, for example, the pleasure from retention and expulsion stays with the individual into adulthood. Whilst the developing child will pass through each of Freud's psychosexual stages, fixations at one or more of the stages may occur along the way.

Regression is where an older child, teenager or adult, when faced with a traumatic or stressful situation, regresses or returns to one of the psychosexual stages. For example, an older child who finds school unpleasant may regress to the oral stage by sucking his or her thumb. Where a child has developed a fixation at a stage regression back to that stage is the most likely response to traumatic or unpleasant experiences. Regression offers comfort and pleasure associated with the stage when actually in it as a child.

When fixation occurs at a particular stage there may be a wide-ranging effect on the older child/adult and a **personality type** may be present. This may result in an oral personality, anal personality or phallic personality.

Fixation at the oral stage leads to an oral personality. The main characteristics of oral types are that they are selfish, takers, hungry and aggressive. If oral stimulation as a child was plentiful oral types will be overdependent on others, but optimistic. If oral stimulation was insufficient they will be depressive. The anal personality results from fixation at the anal stage and occurs from conflicts resulting from potty training. The anal type has three related characteristics: orderliness, parsimony or miserliness, and obstinacy. Considerable research has been devoted to the anal personality, and has shown that these three traits do occur together in a person. Whether or not they occur as Freud explains it is another matter.

3.8 FREUD'S THEORY OF DREAMS

Now we have an understanding of levels of awareness, personality structures, the ego's mechanisms of defence and psychosexual stages of development we can see how they all come together in Freud's theory of dreams, and how dreams, are to be interpreted.

In 1900, in his book *The Interpretation of Dreams*, Freud stated that: 'The interpretation of dreams is the royal road to a knowledge of the unconscious mind.' Freud regarded all dreams as wish fulfilments, with the wishes coming from the id's instinctual needs. Hence if the dream could be interpreted the unconscious id wishes could be revealed.

Freud distinguished between the latent content and manifest content of a dream. The manifest content is the material that you actually remember upon waking up. The latent content is the hidden, true meaning of the dream. The manifest content often appears silly or meaningless to us because the ego has censored and distorted the latent content. The ego does this to prevent repressions of wishes and desires from the id becoming conscious. The translation or censorship of the dream by the ego Freud called the **dream work**. In the dream work the ego uses mechanisms such as displacement (displacing the true object or idea of the dream on to another one acceptable to consciousness) and condensation (combining two people in real life into just one person in the dream). The ego also uses **secondary revision** to censor the first recollection of a dream that you may have on waking. In terms of interpreting a dream, write down all you can recall about a dream on wakening, then (without reference to what you have written down) write what you can recall three hours later. Then compare the two accounts, what is missing from the second account has been censored out of the first account by the ego. Omissions are a good guide to latent content.

What triggers a dream in the first place? Freud stated that a dream is triggered by some significant event of the preceding day. This may seem trivial at the time but somehow reawakens a repressed childhood memory. The repressed childhood memories are mostly around the psychosexual stages of development, and the Oedipus complex in particular. For Freud the primary reason for interpreting dreams was to understand and uncover the repressions that took place during childhood during the psychosexual stages of development. Freud's theory of dreams is summarised in Figure 3.7.

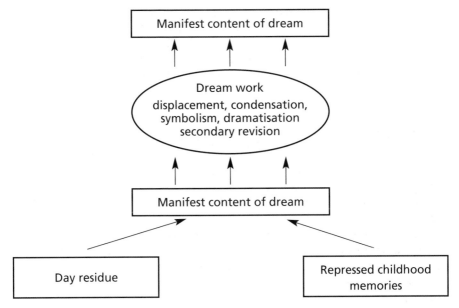

Figure 3.7 Summary of Freud's theory of dreams (Freud, 1900/1976)

An account of Freud's approach to the interpretation of dreams would not be complete without some consideration of symbolism in dreams. The basic maxim that 'if it's longer than it's wide' it must be a phallic symbol, and if you dream of entering a room, for example, it is a vaginal symbol, may generally hold. However, Freud did not claim that there were universal symbols applicable to all people. For Freud a dream had to be interpreted specifically in relation to the person who had the dream and that person's unique life experiences.

One of Freud's case studies, Dora, involved Freud in interpreting two of Dora's dreams. In one of these Dora dreams she is at home and the house is on fire, she has to get out in case she is burnt but is concerned to make sure that she takes her jewel case as well. When Dora is outside the house and safe she wakes up. Freud offers a number of interpretations. For example, dreaming of a fire is symbolic of the love she has for a number of people in her life – her mother, father and a woman who is a close friend of the family. Notice here that one aspect of the dream, the fire, is seen to represent a number of related themes. The jewel case Freud interprets as Dora, who is a young woman, wanting to keep her virginity and concerned not to lose it to the wrong person. The smoke associated with the fire Freud relates to the older men in her life – her father, Freud himself and a man who has made advances to her – because they all smoke cigars. Dora, in Freud's account, is resistant to these interpretations and Freud takes this as a sign of the ego using the defence mechanism of denial.

Freud's theory of dreams does show how all the different elements we have considered so far in this chapter come together. The theory is rich and elegant, however, whether we need to go to these lengths and this level of complexity to understand dreams is debatable. Some psychologists regard dreams as meaningless, brought about by random neural activity when we are asleep.

3.9 FREUD'S CASE STUDIES

Freud's collected works run to 25 volumes (this excludes letters he wrote to friends and colleagues, which also dwelt on psychoanalytic ideas and concepts). In his collected works Freud makes reference to 133 different cases, yet only six are written up in any detail (seven if you include Freud's study of himself in *The Interpretation of Dreams*). The six case studies written up in detail are also a curious mixture. One, 'Judge Schrieber', Freud conducted using an autobiography, since Judge Schrieber had been dead for many years. This was a case of paranoia. The famous 'Little Hans' case study was conducted using Little Han's father as a go-between. On only one occasion did Freud actually meet face to face with Little Hans. Little Hans was five years old at the time and was frightened of white horses with black mouths. He was also obsessed with playing with his penis (widdler) and, to the annoyance of his parents, frequently did this in the presence of other people. Freud analysed and interpreted all this in relation to the Oedipal conflict he thought Little Hans would be going through at that age.

The 'Rat Man' and 'Wolf Man' case studies were so called because of the dreams these men had, and concerned an obsessional neurosis and an infantile neurosis respectively. The 'Female Homosexuality' case study was about an 18-year-old that Freud saw only briefly. Finally, the 'Dora' case study was about an unhappy young woman of 18. We shall look at this case study in a little more detail.

In all, then, the six case studies written up in some detail by Freud are an odd mix. We have to ask why he chose to write up these particular cases? This is an issue we shall come back to after looking at the Dora case in a little more detail.

3.9.1 Dora

The Dora case study was conducted over an 11-week period at the end of which Dora decided to cease therapy with Freud. Dora was an 18-year-old woman who had been referred to Freud by her father. The referral occurred after Dora's father had found a suicide note. Dora's symptoms included depression, aphonia (loss of speech at times), persistent coughing fits and suicidal feelings. Dora's father claimed that Dora's symptoms could be traced back to an incident when she was 16 years of age. This occurred when Dora and her family were on holiday in the Alps with another family, the Ks, with whom they were close friends. Dora accused Herr K of making sexual advances when she was out alone with him on a lakeside walk. Dora said that she slapped Herr Ks face and fled. Since then Dora had pleaded with her father to break relationships with the K's. Herr K denied the incident and Dora's father thought she had made it up, believing Herr Ks version of events.

Dora claimed that another sexual advance was made by Herr K two years later, and this seemed to precipitate the suicide note. Matters were quite complicated, however, since Dora's father was having an affair with Frau K. Dora's mother was characterised as an obsessive-compulsive housewife whom Dora despised. Dora felt that in order to appease her father's guilt about the affair with Frau K she had somehow been 'given' to Herr K in exchange for the hurt her father was causing him. In other ways also the two families were closely intertwined.

Freud was very forceful in his interpretations to Dora, and overinterpreted, forcing conclusions that Dora could not accept. For example, that her rejection and feelings of disgust towards Herr K are a reaction formation where Freud tells Dora that she is really in love with him and desires his sexual advances. Freud also provides interpretations about Dora's incestuous (Oedipal) love for her father, and a lesbian love for Frau K as well. To top it all Freud also says that Dora is in love with him! Freud interprets the various symptoms that Dora presents as evidence of her sexual desires.

Dora was unable to accept, and perhaps even understand, what Freud was saying. Remember this was a famous man forcing interpretations on an 18-year-old. Dora breaks off the analysis with Freud, and for rest of her life rejected anything to do with psychoanalysis. You may think this not surprising!

3.9.2 Freud's use of case studies

A common criticism of Freud's case studies is that their findings cannot be generalised and that, therefore, it is invalid to apply Freudian concepts to all people. A further criticism is that since Freud did not keep notes at the time he was seeing his clients the written accounts may not be accurate. More than this, the accounts may be biased and reflect only what Freud wished to remember. Certainly, Freud only wrote notes about his cases in the evening and not at the time. Another, incorrect, criticism is that he based his theories on middle-class, neurotic, Victorian women. The six detailed case studies refute this criticism, and in the total of 133 cases he refers to there is not a preponderance of such women.

So what are we to make of Freud's detailed case studies? Recent biographies of Freud (such as Gay, 1988) and accounts of the history of psychoanalysis provide two main answers to this question. First, that Freud used case studies to highlight, exemplify and clarify his theories, concepts and ideas. The case studies were not written with the intention of trying to prove his theories, but to make them more immediate and to set them in a human context. Second, you will find if you actually read one or two of them, they actually tell a good story. Freud had an excellent command of German language, and may have used case studies as a means of attracting greater interest in his theories from a much wider audience, including the general public. Whilst some of his theoretical writings are difficult and complicated at times, his case studies, although very detailed are highly readable and comprehensible to lay audiences.

3.10 PSYCHOANALYSIS AS THERAPY

With the theoretical advances that Freud made it is easy to forget that psychoanalysis was developed as a therapy to treat people. Early on, Freud found that his approach was more suited to treating neurotic (anxiety) disorders rather than psychotic disorders such as schizophrenia. The key means by which therapy was conducted revolved around free association, dream analysis, and the analysis of transference and countertransference. We have already considered dream analysis in some detail, so will look at the other elements in what follows.

3.10.1 Free association

The technique of free association requires the person to verbalise all thoughts in consciousness, no matter how trivial, silly or embarrassing they may seem to the person. The idea behind free association is that insights into the unconscious and repressions may be gained. The ego acts as a censor between what we think and what we say. Freud thought that verbalising all conscious thoughts was a way round the censorship of the ego, and hence gave access to the id's instinctual desires and wishes. Dreams, as we have seen, were regarded by Freud as the 'royal road' to the unconscious. Free association to parts of a dream is a commonly used technique.

To be successful at free association is not easy, and some people have great trouble doing it properly. This is because the ego is all the time trying to prevent access to the unconscious. This is shown where somebody is unable to provide any verbalisations of thoughts or where too much verbalisation takes place, thus acting as a smokescreen. In both cases Freud would say the ego is showing resistance and attempts to be in control at all times. Nevertheless, psychoanalytic therapy requires the person to free associate as best as he or she can – practice does show improvement over time.

3.10.2 Transference

One of the first case studies published was in the jointly written book *Studies in Hysteria* by Breuer and Freud. In this book is reported the case study of Anna O, who was a patient of Breuer. Anna O was a young woman whom Breuer treated with hypnosis. Breuer broke off the analysis because he felt that Anna O was becoming too demanding of him and his time. Freud recognised that Anna O had 'fallen in love' with Breuer, and whilst Breuer had run away from this, Freud thought this should be analysed in its own right. The term **transference** is used to describe the strong feelings of love (and hate) that the client or patient feels for the analyst. Freud recognised that the psychotherapist occupies, in a sense, a parental role. Analysis of the transference of the client to the therapist should, therefore, reveal how the person approaches and deals with other close relationships in his or her life. Additionally, and most importantly, the nature of the transference should reveal relationships with both parents during the childhood Oedipal conflict, thus leading to key repressions that are made by the child to escape from the Oedipal conflict.

For Freud, analysis of the transference relationship of the client to the therapist assumed greater and greater significance. Transference can be both positive and negative.

3.10.3 Countertransference

In strict Freudian psychoanalysis there are five sessions a week over a number of years. With free association you would reveal your innermost thoughts to the therapist, probably revealing things you would not to any other person. It is not surprising that a transference develops. On the other side the therapist is listening and interacting with the client, and develops feelings and attitudes as a consequence. The feelings of the psychoanalyst towards the client are called the **countertransference**. The countertransference is not analysed with the client, although the client may wish this. However, the psychoanalyst must analyse the countertransference, usually with another psychoanalyst. This is because the psychoanalyst wants to do his or her best to be neutral and not to treat the client in a biased way because of how he or she feels. For example, suppose as the analyst you come to dislike your client. This cannot be shown, but has to be dealt with.

3.10.4 Effectiveness of psychoanalytic therapy

Freud, in his early writings, thought psychoanalytic therapy could cure people of their neuroses and remove the underlying repressions. Later in his life he changed this view and regarded therapy as a means of strengthening the ego and helping the person to adjust to the ups and downs of life.

Hans Eysenck, who was a long-standing critic of Freud, as long ago as 1952 reported research showing that psychoanalytic therapy had a lower success rate than other therapies (behavioural, drugs) or spontaneous remission (where the person gets better without help). Smith and Glass (1977) conducted an analysis of a large number of studies on the effectiveness of psychoanalysis and found little evidence that it was any more successful than other therapies (in fact it was slightly less successful, but not by much).

Scientific study of psychoanalysis as a treatment is problematic. Therapy usually lasts between two and five years, and it is often found that the client gets worse in the first year. Also, if it is not intended to cure anything but to strengthen the person's ego, how is this to be measured? Psychoanalysis remains a popular therapy for those who can pay for five sessions a week over a number of years and can find the time!

3.11 EVALUATION OF FREUD

Whatever you think of Freud's theories, concepts and ideas he has been enormously influential for the development of psychology. Psychoanalytically oriented theorists, as we shall see in the next chapter, disagreed with much of what Freud said and developed their own ideas. The Behaviourists (such as Watson and Skinner – see Chapter 7) reacted against the subjective nature of psychoanalysis and the focus on inner mental processes. The Behaviourists wanted to be able to observe, measure and predict human behaviour by using objective methods of investigation. However, Freud occupies an important place in personality psychology because he was the first psychologist to produce a comprehensive theory about human thought and behaviour. Also, he was the first to develop a systematic psychotherapy for the treatment of people suffering from mental disorders. Finally, Freud popularised psychology and made it accessible to all who were interested (before Freud, much of the written material on human sexual behaviour had been in Latin and only accessible to scholars).

3.11.1 View of humanity

Freud's theory of personality structure and the ego's use of defence mechanisms paints a negative and conflict-ridden picture of the human condition. The ego is constantly battling with the demands of the id and superego, and trying to manage these in relation to the opportunities and demands of reality. In a sense the mind is constantly at war with itself, with the ego constantly trying to win battles but always unable to win the war. In Freudian theory pleasure is the absence or reduction of tension *not* the presence of something. The ideal state of the human mind is all wishes gratified and anxiety absent. This is never achieved except at death. Even in our sleep, when the ego relaxes its control, unfulfilled and repressed wishes in the id manifest themselves and determine the hidden meanings of our dreams.

Freud's theories also lead us to view human thoughts and behaviour as deterministic. This is because most of what we think and do is determined by past events, largely resulting from childhood. Not only this, these past childhood events are mostly repressed into our unconscious – consequently we have little or no knowledge of them either.

Finally, because the id is the source of all psychic energy, and governed by irrational and illogical forces operating according to the pleasure principle, humans may be seen as only a small step up from other animals. People can be hugely destructive – as evidenced by wars, murders and general anti-social behaviour.

The one bright spot in all this negativity and pessimism is Freud's idea of the ego's defence mechanism of sublimation. The transformation of sexual energy into work has resulted in civilisation, great works of art and the advancement of science.

3.11.2 Scientific status and evidence

At the time Freud was developing his theories he regarded himself as a scientist and claimed that psychoanalysis was a science. However, in the light of modern conceptions of science this is highly questionable. Popper's (1968) influential view is that for a theory to be regarded as scientific it must, even if only in principle, be capable of being refuted. By this is meant that the theory must be able to generate hypotheses that are refutable. Now this is a problem for psychoanalysis. For example, take the Oedipal complex and Freud's claim that the love of the boy for the mother and hatred of the father are repressed into the unconscious. What testable hypothesis capable of refutation may be derived from this? One hypothesis may be that as a result of the repressed desires for the mother the male will seek someone to love who is similar to his mother. Personality assessments and physical features of the mother could be made and compared to the woman the male loves. Similarities could be determined and the hypothesis upheld. But what would refute the hypothesis? If the woman was exactly the opposite to the mother? In this case Freud might bring in the defence mechanism of reaction formation and say that the reason the male has chosen someone so different from his mother is because this protects him from becoming aware of his Oedipal desires for his mother. Either way, Freudian theory can offer a seemingly plausible explanation. This basic problem of Freudian theory explaining events either way is common for whichever concept or idea you look at. Partly for this reason Popper and many others (e.g. Eysenck, 1985b) regard psychoanalytic theory as a pseudo-science at best.

Many psychologists have attempted to investigate experimentally some of Freud's claims (Westen, 1990, provides a review of much of this research). Many concepts and ideas have received empirical support – for example, the oral and anal personalities (Kline, 1972), the repressive coping style (Myers, 2000), perceptual defence (Bruner and Postman, 1947) – however, what is in question is whether all the cumbersome theory of unconscious repressions, the Oedipus complex, is needed to explain such findings.

Hall and van de Castle (1963) studied the content of over 900 dreams to see if sex differences in symbols was present. They hypothesised that male dreams should demonstrate castration anxiety and female dreams penis envy. They developed a coding system for the content of the dreams (for example, in men loss of part of the body, symbolic of castration; and in women standing by a lamp-post, symbolic of acquiring a penis). Coders were used and showed good levels of agreement. Generally it was found that male dreams related more to castration anxiety rather than penis envy, and the reverse for females. But to take the next step and say this results from the Oedipus complex would not be justified by such research.

Space constraints prevent more examples of research being given here, but most follow this general pattern. That is, some support is found for some of Freud's claims but the underlying Freudian explanation is not capable of scientific enquiry because it is not refutable, and hence not scientific.

3.11.3 Personality assessment

Freud did not produce any formal methods for measuring different personality types or for understanding the personality in more depth. Other followers of the psychoanalytic approach did however, the most commonly used and referred to are the Rorschach Inkblot test, the Thematic Apperception Test (TAT) and the Blackie test. These are also examples of projective tests (see Chapter 2) and draw upon the idea of free association. Ambiguous pictures of people, ink blots or, as in the case of the Blackie test (Blum, 1968), white and black dogs are presented and the person, upon seeing the picture, is asked what he or she sees or to make up a story. One example of a card used in the Blackie test is shown in Figure 3.8. This shows a dog, Blackie, holding a collar in its mouth with the word 'MAMA' written on it. This picture is designed to relate to the Oedipal conflict. Try to make up a story, or get a friend to, about the picture on the card, then provide a Freudian interpretation.

Cranner (1991) conducted a full review of psychometric tests measuring defence mechanisms. Such tests include scales on the widely used Minnesota Multiphasic Personality Inventory and the California Psychological Inventory. More specialised self-report-type tests have also been developed – for example, the Defence Style Questionnaire (Bond *et al.* 1983) and the Defence Mechanism Inventory (Gleser and Ihilevich, 1969).

Figure 3.8 Example of a stimulus card from the Blackie test

3.11.4 Applications

Freudian theory has enjoyed widespread application; we have already seen this with respect to dream analysis and psychotherapy. Application has also been made to anthropology, history and interpreting fiction. Freud made application to understanding human mistakes – such as slips of the tongue, incorrectly hearing what another person has said, misplacing objects, forgetting and accidents. All these he called paraproxes or, as is used in common language, Freudian slips. Freud believed that all human behaviour, even the most trivial or seemingly accidental, has an unconscious cause. Indeed Freud regarded human behaviour as overdetermined, this means that one behaviour is capable of a number of causal explanations. Paraproxes or

Freudian slips can be likened to dreams in that there is serious unconscious content and that somehow the ego's defence mechanisms have allowed the Freudian slip to occur. Freud claimed that, because people often strongly derive an unconscious meaning from the mistake, this meant there was such a meaning. One of Freud's most popular books with the general public was his *Psychopathology of Everyday Life*, published in 1901.

Interpretation and analysis by people who have not been trained may be a dangerous pastime. However, because many Freudian terms have entered common language, informal analysis happens all the time. We use words such as unconscious, defence, denial, projection, in many social contexts when trying to explain our own or another person's behaviour. A friend may deny an assertion, or we may deny to another having certain thoughts that we actually did have. It is a tribute to Freud that many of his ideas and concepts have been adopted in common speech – even if they are not usually used in the way Freud would have liked!

3.12 SUMMARY

- Freud is an important figure in personality psychology; his theories, concepts and psychoanalytic therapy have had an enormous and lasting influence on psychology and psychiatry.
- Instincts are fundamental causes of behaviour. Instincts have a source, aim, object and impetus. Freud proposed two main instincts: the sex (or life) instinct and the death instinct. Instincts create unconscious wishes which, if unfulfilled, may cause a person to feel anxiety.
- Freud proposed three levels of awareness: the unconscious, conscious and preconscious. The unconscious represents the largest part of the mind, and contains instincts and drives. The preconscious refers to thoughts and memories that can be brought to consciousness. The conscious part of the mind is what we are actually aware of at any time.
- Freud proposed three personality structures: the id, ego and superego. The id, the original system, is unconscious and contains instincts. The id operates according to the pleasure principle. The ego operates according to the reality principle and uses defence mechanisms to cope with the demands of the id and superego. The superego contains two sub-systems: the ego-ideal and conscience. The superego attempts to deal with the conflicting demands of the id and ego, and is in touch with reality.
- The ego employs defence mechanisms, of which repression is of key importance. Repression is unconscious-motivated forgetting of disturbing thoughts. Defence mechanisms fall into three broad categories: those that deny, those that falsify, and those that distort reality. Other defence mechanisms include sublimation.

- Freud characterised psychosexual development through a series of stages: oral stage, anal stage, phallic stage, latent stage and genital stage. The most important aspect of the phallic stage is the Oedipus complex. Successful resolution of the Oedipal conflict results in appropriate gender identity.
- Dreams, for Freud, provide insight into the unconscious. All dreams in the end, for Freud, can be traced back to id wishes and childhood repressions. Freud distinguished between the latent and manifest content of a dream. The manifest content is what you actually remember, the latent content the true, hidden meaning of the dream. The technique of free association was used by Freud to get at the latent content of the dream.
- Freud published six detailed case studies including those of Dora, Little Hans, the Rat Man and the Wolf Man. Freud did not use case studies in an attempt to prove his theory but to highlight and exemplify his concepts and ideas.
- Psychoanalysis as a therapy requires people to use the technique of free association to uncover unconscious thoughts, repressions, etc. Transference describes the strong feelings (positive and negative) that the client feels for the psychoanalyst. Countertransference describes the feelings of the psychoanalyst for the client. Analysis of the nature of the transference will reflect the client's relationships with others, particularly his or her parents.
- Freud's theory of personality presents a negative and conflict-ridden view of human beings. Freud's theory also regards human behaviour as deterministic, and largely driven by conscious childhood memories. Many regard Freud's theories and concepts as not scientific and not open to empirical enquiry. Freud's concepts have been used in psychoanalytic therapy around the world and have enjoyed widespread application outside psychology.

3.13 FURTHER READING

Freud, A. (ed.) (1986) *The Essentials of Psychoanalysis: the definitive collection of Sigmund Freud's writing*. Harmondsworth: Penguin Books. This is a collection of the writings of Sigmund Freud selected to provide coverage of his key ideas, concepts and theories. Each extract is introduced by Anna Freud and provides context. It is valuable and important to read Freud's own writings.

Ward, I. and Zarate, O. (2000) *Introducing Psychoanalysis*. Cambridge: Icon Books Ltd. This provides a comic-strip type approach to Freud's ideas and theories. Good fun to read whilst providing a fuller introduction than that offered in this chapter. Ivan Ward works at the Freud Museum in London.

Breger, L. (2000) *Freud: darkness in the midst of vision*. New York: John Wiley & Sons. Most recent and authoritative biography of the life and work of Sigmund Freud. Provides a balanced and part-critical view of Freud and psychoanalysis.

4 Post-Freudian Developments and Ego Psychology

4.1 INTRODUCTION

Throughout Freud's life as a psychoanalyst, and until his death in 1939, the primacy of the sexual dogma was adhered to consistently and strongly. If anyone disagreed with this basic tenet of psychoanalysis Freud took a dim and harsh view. This meant that you were either with Freud or against him. Some of Freud's early supporters found this too restrictive and, in the end, broke away to develop their own ideas. In this chapter we will take a look at the work of Carl Jung and Alfred Adler, two early adherents to psychoanalysis, who developed and extended the concepts of the unconscious and conscious respectively. Other psychologists took a different tack and focused much more on the ego and its role in helping the person to adapt and change according to the different challenges presented by relationships, work and the general engagement with the world in which we live. In this chapter we will also consider the theories and applications of two ego psychologists: first, Freud's own daughter Anna Freud and, second, Erik Erikson. Each developed the idea of the ego quite differently; Anna Freud within the general framework of Freudian theory, and Erik Erikson by taking a lifespan perspective from birth to old age.

In our relatively brief consideration of these four important psychologists, we will look at concepts and practical applications of their ideas, and offer an evaluation of their contribution to understanding the human personality.

4.2 JUNG AND ANALYTIC PSYCHOLOGY

Jung's theory of personality and approach to therapy is called **analytic psychology** and represents perhaps the most complex and esoteric approaches we will consider in this book. Jung read widely and was interested in topics ranging from alchemy (the medieval 'science' that attempted to turn base metals into gold), witchcraft and the Mandala art form of Buddhist religion, to eastern religions, which were little heard of in the West at the time Jung was writing. Perhaps because of this unusual range of sources for his writings Jung's ideas have attracted little interest from mainstream, experimental psychology. Perhaps the more so because Jung put forward the concept of *synchronicity* (Jung, 1960) which he described as an 'acausal connecting principle'. Basically what Jung claimed was that at times in everyone's life coincidences occur that we find very difficult to explain by chance. Jung claimed that these coincidences were connected by his principle of synchronicity, but that no causal or scientific explanation could be given. With such a concept it is hardly surprising that scientists had little time for Jung's wider theoretical ideas.

4.2.1 Biographical sketch

Carl Gustav Jung was born in Switzerland in 1875 and lived in that country all his life. Jung's father was a Pastor in the Swiss Reformed Church, which might help explain Jung's life-long interest in religion in general and the different religions of the world. By all accounts, Jung's father was weak and dominated by his wife. Jung's mother comes across as a powerful and dominating personality who had suffered emotional disturbances throughout her life. Jung characterised his childhood as lonely (Jung, 1961) and, perhaps as a result, developed an introverted personality. Jung studied medicine at the University of Basel, although he also had strong interests in archaeology, philosophy, religion and science. Jung's first post was as an assistant in a mental hospital in Zurich. Here he worked with the famous psychiatrist Eugen Bleuler, who coined the term 'schizophrenia'. Both Jung and Bleuler worked extensively with people diagnosed as schizophrenic. This is an important contrast to Freud, who mainly worked with people suffering from neurotic or anxiety disorders. Jung studied, like Freud, for six months in Paris and returned to take up post at the University of Zurich.

Jung began reading Freud's writings upon the publication of the latter's *The Interpretation of Dreams*. Gradually, they began to correspond with each other and met in 1907. For the next six years an intense relationship developed between the two men, with Freud regarding Jung as his successor.

They toured the United States of America together in 1909, but tensions developed as Jung increasingly became unable to accept the primacy of the sexual instinct in his theoretical development. A complete break between the two men occurred in 1913, which precipitated a crisis for Jung. This journey into self-analysis (Jung, 1961; Goldwert, 1992) resulted in Jung developing his own theory of personality.

In 1944 Jung was appointed Professor of Medical Psychology but resigned his post due to poor health. He lived to the grand age of 86 years and died in 1961. Many people have regarded Jung as one of the great thinkers of the twentieth century (Ellenberger, 1970).

4.2.2 Structure of the personality

Jung proposed three interacting systems of the personality: the ego, the personal unconscious and the collective unconscious. Unlike the Freudian system where the id, ego and superego are in conflict, the three interacting systems of Jung are to be seen as having complex interactions, but as striving towards harmony and unity of the personality. Jung used the word psyche to refer to all psychological processes, including thoughts, feelings and sensations. For Jung the unconscious (whether personal or collective) was not full of repressed material, as with Freud, but a mixture of one's conscious thoughts and predispositions to experience the world in certain ways.

The ego
Jung conceived the ego as the conscious part of the psyche that provides us with our conscious 'here and now' experiences of thoughts, emotions and sensations. The ego also provides the individual with a sense of continuity and identity. The ego, for Jung, provides us with our conscious sense of ourself and how we perceive ourselves. Of the three systems, the ego was regarded as less important than the personal and collective unconscious in terms of determining how a person thinks, feels and behaves.

The personal unconscious
Jung used similar imagery to Freud in that the psyche (mind with Freud) is like an iceberg with most of it hidden from view. The personal unconscious contains thoughts, perceptions and feelings that have been suppressed or ignored. Essentially, the personal unconscious contains all those memories we can recall that have a basis in our experience of and interaction with the world. Because our consciousness can only contain a limited amount at any one time, the personal unconscious holds all that can be brought to consciousness. For example, at this particular moment you have not been thinking of your telephone number; but now this has been mentioned you can

readily bring it to mind. Other memories may require more effort or association to retrieve them, but are also contained within the personal unconscious.

For Jung the most important and interesting aspect of the personal unconscious are what he called complexes (Jung, 1964). **Complexes** are groups of thoughts, feelings and memories organised around a particular theme and exert a strong influence on the thoughts and behaviour of a person. Some complexes may be beneficial – for example, perfection or spirituality. Others may be potentially harmful, such as a power complex or a complex about sex. Complexes may also be organised around other people, such as the mother or father. Jung (1954) was particularly interested in the mother complex – our memories and experiences of being mothered. In the extreme, a complex may come to dominate the personal unconscious, resulting in a personality dominated by the mother and exerting strong control over the person. Potentially a person can have a complex about any object or person.

The collective unconscious

The collective unconscious, along with Jung's idea of synchronicity mentioned earlier, represents the most controversial aspects of his theory of personality. They are also those aspects that are most difficult, some would say near impossible, to investigate scientifically. The collective, or transpersonal, unconscious Jung regarded as a product of evolution, which is shared across all people and back down the generations. For Jung all human beings shared the same collective unconscious, which consists of memories (unconscious) the individual inherits. These memories represent experiences that all people have in common, such as mothering, birth and fear of death, fear of the dark, worshipping a power or a god, fear of evil, etc. Jung regarded evidence of the collective unconscious to come from his wide and varied reading on religion, art, the occult and mythology. Evidence also came from the interpretation of dreams. The collective unconscious, therefore, represents the shared experiences, emotions and memories we inherit from previous generations. This means that we come into the world predisposed to experience the world, think and feel in certain ways.

Just as complexes in the personal unconscious represent organised themes around an object or person, organised themes also exist in the collective unconscious. These Jung called archetypes (Jung, 1936).

4.2.3 Archetypes

According to Jung (1936), 'The archetype is a kind of readiness to produce over and over again the same or similar mythical ideas'. Archetypes represent predispositions, around specific themes, to experience and respond to the world in certain ways. Jung suggested that the number of archetypes within our collective unconscious was large. Which ones exert a strong unconscious influence on a person will depend upon such factors as the type of culture, time in history, and the particular interests and concerns of the person. Archetypes include the magician, the hero, the wise man and god. The archetype of the magician may exert an influence on a person if he or she has developed a particular interest in the arcane art of magic (for example, through using tarot cards) and/or lives in a time or culture where magic is commonly practised. Some archetypes are more universal, such as the archetype of the mother, which predisposes the child to come to experience and respond to mothering in a particular way. Archetypes may also interact – for example, the wise old man and hero archetypes resulting in the philosopher-king type person. Archetypes, for Jung, are represented in dreams, myths, religions and religious art. The analysis of dreams allowed Jung to understand the archetypes that operate at a particular time to influence the thoughts (conscious) and behaviour of a person, and so reflect their personality.

Jung claimed that some archetypes had evolved so much that they could be regarded as almost separate systems of the personality. Four archetypes fall into this category; these are the persona, anima and animas, the shadow, and the self. The persona archetype is the mask adopted by everybody in response to our interaction with other people – we have a private side and a public side to our personality. How much of our private side we will reveal to another depends on the degree of intimacy of the relationship.

The anima and animas archetype represents the male and female sides of our personality. Jung claimed that everybody exhibited male and female psychological characteristics, with the balance in each person being different.

The shadow archetype represents our animal instincts inherited and passed down through evolution from lower forms of life. Part of the shadow archetype would be the sexual instinct, another part would be aggression. The shadow archetype may, at times, be responsible for unpleasant and socially unacceptable behaviour on the part of the individual. Archetypes can interact – for example, the persona archetype can act to hide from public view the darker and more instinctual side of the shadow archetype.

The self archetype represents the person's striving for unity of the personality, and, as a consequence, it is a central system in Jung's theory. Jung said that this archetype usually only emerged in middle age when other systems of the personality had developed. When it does emerge the person becomes concerned with wholeness and self-fulfilment. The self archetype has the potential to provide stability and unity for the individual. As we shall see later in this book (Chapter 8), the humanistic psychologists, such as Rogers and Maslow, developed the idea of the self archetype to be a much more conscious search for self-fulfilment on the part of the individual. Figure 4.1 summarises what has been said above about archetypes.

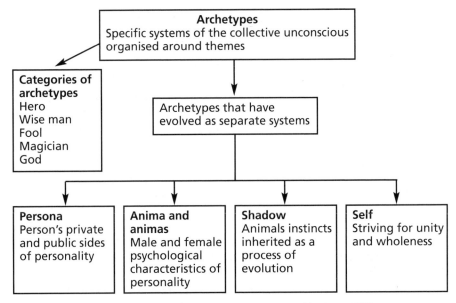

Figure 4.1 Archetypes in the collective unconscious as suggested by Jung, 1954

4.2.4 Attitude and psychological type

The systems and processes of the ego, personal unconscious and complexes, and the collective unconscious and archetypes paint quite a complicated picture of the psychological functioning of the individual. Overarching all this is, Jung suggested, a general aspect of personality called an attitude. The attitude of a person, in the technical sense of Jungian theory, is along a continuum ranging from introversion to extroversion. For Jung, both are present in the personality such that if a person is extrovert publicly and in interaction with other people, he or she is introvert privately (recall the persona archetype); and the other way round – if introvert with others then extrovert privately. For Jung, introverts turn their psychic energy inwards to their subjective world. Introverts prefer to think about ideas and concepts rather than interact with people. By contrast, extroverts turn their psychic energy towards the external world and towards the objective. Extroverts are more in tune and influenced by their outer world than inner world.

The general attitude of the person, as introvert or extrovert, is also related to four functions – thinking, feeling, sensing and intuiting – which combine to form a psychological type. The function of thinking is concerned with the intellect and logical, scientific modes of thought. By contrast, the function of feeling is to do with effect and our emotional response to people, objects and situations. The sensing function is to do with the information we receive

Table 4.1 Eight psychological types resulting from the introvert–extrovert attitude and four modes of functioning

	Attitude	
	Introversion	**Extroversion**
Thinking	Need for privacy. Theoretical intellectual, impractical. Not comfortable with people. Philosophers, theoretical scientists	Live by rules, objective in approach and practical. Comfortable with people. Mathematicians, accountants
Feeling	Quiet, thoughtful and sensitive, tend to ignore the objective world. Art critics, some types of writers	Social, like to get on with others and avoid conflict. Traditionalists, emotional
Sensing	Passive, calm and focused on sensations from the outside world. Artists, musicians	Pleasure seeking, enjoy new experiences. Oriented towards reality. Party-goers, travellers
Intuiting	Dreamers who tend to be interested in occult/mystical matters. Focused on the subjective. Prophets, mystics, religious fanatics	Creative and like new ideas. Take decisions based on intuition rather than fact. Inventors

about reality through our various senses – primarily vision, hearing, smell, taste and touch. The intuiting function is about unconscious perception and creativity. Jung said that each of these four functions is not equally developed in the person – for example, western society tended to develop the thinking and sensing functions (science and technology) often at the expense of the other two functions. The self archetype, in striving for unity, is about developing all four of these functions, and not emphasising one or two to the detriment of others.

With the introvert–extrovert attitude and these four functions eight psychological types can be described. These are summarised in Table 4.1.

4.2.5 Myers-Briggs Type Indicator

Most of Jung's theories, concepts and ideas have failed to attract scientific research from psychologists. However, the personality characteristic of introversion–extroversion was developed by Eysenck, as we shall see in Chapter 6. Also, much research has gone into the psychological types and four functions shown in Table 4.1. The Myers-Briggs Type Indicator (MBTI), developed originally by Myers (1972), is a well-established questionnaire based on four bipolar personality dimensions in which each dimension represents two opposites. These are:

extroversion	–	introversion
sensing	–	intuition
thinking	–	feeling
judgement	–	perception

The fourth dimension is to do with a person's lifestyle and whether they are taking a judging attitude and live in a planned, orderly way, or prefer perceptive processes and live in a more flexible, spontaneous way. The first three dimensions are similar to Jung's attitude and functions, the fourth was added by Myers. With two poles on each of the four dimensions 16 different types are produced. The Myers-Briggs questionnaire measures personality preference. One such type is extrovert, intuition, thinking and judgement. A person with this preference would be characterised as a decisive leader who is good at logical tasks and good at public speaking. Such a person is usually well informed and enjoys knowledge. On the negative side this preference may reflect a person who is more confident than may be warranted.

The MBTI has been used extensively to investigate the type of person attracted to particular areas of psychology (Schacht and Howe, 1989), For example, behaviourists tend to be thinking types, whilst humanistic psychologists are more feeling types. The MBTI has been used extensively in the business world to identify different types of decision-makers (for example, logical versus intuitive). It has also been used to investigate how people choose a partner in life. Cohen (1992) found that sensing and intuiting types attract one another, as do feeling and thinking types.

4.2.6 Evaluation of Jungian theory

Jung presents a complex and complicated theory of personality that has largely been ignored and rejected by mainstream experiment psychologists. In part this may be due to the problem that many of the concepts and ideas are not empirically testable. As with Freudian theory, it is difficult to generate specific hypotheses and then subject a hypothesis to scientific research. For example, just how might you go about attempting to establish scientifically the existence of the collective unconscious? Jung himself did use an empirical and scientifically precise word association technique to determine complexes in an individual; but with Jung's word association technique the problem of interpreting the meaning of a set of word associations is very subjective. The area that has attracted most research is the idea of psychological type and the MBTI, but here we see that the dimensions used in this approach do not reflect Jung's conception accurately.

The view of humankind that is reflected in Jung's theory is positive, especially in contrast to Freud's theory of the personality. Jungian theory is not about conflict but about the balance of different aspects of the personality and how all the different parts and processes may come together to achieve unity through the self archetype. Jung's use of a wide range of material, both present-day and historical, captures the richness and diversity of people and culture. Religion, mysticism and the occult are also positive aspects of the human psyche that fascinated Jung and, for him, demanded understanding.

In terms of application analytic psychology is not only a theory but represents a therapy that is practised to this day. The training necessary to become a Jungian analytic psychologist is long and demanding. This type of therapy is regularly used with the more intractable and difficult mental disorders of schizophrenia and other affective disorders – areas that Freudian theory struggled to deal with.

In overall evaluation, Jungian theory represents a rich, complex and fascinating account of human personality. Whilst largely rejected by scientific-minded people Jungian theory appeals to many people who wish to find a deeper understanding of themselves, their cultures and their spirituality. Jung's theories offer an alternative to what many regard as the materialism of western and more technologically advanced societies.

4.3 ADLER AND INDIVIDUAL PSYCHOLOGY

In 1902 Alfred Adler was asked by Freud to join a weekly meeting with other psychoanalysts. This group became known as the Vienna Psychoanalytic Society and Adler becomes its first president. However, Freud and Adler did not develop a good friendship or working relationship and Adler resigned from the Society in 1911. This resignation was the culmination of growing disagreements that Adler had with the primacy of the sexual instinct, the nature of the Oedipus complex and the importance of unconscious mental processes. Given that all three of these are fundamental to Freudian psychoanalysis it is hardly surprising that the two men fell out. Adler went on to develop his own theories and therapeutic treatments which he called 'individual psychology' (Adler, 1935).

4.3.1 Biographical sketch

Alfred Adler was born in Vienna in 1870. He was the second of six children and suffered poor health in early childhood. He had rickets, which affected his bones and made him weak and clumsy. By contrast his younger brother was strong and healthy resulting in Adler feeling a sense of inferiority. His father was a successful Jewish merchant and hence Adler enjoyed a fairly affluent childhood.

Adler studied medicine at the University of Vienna and trained as an eye specialist initially. He later specialised in neurology and qualified as a psychiatrist. Whilst studying at university, Adler became interested in socialist politics and saw equality and democracy as essential to humanity. After his break with Freud in 1911, he coined the term individual psychology to emphasise the importance of considering the whole person in order to understand personality and offer effective treatment for mental disorders (Hoffman, 1994). Adler served as an army doctor the Austrian–Hungarian empire in the First World War. Afterwards he established clinics, and trained teachers in Vienna. In the 1920s he spent increasingly longer times in the United States of America, and moved there permanently in 1932. He worked in New York and established a successful academic and clinical career there. In May 1937, whilst on a lecture tour in Scotland he died of a heart attack in Aberdeen. As a person Adler was optimistic, extremely competitive, friendly and sociable, and held strong socialist beliefs as well as beliefs about the equality of the sexes and the rights of women.

4.3.2 Inferiority and superiority

Whilst Adler did not totally reject the idea of unconscious mental processes, his general approach to understanding the person was to emphasise interpersonal relationships and the importance of human culture and society. Hence Adler saw intra-psychic processes, which Freud almost exclusively focused on, as less important. This emphasis by Adler led to the development of two important concepts: social interest and fictional finalism (Adler, 1931). Social interest is to do with the feelings and interest we have in others and the culture or community in which we live. Recent research has shown that people high in social interest are, for example, trustworthy, socially well adjusted and experience fewer mental disorders than people low in social interest (Watkins, 1994). Fictional finalism refers to the goals people set themselves in life. He used the word 'fictional' not to represent make-believe but to emphasise that we create goals for ourselves that reflect important achievements we work towards in life. Hence, in Adlerian theory, future goals motivate present behaviour.

One of the most important goals that a person strives to achieve is the goal of superiority. This is not to do with trying to be better than other people, but with being competent and effective in our personal lives. The term also refers to trying to create a better or superior society. For Adler what motivates this striving for superiority is the overcoming of feelings of inferiority that he claims we all possess, and that originate in early childhood.

The primary goal for each individual, according to Adler, is that of striving for superiority (or self-perfection), this is motivated by the feelings of inferiority that a child develops due to the total dependence of the infant on parents or caregivers (Adler, 1973). Everybody grows up with some feelings of helplessness, but certain experiences or conditions may result in these feelings developing into an inferiority complex. A person is said to have an inferiority complex when he or she is unable to compensate for or overcome normal feelings of inferiority. An inferiority complex may originate in three main ways, as shown in Figure.4.2. Adler was one of the first psychologists to recognise the effect of physical disability, and that how a disabled person is

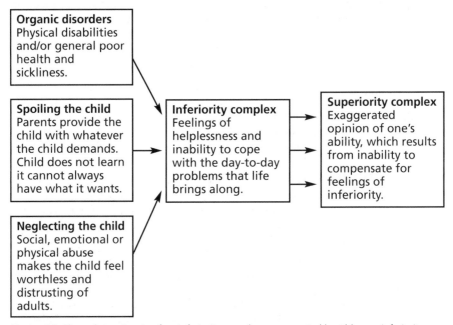

Figure 4.2 Three determinants of an inferiority complex as suggested by Alder; an inferiority complex may result in a superiority complex, which represents an attempt by the person to compensate

treated by society affects that person's psychological development and personality.

Sometimes, Adler claimed, people who experienced difficulty overcoming feelings of inferiority overcompensated by developing exaggerated opinions of their abilities and so demonstrated a superiority complex. Behaviours associated with a superiority complex include boasting, vanity, self-centredness and the denigration of other people.

With most people, as they move from childhood to the teenager years to adulthood, feelings of inferiority are overcome or compensated for through striving for superiority. Social interest and fictional finalism help the individual in this quest for feelings of self-competence through contributions to the community, society or culture in which they live (Adler, 1964).

4.3.3 Style of life

Adler's concept of fictional finalism concerns life goals that an individual strives to achieve. How that individual approaches life, interacts with others and relates to society is called their style of life (Adler, 1931). For example, a person may attempt to achieve goals through intellectual competency and through developing superior intellectual skills. Another person may develop physical strength and physical skills in order to achieve life goals. Adler stated

Table 4.2 The four primary styles of life with a brief description of each, as suggested by Adler, 1927

Style of life	Description
Ruling type	Dominating, aggressive behaviours. Person has little regard for others, little social interest and is only interested in society for what he or she can get from it.
Getting type	This is most common style of life. Here people get and take from others without giving. This type is dependent on others for fulfilment of needs and goals.
Avoiding type	With this style people try to avoid the problems and challenges of life, and may deny difficulties exist or need to be resolved. Not socially constructive.
Socially useful type	People cooperate with others to mutually achieve goals. Interest in others and society is shown. Alder regarded this as the style of life we should all work towards.

that each individual has a unique style of life; however, he thought that four primary styles of life could be differentiated. These are the ruling type, the getting type, the avoiding type and the socially useful type. A brief description of each is given in Table 4.2. These four primary styles of life not only facilitate achievement of life goals but reflect how a person copes with and adjusts to the daily problems and challenges that life presents us with. Adler (1927) regarded the first three of these styles of life as maladaptive both to individuals and the society in which they live. The socially useful style of life Adler regarded as adaptive and desirable to develop in people since he regarded this style as that which humanity should strive to achieve.

Another concept Adler introduced was that of the creative self. Perhaps as an adverse reaction to Freud's deterministic theory of personality, and the more mechanistic explanations of biology, Adler wanted to emphasise how individuals can control and create their own lives. Hence the idea of the creative self refers to Adler's belief that we can create and change our style of life, and that people have freedom to choose how they want to be. In short, for Adler, people are free to choose their own life goals and how they go about trying to achieve them.

For Adler a person's style of life as a teenager or young adult develops from early childhood, from social interaction with parents, significant others and other children. Also important is the birth order of the child in the family, and it is to this that we now turn.

4.3.4 Birth order and personality

Adler regarded early childhood and interaction with parents in particular as important influences on the personality developed and style of life (Adler, 1964/1933). Whilst Adler did not think that a child went through different stages of development he did think that birth order had important psychological consequences for the child. This is because he regarded the treatment of each child in the family, according to the order in which he or she was born, by parents and significant others (friends, relatives, etc.) as unique.

The first-born, or eldest child, is in a unique and enviable situation in that this child receives the full attention of the parents. The first-born has a happy and secure existence until the second child is born; this causes the first-born to feel 'dethroned'. Because of this Adler claimed that the first-born is likely to be locked into the past, pessimistic about the future and concerned with trying to achieve power in life. In essence, the dethroned first-born tries throughout life to regain the former supremacy and position as centre of attention experienced before the next child came along. In adult life the first-born is concerned with authority and power, and supporting the status quo.

The second-born is also in a unique position since this child has never experienced the power of being the centre of attention, as did the first-born. Hence, the second-born does not feel any strong sense of dethronement should another child come into the family. The second-born is competitive, trying to catch up with the first-born, and optimistic because not locked into the past. The second child is competitive and ambitious, but may set him or herself standards or goals that are too difficult to achieve. It is of interest to note that Adler himself was a second-born child.

The last-born may sometimes be the baby or 'pet' of the family, and likely to develop at a fast rate to catch up with the other siblings. The last-born is likely to be a high achiever. However, if spoiled as a child, where the parents give in to all demands, the last child in the family may become helpless and overdependent on others when older. Because the last-born may have been unaccustomed to striving as a child, he or she may have difficulty in coping with life's challenges and disappointments as an adult.

The only child is like the first-born who never loses the position of primacy and power in the family. As such the only child may find it difficult to share with others and take second place as an adult. The only child, according to Adler, is likely to mature early.

Much research has been conducted by psychologists on the effects of birth order on personality, and has generally found that birth order can have certain psychological consequences (Plomin and Daniels, 1987), But the evidence supporting the claims made by Adler and described above is mixed. First-borns do seem to show high intellectual and academic achievement, which is consistent with Adler's views since power and authority may be achieved through high intellect. Belmont and Marolla (1973), for example, sampled almost the total male population of The Netherlands who attained the age of 19 years between 1963 and 1966. They found first-borns to show strong intellectual achievement compared to others born in the family. More recently, Newman and Taylor (1994) analysed the birth order of US state governors in office in 1988 and found first-borns to be disproportionately represented.

Zajonc and Mullaby (1997) developed a theory to explain why first-borns show greater intellectual achievement. This theory concerns the effects of the immediate family environment on the child. Over 20 years of research has consistently shown the first-born to exhibit greater intellectual development than the others born in the family.

Most of the research on birth order has focused on intelligence and intellectual achievement. Other research investigating Adler's claims about personality and birth order has not generally provided support (Ernst and Angst, 1983; Sulloway, 1996; Watkins, 1992).

4.3.5 Evaluation of Adler's theories

Adler's theories present a very positive view of humankind in which people are able to control and change their lives, alter their style of life and change their personality. Adler emphasised the importance of other people, our interactions with them and the society in which we live. More psychoanalytically oriented psychologists criticised Adler for largely ignoring unconscious forces and downplaying the role of biological factors such as inheritance and the sex instinct. Whilst Adler does present a positive view of humankind, the fundamental and underlying motive of striving for superiority over feelings of inferiority does seem to start from a negative position. This motive can also be seen as reducing all human behaviour to one underlying explanation.

Evidence for Adler's theories has been mixed. As we saw in the previous section on birth order, much attention has been given to intelligence and intellectual achievement in this respect, but largely at the expense of the other claims Adler made about birth order and personality. Over the last 20 years research into Adlerian concepts and ideas has grown – the areas that seem to be attracting the attention of research psychologists are social interest, early childhood recollections and style of life (Watkins, 1992; 1994). For example, Manaster and Perryman (1979) developed a system for scoring early childhood recollections based on seven general categories: memory of people, themes or topics, visual or auditory detail, location or setting, active–passive, control, and effect. This scoring system has been used to examine differences in birth order, as well as people with different careers. Generally, this research provides some support for Adler's claims about different styles of life and their basis in childhood.

Psychotherapy based on Adlerian principles seeks to analyse the life goals, style of life and degree of social interest a person shows. The objective of Adlerian therapy is to help an individual set realistic life goals, encourage a socially useful style of life and further the social interest of the person. Dreams, for Adler, are to be analysed in terms of the style of life of the person. Dreams can also be forward looking rather than, as with Freud, based on infantile wishes.

Adler's theories and ideas are generally regarded as subjective and reflect Adler's own experiences. However, his focus on child-rearing styles, the potential effects of neglect of the child and disability brought these social issues to the attention of people. There has been a resurgence of interest in Adler's ideas and claims over the past 20 years.

4.4 ANNA FREUD AND EGO PSYCHOLOGY

Anna Freud, the sixth child of Sigmund Freud, devoted her adult life to both her father, until he died in 1939, and psychoanalysis. Anna Freud remained true to the Freudian principles and tenets that her father had established; however, her focus of attention was different. She also developed and clarified areas of psychoanalysis that her father had paid less attention to. In this brief consideration of Anna Freud's contribution to the development of psychoanalysis we will see that her focus was on the ego as the executor of the personality. Anna Freud also pioneered child analysis and investigation into how the child's ego overcomes and masters problems set by life (called developmental lines).

4.4.1 Biographical sketch

Anna Freud was the sixth and last child of Sigmund and Martha Freud; she was born in December 1885 and would become the person to take psychoanalysis forward after her father's death. Biographies of Anna Freud depict her as a shy and introverted young woman in adolescence (Roazen, 1971; Young-Bruehl, 1988), with a very strong attachment to her father and not a lot of interest in men of her own age. In her early twenties her father broke the rules of psychoanalysis that he had laid down and took his daughter into analysis. Anna's analysis by her father lasted for around two years (Young-Bruehl, 1988). At the same time Anna began attending her father's lectures and joined the Vienna Psychoanalytic Society. In 1923 Anna began practising as a psychoanalyst and made important contributions to the development of psychoanalysis.

Sigmund Freud developed cancer of the upper palate in his mouth in 1923, and it was Anna Freud that nursed and cared for her father until his death in 1939. It was Anna who persuaded Freud to leave Vienna in 1938, because of the persecution of Jews by the Nazis, and made the arrangements to move to Hampstead in London where Freud died a year later. Anna remained in the house they had moved to in Hampstead until her death at the age of 87 in 1982. In this time Anna became a famous psychoanalyst both as a practitioner and through her writings. Anna's interest in child analysis made her influential in areas of child care, education, family law and paediatrics. Her work influenced how we think about children and the type of child care that is most appropriate.

4.4.2 The ego and mechanisms of defence

In 1946 Anna Freud published a book with the above title. In it she developed and systematised her fathers ideas on the defence mechanisms employed by the ego. Whilst Sigmund Freud had concentrated on exploring the unconscious drives of the id, Anna was concerned with the operation of the

Table 4.3 Ego defence mechanisms detailed by Anna Freud, 1936

Defence mechanism	Description
Repression	Motivated forgetting, primary defence mechanism.
Denial	Preventing external events entering awareness.
Asceticism	Renunciation of needs, e.g. desires, pleasures.
Projection	External displacement of impulse, wish on to another person of object.
Altruistic surrender	Self-sacrifice, allowing others to succeed and achieving satisfaction from their success.
Displacement	Redirection of impulses, often aggressive impulses, on to another person or object.
Turning against self	Redirection of impulses, inappropriately, to self. Results in masochistic and inadequacy feelings.
Reaction formation	Changing unacceptable impulses into their opposite.
Reversal	Changing active impulse into passive impulse.
Sublimation	Transforming unacceptable impulse into a socially acceptable and productive behaviour, e.g. sex to work.
Introspection	Incorporating beliefs and behaviours into oneself.
Identification with the aggressor	Taking on the traits and behaviours of a person or object that is feared.
Isolation	Removing emotional content from thoughts and behaviours.
Undoing	Cancellation of an unacceptable thought once that thought has been acted on.
Regression	Developmental retreat to a childhood mode of response in the face of threat.

ego and the observable behaviour resulting from the use of different defence mechanisms. Anna identified and detailed three sources that cause the ego to respond defensively. First, displeasure (guilt or conscience) deriving from the superego knowing that the id has been gratified – for example, through sexual behaviour. Second, from danger in the outside world – this is objective or realistic anxiety because of its basis in reality. Third, the ego's attempts to ward off or defend against the strength of unconscious impulses coming from the id. To stop itself from being overwhelmed or rendered helpless, the ego has a range of defence mechanisms it can use and thus regains control as the executor of the personality.

Anna Freud identified and described 10 ego defence mechanisms that were mentioned by her father and added another five of her own. These are shown in Table 4.3

Anna Freud used her knowledge of these different ego defence mechanisms to develop her approach to child analysis and to understand how the ego develops in childhood. Her focus on the ego and its mechanisms of defence laid the ground for other psychologists to study and work on the ego. Perhaps most notably her work gave force to ego psychologists such as Erik Erikson, who we shall look at in the next section of this chapter, and Heinz Hartmann (1964) who regarded the ego as an autonomous force in our personality. Freud regarded the ego as dependent on the id for its energy, hence the development of ego psychology represented a break from Freudian principles.

4.4.3 Child analysis

Both Anna Freud and Melanie Klein (see Chapter 5) developed methods of psychoanalysis specifically for children. Their methods differed, as did their theoretical perspectives, and both were working in London at the same time, becoming rivals. The first problem Anna Freud had to overcome was to find some criteria to work with to determine when her analytic treatment of children was appropriate. Unlike the adult, who generally comes to psychoanalytic treatment voluntarily and seeking help or understanding, children as young as four years old do not comprehend the need for analysis and are usually brought by their parents. Anna Freud's solution to this difficult matter is captured in a quotation from her writings: 'In childhood there is only one factor of such central importance that ... calls for immediate action; namely, the child's ability to develop, not remain fixated at some stage of development' (Freud, 1945).

To help her determine if a child was not developing psychologically Anna Freud developed what she called a Diagnostic Profile (Freud, 1965). This is shown in Table 4.4. As you can see this profile has nine major sections and provides insight into the general functioning of the child in the family, the

Table 4.4 The Diagnostic Profile that Anna Freud used with children (adapted from Freud, 1965)

Diagnostic Profile
1. Reason for referral – behaviour problems, development arrest.
2. Description of child – personal appearance, moods, manners.
3. Family background and personal history.
4. Possibly significant environmental influences.
5. Assessment of development: • expression of drives and libido. • development of ego and superego.
6. Genetic assessments – signs of regression to or fixation at developmental stages.
7. Dynamic and structural assessments – signs of id–ego, superego–ego or reality–ego conflicts.
8. Assessment of general characteristic: • frustration tolerance • sublimation potential • attitude to anxiety • progressive versus regressive tendencies.
9. Diagnosis – integration of the above into an assessment.

developmental appropriateness of the child's behaviour, and the application of psychoanalytic concepts.

With this profile Anna Freud was able to move to the next problem – how to gain the trust, confidence and openness of the child towards the psychoanalyst. Anna Freud undertook a 'preparatory phase' in which psychoanalytic interpretations of the child's thoughts and behaviour were avoided. In this phase the objective was to help the child see the need for help, see the psychoanalyst as a friend and someone to be trusted and confided in, and as an ally who could provide help. In many ways Anna Freud had to become, in effect, another parent figure for the child. Once this had been established, or established as best as possible, Anna Freud could move on to child analysis. But what does the analyst interpret in young children?

Melanie Klein, as we shall see in the next chapter, used the child's play behaviour to make psychoanalytic interpretations. Anna Freud did not agree with this approach because she did not see children's play as equivalent to the verbal free associations the adult makes when undergoing analysis. Instead Anna Freud focused on two things: first, the child's verbal reports on dreams and fantasies (fantasies are to be seen as conscious thoughts the child has when awake); and, second, the interpretation of the relationship the child had with her as an analyst. The latter is equivalent to analysis of the transference between patient and analyst in adult analysis.

Analysis of the dreams and fantasies of the child, and the nature of the transference allowed Anna Freud to understand the development of the child and how the ego may be blocking development through overemployment of defence mechanisms. Analysis aimed at strengthening the ego helps reduce dependence on defences and so allows psychological development to take place.

4.4.4 Developmental lines

Anna Freud's focus on the ego led her to consider how the ego attempts to master the problems and challenges presented by life, and how the ego successfully adapts to change. She used the term developmental lines to refer to the six developmental stages of id–ego interaction the child goes through on the path to ego mastery. Ego mastery is to do with a child's maturation and development from dependence on others to independence. Also important are rational thought and active engagement with reality. For Anna Freud the problems and challenges that children have, typically, to deal with and adjust to are: separation from the mother, birth of a brother or sister, illness, school and friends. Also with the onset of adolescence the older child or young teenager has to cope with sexual awareness and interest, and love (Freud, 1962). The six developmental lines are as follows:

1. from dependency to emotional self-reliance
2. from sucking to rational eating
3. from wetting and soiling to bladder control
4. from irresponsibility to responsibility in body management
5. from play to work
6. from egocentricity to companionship.

These six developmental lines follow the Freudian stages of psychosexual development quite closely – oral, anal, phallic and genital (the latter occurring at the age of puberty). Whilst Sigmund Freud focused on the unconscious, instinctual aspects of the psychosexual stages of development, Anna Freud was concerned to understand the tasks, challenges and adaptations that had to be made in normal ego development for the child and young teenager.

These developmental lines enabled Anna Freud to understand and determine normal and abnormal (fixated or regressed) child development. They could be employed in her analysis of children and used to guide how the child should be helped to develop and the specific aspects of ego mastery associated with each developmental line.

Finally, Anna Freud provided insight into the conflicts and disharmonies often shown by teenagers, and so laid the foundations for Erik Erikson to develop the idea of identity and identity crisis as a major consideration of the teenager.

4.4.5 Evaluation of Anna Freud

As can be seen from what has been said above, Anna Freud stayed very much within the framework of psychoanalysis established by her father. Her contribution was to focus on the functioning of the ego and, as a consequence, she laid the foundations for the development of ego psychology, albeit outside the Freudian framework of concepts and ideas.

Of equal, and perhaps greater, importance was the work she contributed to the analysis and greater understanding of young children. This laid the foundation for our understanding of the effects of child abuse, the attachment of the child to its mother and father, and the consequences of separation and loss for the child. Whilst Anna Freud's ideas and theoretical contributions have not attracted research on the part of experimental psychologists, the growth and establishment of developmental psychology was, in part, a result of her work with and dedication to young children. Anna Freud never married and did not have any young children of her own; her work with children, over 60 years, clearly provided many compensations and rewards of its own.

4.5 ERIKSON AND EGO PSYCHOLOGY

Broadly speaking, Erik Erikson subscribed to the general Freudian principles of id, ego and superego, and the existence of strong, instinctual unconscious forces. Erikson also built upon Freud's epigenetic principle of personality developing through predetermined stages. Whilst Freud conceptualised development as psychosexual and taking place in the first five years of life, Erikson conceptualised development as psychosocial, i.e. taking place over the full lifespan of the individual. Additionally, Erikson focused on the development of the ego and how the ego helps a person adapt and adjust to culture, society and the challenges that life presents. Erikson regarded the ego as a powerful agent in its own right and an agent that can operate independently of the id (Erikson, 1974).

Erikson emphasised the importance of culture and society, as well as our interaction with other people as important determinants of ego development throughout our life. This contrasts with Freud's more biological view. Different cultures and cultural practices had, Erikson claimed, profound effects upon the personality. For example, Erikson studied the Sioux and Yurok American Indians (Erikson, 1963), and observed that the extended and permissive child-rearing style of the Sioux resulted in an oral personality, as conceived by Freud. By contrast, his study of the Yurok, with strict toilet training requirements, resulted in an anal personality. Erikson also studied other cultures and attempted to show that individuals in each go through the same developmental stages.

4.5.1 Biographical sketch

Erik Homburger Erikson was born in Frankfurt, Germany in 1902, and raised for the first three years of his life by his mother. Erikson's birth name was Erik Abrahamson, but he never knew his father and biographies claim that he was conceived in an extra-marital relationship (Roazen, 1976). In 1905 his mother married a paediatrician, Theodor Homburger, and Erikson took his surname. It was not until Erikson was 34 years of age, and living in the United States of America, that he added the surname Erikson to Erik Homburger. Why he did this seems a mystery and is not explained in his autobiography (Erikson, 1975).

At 18 years of age he went to art school in Germany, and whilst teaching art his friend, Peter Blos, who later became a well-known psychoanalyst, invited Erikson to Vienna to teach in a children's school. At the age of 25 Erikson was taken into analysis by Anna Freud and studied psychoanalysis for the next seven years. With the rise of Nazism, Erikson and his wife, Joan Serson, who had also undergone psychoanalysis, moved to Denmark and shortly afterwards to Boston in the United States.

Erikson had posts at a number of prestigious American universities, including the Harvard Medical School, Yale and the University of California at Berkeley. He finally returned to Harvard at the age of 48 and remained there until retirement in 1970. In 1987 he moved to Cambridge, Massachusetts, where he founded the Erik Erikson Person Centre. He died in 1994 at the age of 91.

Some of Erikson's books have become regarded as influential and important twentieth-century writings on humanity; most notably *Childhood and Society* (1963), *Identity, Youth and Crisis* (1968), *Gandhi's Truth* (1969) and *Identity and the Life Cycle* (1980).

4.5.2 Psychosocial lifespan development

Erikson claimed that the development of the ego over the lifespan of the individual, literally from birth to old age, follows an *epigenetic principle*. This is a term borrowed from biology and is to do with how the embryo develops in the womb. In psychological terms Erikson used the description to refer to human psychosocial development occurring in a series of stages: that the sequence of stages was the same and universal to all human beings regardless of culture; that ego development occurs throughout life; and that each stage is marked by a critical point. Erikson proposed eight psychosocial stages of development, the first occurring in very early childhood and the last in old age. As a person moves from one stage to the next the previous stage acts as a building block to help the person through the next stage. A simple physical analogy of child development provides an analogy – the child has to learn to crawl before walking, and to walk before running.

The eight stages of lifespan development are called psychosocial stages, both to distinguish them from Freud's psychosexual stages and to give emphasis to the importance of society/culture and our relationships and interactions with other people in the development of our ego. For Erikson the young child possesses a relatively weak and ill-formed ego and each of the stages serves to strengthen the ego in a particular way.

The eight psychosocial stages of development have a number of things in common. First, each stage is characterised by a conflict or tension between opposites – for example, in the first stage the opposites are trust and mistrust. Second, each stage provides, if successfully completed, a 'basic strength' to the ego – for example, with the first stage the desired outcome of the conflict between trust and mistrust is the ego strength of hope. Third, the tension and conflict at each stage present a crisis to the individual, which must be resolved in order to move on to the next stage successfully. Fourth, and finally, whilst the individual is experiencing the specific crisis at each stage the ego is vulnerable and may call upon a range of defence mechanisms to protect it (see the section on Anna Freud in this chapter for the defence mechanisms available to the ego).

The eight psychosocial stages of development suggested by Erikson are detailed in Table 4.5. For each stage, the table shows the typical age of occurrence of the stage, the crisis for the ego to resolve, the ego strength and the important relationships that relate to the stage of development. Although space constraints do not permit a detailed consideration of each stage, in the next two sections we will look more closely at the first stage (trust versus mistrust) and the fifth stage (identity versus identity diffusion) more closely.

Table 4.5 Eight stages of psychosocial development proposed by Erikson, 1950; the table shows the 'crisis' at each stage, the successful outcome for the ego and the social relationships of prime importance at each stage.

Stage	Rough age	Psychological crisis	Description of the crisis	Ego strength	Important relationships
1	0–1 yrs	Trust vs mistrust	Learns to feel comfortable and trust parent's care; or develops distrust of the world.	Hope	Maternal person
2	1–3 yrs	Autonomy vs shame	Learns sense of competence by learning to feed oneself, play alone, use toilet; or feels ashamed and doubts own abilities.	Will	Parents
3	3–5 yrs	Initiative vs guilt	Learns to use own initiative in planning behaviour; or develops sense of guilt over misbehaviour.	Purpose	Basic family
4	5–11 yrs	Industry vs inferiority	Learns to meet demands imposed by school and home responsibility; or comes to believe he or she is inferior to other people.	Competence	Family, neighbours, teachers
5	11–18 yrs	Identity vs identity diffusion	Acquires sense of identity in terms of vocation, etc.; or falls achieve identity.	Fidelity	Peers, ingroups and outgroups
6	18–40 yrs	Intimacy vs isolation	Engages in successful intimate relationship, joint identity with partner; or becomes isolated.	Love	Friends, lover
7	40–65 yrs	Generativity vs stagnation	Helping others, allowing independence to children; or self-centred and stagnant.	Care	Spouse, children

8	65–70 yrs	Integrity vs despair	Reaps benefits of earlier stages. Develops acceptance of temporary nature of life; or despairs over ever being able to find meaning of life.	Wisdom	Spouse, children, grandchildren

4.5.3 The stage of trust versus mistrust

The first stage of psychosocial development occurs in the first year of life and is closely related to Freud's oral stage of development (see Chapter 3). The important relationship is with the mother or primary caretaker of the child. For Erikson the mother's approach to looking after her child is strongly influenced by society and prevailing cultural values. The child develops the ego strength of basic trust as a result of a mothering style that is caring and responsive to the child's needs, with love given willingly (Erikson, 1963). Evidence of basic trust for Erikson comes from observations of the young child not showing signs of anxiety or distress when the mother is out of sight. This very much brings to mind the idea of attachment, with the mother–child bond and separation anxiety (Ainsworth, 1989) when a mother leaves the child.

At the other extreme is the young child who has not experienced a caring, loving and responsive mother or caretaker and where needs have not been met. This results in the ego developing a sense of basic mistrust. Erikson recognised that a mother cannot provide for and meet all the needs of the child all the time. Therefore the child develops both trust and mistrust. The successful resolution of this crisis comes when the basic sense of trust is stronger than the basic sense of mistrust. In this case the ego strength that develops as a result is that of hope. This Erikson characterises as: 'The enduring belief in the attainability of fervent wishes, in spite of dark urges and rages which mark the beginning of existence' (1963). The basic sense of trust or mistrust that the ego acquires from this stage influences the child for the rest of its life and the way in which each of the seven subsequent psychosocial stages of development are approached. Acquiring the ego strength of hope means the child, teenager and adult enter most situations with a deep-seated belief in a positive outcome. For the child whose basic sense of mistrust is stronger than that of trust, the ego throughout life will approach situations more pessimistically, and in the extreme may suffer feelings of failure and depression.

4.5.4 The stage of identity versus identity diffusion

This fifth psychosocial stage of development typically occurs during the teenage years with the development of an identity crisis. The term identity crisis is used commonly in everyday life and is applied rather indiscriminately to any situation where a difficult decision or choice has to be made. Erikson (1963) used the term in a more precise and restrictive way, with the teenager asking him or herself the question 'Who am I?' Or, more appropriately in terms of Erikson's theory, 'What should or could be my roles (work, relationships, political, etc.) in life and what roles would I like to develop into?' The identity crisis is about role confusion, which is precipitated by the transition from teenager towards adulthood. To quote Erikson: 'The prime danger of this age, therefore, is identity confusion, which can express itself in excessively prolonged moratoria' (1963).

The task of the ego at this stage is to establish a set of identities related to different aspects of our lives and which we can hold on to as we move into adulthood. The ego strength obtained from achieving positive identity is that of *fidelity* – 'the ability to sustain loyalties freely pledged in spite of the inevitable contradictions of value systems' (Erikson, 1964). Fidelity is important in sustaining both intimate relationships and friendships, in work and our approach to work and, more widely, in how we relate to and act in the society or culture in which we were brought up.

This psychosocial stage of development has attracted the most research from psychologists. For example, Marcia (1966; 1994) characterised the identity crisis as one in which the individual actively explores and experiments with different identities before giving commitment to one identity. Marcia (1980) then went on to show that four main identity statuses could be observed. These are:

1. identity achievement   –   successful resolution of the identity crisis
2. identity diffusion   –   failure to resolve the identity crisis or still actively looking
3. foreclosure   –   the individual has not experienced identity crisis because identity has to be adopted beforehand
4. moratorium   –   suspension of active search for an identity.

The desired goal is identity achievement. Foreclosure is unsatisfactory because here an identity has been imposed on the teenager without the person actively exploring and deciding upon an identity for him or herself. Events later in life might disturb the foreclosure and precipitate an identity crisis as an adult.

Ochse and Plug (1986) developed a questionnaire to test the extent to which a person has successfully (or not) passed through each of the eight

Table 4.6 Some items from the questionnaire developed by Ochse and Plug (1980) to measure identify formation versus role confusion; the items marked * should having the scoring reversed; total up your score; a low score indicate role confusion and a high score identity formation

```
        1 =   Never applies to me
        2 =   Only occasionally or seldom applies to me
        3 =   Fairly often applies to me
        4 =   Very often applies to me
_____  1. I wonder what sort of person I really am.*
_____  2. People seem to change their opinion of me.*
_____  3. I feel certain about what I should do with my life.
_____  4. I feel uncertain as to whether something is morally right or
              wrong.*
_____  5. Most people seem to agree about what sort of person I am.
_____  6. I feel my way of life suits me.
_____  7. My worth is recognised by others.
_____  8. I feel freer to be my real self when I away from those who know
              me very well.*
_____  9. I feel that what I am doing in life is not really worthwhile.*
_____ 10. I feel I fit in well in the community in which I live.
_____ 11. I feel proud to be the sort of person I am.
_____ 12. People seem to see me very differently from the way I see
              myself.*
_____ 13. I feel left out.*
_____ 14. People seem to disapprove of me.*
_____ 15. I change my ideas about what I want from life.*
_____ 16. I am unsure as to how people feel about me.
_____ 17. My feelings about myself change.*
_____ 18. I feel I am putting on an act to do something for effect.*
_____ 19. I feel proud to be a member of the society in which I live.
```

stages of development. The questionnaire for the identity stage attempts to measure identity formation versus role confusion. Some items are shown in Table 4.6. Another scale to measure the eight stages has been developed by Domino and Alfonso (1990).

Research into identity has looked at the consequences of identity achievement or the failure to achieve a strong sense of identity in relationships. For example, Kahn *et al.* (1985) investigated identity status and marriage. This was a longitudinal study in which the identity status of men and women were assessed at the age of 18. When the same people were contacted at the age of 36, Kahn and his colleagues found that women with a strong identity at the age of 18 were less likely to be divorced than those with a weak identity or role confusion at 18. Kahn also found that men with a strong sense of identity at 18 were more likely to have got married than those showing role confusion.

Whilst Erikson suggested that the teenager usually experienced identity crisis and role confusion, traumatic events later in life (such as divorce, redundancy from work, death of a close friend) may cause the person to question their identity and actively explore new identities, and hence go back into a period of role confusion. This will then normally be resolved and in some cases a new set of identities taken on. In the pop music world we might liken this to a pop star 'reinventing' him or herself.

4.5.5 Psychohistory

Erikson developed and pioneered a technique for the intensive study of individuals, particularly historical figures, called psychohistory. This represents a combination of using psychoanalytic Freudian concepts with methods of historical study. Erikson defined psychohistory as: 'the study of individual and collective life with the combined methods of psychoanalysis and history' (1974).

Erikson thought that historians did not pay sufficient attention to the role of the development of the historical figure to explain their influence on other people. Erikson applied his psychosocial theory of ego development in an attempt to gain deeper insight into important figures in history – both alive and dead. Psychohistory has a focus on ego development of the person but also attempts to take into account the influence of political, economic, social and cultural forces on that person. Thus the development of the ego is seen and understood within the wider society and culture in which the person lives or lived.

Erikson conducted a psychohistorical study of people such as Martin Luther (the German Protestant theologian) and Mahatma Gandhi (a leader of India), and published these accounts as books (Erikson, 1975; 1969). For example, Erikson's analysis of Gandhi attempted to show how the ego strength of this leader was able to resolve political conflicts. The focus of psychohistory is to examine the psychological strengths of the person, rather than weaknesses. Erikson's analysis of Gandhi looked at all eight psychosocial stages of development, but dwelt on a crisis that Gandhi experienced in early middle age, which revolved around identity and identity achievement. The question for Gandhi was what role he should adopt when faced with conflict and authority figures making unreasonable, or from his perspective immoral, demands. Gandhi adopted the role of passive resistance and, for example, used fasting for long periods as a political weapon to change the behaviour of his opponents.

Psychohistory has become an established and quite widely used technique for analysing an individual using Erikson's psychosocial stages of development of the ego. It has been applied to such historical figures as Thomas Jefferson, George Bernard Shaw and Adolf Hitler, to name but a few (Erikson, 1974; 1975).

4.5.6 Evaluation of Erikson

Erikson's theory of ego development through the eight psychosocial stages is, perhaps, one of the most widely referred to theories outside Freudian theory. Because Erikson considers the lifespan of the individual from birth to old age his work has been seen to be relevant in the fields of personality, child development, lifespan development and typical psychology. Erikson's focus on the ego and its relationships with other people, society and culture have been seen to be more relevant and acceptable than the focus of Freudian theory on unconscious forces and sexual instincts that are often largely outside the ego's control. Because of this the view of humanity that emerges from Erikson's work is a positive one and one where the ego can have control and influence how it develops. By contrast with Freudian theory the ego is in a perpetual 'middle ground' trying to cope with the demands of the id, superego and external world. Within this there is little sense of how the ego develops and grows over the life of the individual.

Erikson's psychosocial stages of ego development have attracted a considerable amount of empirical research. Psychologists have mainly concentrated their efforts on the latter four stages of development. Much of this research has produced evidence generally in support of Erikson. For example, cross-cultural research has explored the presence of the psychosocial stages in different cultures, such as Mexican Indians, and offered supporting evidence (Bernal *et al.* 1990; Markstrom-Adams, 1992). Erikson's work has also been extensively applied to the psychology of later life and old age with, for example, Zuschlag *et al.* (1992) characterising the 1990s in the United States of America as not having a positive effect on the resolution of ego integrity versus despair.

Generally, empirical researchers in psychology have readily been able to investigate Erikson's theories, and have been able to develop testable hypotheses resulting in considerable support.

In terms of application Erikson's theories have been used across different cultures and to develop a form of therapy aimed at strengthening the ego. Erikson's ideas have been applied to the areas of child psychology, education, social work and business contexts. McAdams (1997) has used Erikson's ideas to suggest that each of us creates a conscious narrative or story for ourselves, and this 'self-story' develops as we go through the different psychosocial stages of development. This self-story provides each of us with our unique identity and understanding of ourself.

4.6 SUMMARY

- In this chapter we have looked at alternative approaches to Freudian theory; these included the analytic psychology of Carl Jung, and the individual psychology of Alfred Adler. Two approaches to ego psychology were also considered, those of Anna Freud and Erik Erikson, both of which can be seen as extensions to or developments of Freudian theory.

- Jung's theory of personality proposes that the ego, collective unconscious and personal unconscious form the structure. The collective unconscious includes racial memories, some of which are organised around specific themes called archetypes. The personal unconscious contains material from experience with some memories around specific themes called complexes. Overarching these structures is a general aspect of personality concerning introversion–extroversion. Related to this are four functions – thinking, feeling, sensing and intuiting; these combine to form a psychological type. The Myers-Briggs Type Indicator is based on introversion–extroversion and functions of personality.

- Adler developed individual psychology in which the basic motive for an individual is to overcome the feelings of inferiority that develop in early childhood. Adler's theory deals more with our relationships with other people and the society in which we live. This is reflected in his concept of social interest. Adler described how a person related to others as a style of life, and said four primary styles existed – ruling type, getting type, avoiding type and socially useful type. The latter is the most adaptive and useful to be developed in a person. Adler claimed that birth order has an effect on personality because each child is treated differently according to the order in which it is born into the family. The idea of birth order and personality has attracted much research in psychology. Adler put forward a positive view of humankind; however, evidence for his theories is mixed.

- Anna Freud extended her father's theoretical frameworks by developing a greater understanding of the operation of the ego. She detailed the range of different defence mechanisms that the ego employs to cope with competing demands, adding to those her father identified and describing 15 defence mechanisms in all. Anna Freud pioneered child analysis through gaining the trust of the child to enable her to analyse the dreams and fantasies a child reported. She also analysed the nature of the transference relationship between the child and the analyst. Anna Freud identified six developmental lines, which occurred in sequence and identified the key challenges facing the ego at different ages.

- Erik Erikson adapted the epigenetic principle to develop eight psychosocial stages across the lifespan. Each stage presents the individual with a different crisis to resolve and, where successfully resolved, provides a different ego strength. The stage of trust versus mistrust is the first to face the child, and successful resolution leads to the ego strength of hope. The fifth stage presents an identity crisis to the ego about the roles to adopt in life. The ego strength from successful resolution is fidelity; if not successful role confusion may continue. Erikson developed and pioneered the technique called psychohistory. This brings together concepts of ego development, psychoanalytic techniques and historical methods. Erikson conducted psychohistory studies on famous people such as Gandhi, Martin Luther and George Bernard Shaw.

4.7 FURTHER READING

Jung. C.J. (1964) *Man and His Symbols*. Gorden City, New York: Doubleday and Company. Jung wrote this book for a wider and more general audience; it is probably the best introduction to Jung's ideas and has many lavish illustrations to help demonstrate his key ideas.

Fordham, F. (1973) *An Introduction to Jung's Psychology*. Harmandsworth: Penguin Books. Highly readable and classic account of Jung's ideas and theory. Authoritative and provides a good introduction.

Adler, A. (1956) *The Individual Psychology of Alfred Adler: A systematic presentation in selections from his writings* (ed. H.L. Ansbacher and R.R. Ansbacher). New York: Basic Books. A collection of writings representing the major ideas and concepts of Adler. Compiled by editors who promote Adler and have a deep understanding of his work.

Monte, C.F. (1999) *Beneath the mask: an introduction to theories of personality* (6th edn), Chapter 8, 453–91. New York: Harcourt Brace. Provides an excellent chapter on Adler, which covers all of his main ideas in a reasonable level of detail. College Publishers.

Freud, A. (1965) *Normality and Pathology in Childhood: assessment of development*. Volume 6 of the *Writings of Anna Freud*. New York: International Universities Press. This book pioneered the development of child analysis and details the work Anna Freud had conducted with children over a number of decades.

Monte, C.F. (1999) *Beneath the Mask: an introduction to theories of personality*. (6th edn), Chapter 4, 162–208. New York: Basic Books. A useful chapter providing coverage of Anna Freud's ideas and clinical work with children.

Erikson, E.H. (1963) *Childhood and Society*. (2nd edn). New York: Norton. Most of Erikson's books are accessible and readable. This classic text reports on his work with the Sioux and Yurot American Indians, details the eight psychosocial stages of development and discusses the development of ego strength and ego identity.

Monte, C.F. (1999) *Beneath the Mask: an introduction to theories of personality* (6th edn), Chapter 6, 368–405. New York: Basic Books. Another detailed chapter of this book, which offers full coverage of the range of ideas and work of Erikson. Plenty of up-to-date research on the psychosocial stages of development.

5 Psychoanalysis and Object Relations

- Introduction
- Melanie Klein and the British tradition
- Klein's influence
- Heinz Kohut and the American tradition
- Kernberg and the borderline personality
- Evaluation of object relations approach
- Summary
- Further reading

5.1 INTRODUCTION

Pause for a moment and think about the things that make you happy. Now list the three things that give you the greatest happiness and pleasure. Most people will have relationships with other people in their top three, and may even have all three in their list as different relationships that they have with people – relationships with parents, a best friend and an intimate partner, say. Myers (1992) confirmed this in his research on what makes people happy. **Object relations theory**, of which there are a number of versions, takes the relationships people have with other people as of central concern. In particular, object relations theorists seek to understand how young children develop relationships with other people and, importantly, represent these relationships mentally and at an unconscious level. The term 'object relations' is perhaps a little unfortunate since on first reading people often associate object with inanimate, physical objects. Here, however, the word 'object' refers to people as well, and hence object relations refers to relationships that a person has with other people.

Object relations theory was developed from Freudian psychoanalysis by Melanie Klein in Great Britain and Heinz Kohut in the USA. It differs from traditional Freudian theory (see Chapter 3) in three ways. First, less emphasis is placed on the biological drives of sex and aggression and how the ego copes with conflicts, and there is more emphasis on personal relationships. Second, in contrast to the dominant role played by the father in the Oedipal complex much greater emphasis is placed on the relationship between child and mother. Of great importance in object relations is how the young child in the first year or so of life internalises the mother, at an unconscious level. Third, the nature of the relationship between child and mother, and how this is internalised by the child, serves as a basis and influence on all future relationships for the individual both as a teenager and adult.

Object relation theorists are less concerned with id–ego–superego conflicts and how the ego attempts to resolve such conflicts; they are more concerned with how human relationships and the need for relationships with other people motivate and determine behaviour. As you can probably imagine, object relations theory had an important influence on **attachment theory** (the mother–child bond) as developed by John Bowlby (1969) and Mary Ainsworth (1989).

In what follows in this chapter we shall first look at the British tradition of object relations theory. The main influence has come from Melanie Klein, who we will consider in some detail. Her influence on later theorists such as Bowlby and Winnicott will be considered briefly. Next we will look at the main influence in the American tradition, Heinz Kohut, and his influence on other theorists such as Kernberg.

5.2 MELANIE KLEIN AND THE BRITISH TRADITION

Melanie Klein regarded herself as working within but extending the Freudian approach to psychoanalysis. However, the work of Anna Freud (see Chapter 4) on child analysis and ego development in the young child was regarded as following the Freudian line more closely. Whilst Klein was younger than Sigmund Freud she did develop and publish her theories ten or so years before Freud died. Freud seems to have paid little attention to Klein's work except to say it had raised doubt and controversy in the Vienna psychoanalytic circle (Steiner, 1985).

5.2.1 Biographical sketch

Melanie Klein was born in Vienna, Austria, in 1882, being the youngest of four children. Her childhood and teenage years were marked by death and loss of people close to her. Melanie Klein was fond of her older sister Sidorie; unfortunately Sidorie died when Klein was four years old. At 18 her father died and just two years later her eldest brother, Emmanuel, died. Emmanuel's death was particularly difficult for Melanie Klein since she had become strongly attached to him after the death of her sister Sidorie. Whilst growing up Melanie Klein felt rejected by her parents and also observed them engaged in forms of work that neither of them enjoyed.

Klein married at the age of 21. This was not a happy marriage, all the more so since it has been reported that she disliked sex and abhorred pregnancy (Grosskurth, 1986). Nevertheless she had three children, one of whom, Melitta, went on to be a psychoanalyst like her mother. Klein separated from her husband in 1919, after 16 years of marriage, and moved to Berlin to set up a psychoanalytic practice in which she analysed young children. In 1926 she moved to London, England, where she lived until her death in 1960.

Klein's theoretical views were highly influential within British psychoanalysis, but so too were those of Anna Freud, Sigmund Freud's daughter. Anna Freud had moved to London with her father in 1938. Hence, for over 20 years, Anna and Melanie Klein argued and disagreed over the importance of ego conflicts and how children were to be analysed. Disagreement and antagonism between the two continued until, in 1946, the British Psychoanalytic Society allowed three approaches to psychoanalysis. These were the Kleinian approach, Freudian approach and a middle group that was more eclectic and independent of the former two approaches. These divisions exist to this day.

Melanie Klein was a colourful figure who suffered from depressive episodes. At times she would ring up friends at any time of the night or day and demand to be taken out somewhere to distract her (Grosskurth, 1986). Melanie Klein has had a lasting and important influence on psychoanalysis.

5.2.2 Early defence mechanisms

Klein (1932) regarded the first six months of a child's life as of crucial importance to its future functioning as an adult, especially in terms of relationships with other people. Klein suscribed to Freud's tripartite division of the personality into id, ego and superego, and to the fundamental importance of the unconscious and unconscious mental processes. At birth the unconscious id is made up of two biologically given instincts: the life instinct and the death instinct. The life instinct, or Eros, is identical to Freud's concept of the sex instinct, for Freud this was the primary instinctual drive for a person. The death instinct, or instinct for aggression and destruction, was acknowledged by Freud in his later writings but developed more fully by Klein. For Klein the life and death instincts had an equally powerful influence on the unconscious psychic life of the infant and continued to exert their influence throughout a person's life.

For Klein the young child is born with an instinctual id and a primitive ego, with the superego developing towards the end of the first six months of life. This is different to Freud's view since he said that the ego develops in the first year of life and the newborn baby is all id. Also, Freud regarded the superego as developing during the phallic stage between the ages of four and six years. Klein characterised the basic and fundamental problem for the primitive ego as coping with anxiety and finding ways of not being overwhelmed by feelings of anxiety. The origin of these feelings of anxiety is the two instincts, but particularly the death instinct, which presents threats of destruction to the young child.

Klein regarded the young infant as having a rich, but primitive unconscious fantasy life (Klein, 1932); the fantasies she regarded as reflecting the two instincts of the id. Many of these fantasies are also to do with the child's interaction and relationship with the mother.

The primitive ego employs primitive defence mechanisms to ward off anxiety. These are learned before the child has acquired language and when the superego is mainly non-existent. As a consequence these early defence mechanisms endure into adulthood and become important in our relationships with other people. Klein (1946; 1955) proposed four main defence mechanisms that the child used in the first six months of life. These are splitting, projection, introjection and projective identification. A brief description of each of these is given in Table 5.1. The defence mechanism of **splitting** is of particular importance since what the child does is to split one

Table 5.1 The four primitive and early defence mechanisms Klein claims are used by a child's primitive ego in the first six months of life (Klein, 1935)

Defence mechanism	Description	Example
Splitting	Object (person) or part object is split into good and bad aspects as a result of experience.	Mother's breast split into good and bad as a result of breast feeding.
Projection	Disown impulse or bad experience/fantasy and project on to another object or person.	Boy's desire to harm another due to death instinct projected on to another person.
Introjection	Internalise aspect or perceived attribute of another person or part person.	Good experience of breast feeding; good breast introjected as a result of splitting.
Projective identification	Project good or bad part of the self on to an external object (person) then subsequently identify with the external object to take back what has been projected.	Destructive impulse projected on to the bad breast. Breast identified with, so allowing control over bad experience.

object or part object (mother or breast, for example) into good and bad parts. This can also be applied to the self so that the ego splits the self into a good self and a bad self.

The purpose of the ego employing the defence mechanism of splitting is to allow the child to be comforted by the good aspects of the object, and hence reduce anxiety. The bad parts of the object (mother, breast, self) are split off and seen as separate and hence not so anxiety-provoking. Splitting may help the primitive ego, but if used rigidly the child, and later the adult, will not be able to bring together the good and bad in one object. It is important that as the child develops, and in adult life, the individual can relate to the whole object and not just selective good parts.

Projection is where anxiety-provoking and destructive fantasies and impulses are projected or attributed to objects external to the child. Both good and bad fantasies or impulses can be projected on to another person. For example, the child may project the death instinct on to another person. However, the consequence of this may be that the child feels persecuted by the person the death instinct has been projected on to, since that person will be seen as wanting to aggress against and destroy the child.

Introjection is the opposite of projection in that the ego takes in or introjects aspects or parts of an external object. Normally, the young child introjects good objects or part objects to allay feelings of anxiety. Introjection of bad objects may also take place if the ego is attempting to get them under control. However, this may initially raise anxiety levels because the introjection of bad objects is threatening to the ego, and may terrify the child if not brought quickly under control.

Projective identification is where the ego first splits off aspects of the object, which may be both good and bad, then projects what has been split off on to another object. Thus far it is the same as projection. The next step, however, involves the ego then taking the split-off aspect back by identifying with it. This allows the infant to first get rid of the bad and threatening aspects of a person, object or part object by projecting outside of themselves. Taking them back in through identification allows the object or part object to be seen as a whole and gives the child a means of coping with the anxiety initially felt.

These four defence mechanisms, Klein claims, are used extensively by the child in the first six months of life. If overused or used rigidly because of unhappy relationships with other people, especially the mother, the foundations of psychotic disorders such as schizophrenia and manic depression may be laid. We will look at this in more detail in Section 5.2.5 of this chapter.

5.2.3 Developmental positions

Klein (1946; 1964) viewed the ego as coping with the life and death instincts and continually seeking to ward off overwhelming feelings of anxiety. In the first six months or so of life Klein suggested that the child experiences two developmental positions. These she called the paranoid-schizoid position and the depressive position. (Klein deliberately chose to call them positions rather than stages since a position can be returned to in later life. To use the word 'stage' implies that something is gone through and not returned to.) Klein saw the adult returning to one of these two developmental positions at times of stress or trauma in their life. Which one would be returned to depended on the nature of the life event.

The **paranoid-schizoid position** occurs in the first three months or so of life where the primitive ego splits off part objects into good and bad to cope with anxiety. The young child has fantasies of persecution from the bad part object into which the child also projects the death instinct. Bad objects or part objects produce a fear of annihilation in the child, and the task of the ego during this position is to overcome these fears. The part object most commonly split into good and bad is the mother's breast. This is because the child has both good and bad experiences of feeding at the breast. The primitive ego in the paranoid-schizoid position is not able to integrate good and bad into one part object. Hence the bad breast is split off and invested with other negative qualities such as aggression and the death instinct. This is where the 'paranoid' comes from – the split-off bad part objects become more anxiety-provoking because they are invested with other persecutory qualities. The 'schizoid' part of the position is to do with the split between good and bad, and the tendency to make this excessive and idealise good and bad as extremes.

The ego has to overcome these fears, and the desired goal or achievement of the ego during this position is to overcome fears of disintegration by introjection and identification with the ideal (good) breast. If the defence mechanisms are overused at this stage to cope with bad or negative experiences with part objects (for example, breast feeding not being satisfying but frustrating for the child) then the infant will not cope with the anxieties of the depressive position. In short, the paranoid-schizoid position is characterised by the child splitting part objects into good and bad. These are then either introjected (good) or projected (bad) to help the ego manage and reduce feelings of anxiety and annihilation. In part, during this position the infant is getting rid of unwanted parts of the self or experiences of others that cannot be coped with by the primitive ego.

The **depressive position** occurs during the second quarter of the first year of life, i.e. between three and six months. The onset of the depressive position is when the infant starts seeing the mother as a whole person rather than a collection of part objects. The infant experiences depressive anxiety due to feelings of guilt, loss and pining. This is because the child realises the mother may go away and abandon the child. Fearing the loss of the mother the child introjects the whole mother, with the result that the mother becomes both a source of gratification and frustration. The splitting of the mother into part objects no longer serves the ego.

The task of the ego in the depressive position is to establish the mother (and other significant people, as appropriate) as a whole object. This means that the ego is exposed to feelings of both love and hate, and has to cope with ambivalence. Failure to establish the mother as a whole object results in paranoia and depression.

The Oedipal complex, for Klein, is part of the depressive position. When the mother is experienced as a whole person, the father comes into the picture. The task of the ego is to see and experience both parents as individuals and a couple. The child gives up Oedipal wishes due to love for the parents and a desire not to hurt them.

Table 5.2 summarises the key aspects of these two positions. How well the ego achieves the tasks in each position will influence how the person relates to and interacts with other people in adult life. Excessive splitting during the paranoid-schizoid stage may result in the adult person only being able to see people in black and white terms. Also, excessive splitting may result in over-idealisation of the good and bad qualities of a person. This will mean that an individual is not able to have a realistic view of another. The disappearance of some objects (death of parent, ending of an intimate relationship) in adult life will reawaken conflicts that were experienced during the depressive positive. So if the ego was not able to establish the mother as a whole person during the depressive position the adult may be unable to accept the death of a parent or the end of an intimate relationship. The consequence may be that the depressive position is returned to and similar feelings to those experienced in childhood re-experienced as an adult.

Table 5.2 The paranoid-schizoid and depressive positions on infant experiences in the first six months or so of life

Position	Ego task	Description
Paranoid-schizoid	Overcoming fear of disintegration by introjection and identification of good part objects.	Ego splits part objects into good and bad as a result of experience. Good objects introjected, bad projected. Result of this is to reduce anxiety.
Depressive	Ego has to establish whole objects (mother and father).	Part objects and splitting into good and bad.

For Klein these first six months of life and how the tasks of the ego in the paranoid-schizoid and depressive positions are achieved or not achieved will have profound effects on relationships in later life. Because all this takes place before a child has command of language it is mostly happening at an unconscious level. Klein developed a method of child analysis in order to understand the conflicts from these positions.

5.2.4 Klein's play analysis technique

Klein's (1932; 1955) approach to child analysis was rejected by Anna Freud, but became an important feature of Klein's work. Basically, Klein regarded a child's free play as the equivalent to free association using language in the adult. The Freudian technique of free association requires the person to try to report all thoughts associated with what you are asked to think about. Freud instructed his patients not to censure anything and to report all that came to consciousness. Klein thought that children's free play was equivalent – and perhaps less open to censorship – to adult free association. Klein would provide each child she analysed with a box of toys that were given to the child. In this box would be toys such as cars, bricks and play tools, as well as a number of toy people. Klein would ensure that the child appreciated these were his or her special toys, and then get the child to play with them. With older children Klein would ask the child to talk and provide a commentary on their play, if they were able to do so. Klein viewed the child's play as expressing preoccupations with conflicts, fantasies and fears. Over a period of time Klein said that the child would transfer his or her relationship with the parents on to the psychoanalyst.

Klein would watch a child in play and listen to what was said. Then she would make interpretations of the play in relation to conflicts arising from one or both of the developmental positions. For example, if the child was playing with a car and toy person, and was continually 'running over' the toy person with the car this might be interpreted as a destruction fantasy. This might reflect the fantasy a child has of powerful and primitive parents, and in revenge the child symbolically destroys the parent, thus removing the threat of punishment, by running over the toy person with the car. Klein observed that children's play can be symbolically violent and destructive, thus allowing her insights into how the ego coped with the destructive forces of the death instinct.

This approach to child analysis has been criticised because it is the psychoanalyst that places the interpretation on the child's play. Since the child is not able to engage in a verbal debate with the analyst the interpretation is difficult to challenge. It is easy to see how two analysts, even from the same Kleinian perspective, may place two very different interpretations on the same play of the child. How the interpretation can be challenged and refuted is quite a difficult matter with Klein's approach.

5.2.5 Understanding psychotic disorders

Sigmund Freud found his approach to psychoanalysis difficult for people who suffered from psychotic disorders such as schizophrenia and manic depression. At times he found that psychoanalysis could precipitate a psychotic episode. Indeed treatment of psychotic disorders by any form of psychotherapy has proved difficult. In considering Klein's two development positions and the primitive defence mechanisms, especially that of splitting, some light is cast on this difficulty.

We have been looking at splitting in terms of the ego splitting part objects, such as the mother's breast, into good and bad. The good is idealised and introjected, the bad projected on to an object external to the person. Splitting can also be applied to the id and the self. For example, the terrifying images and objects resulting from the death instinct can be split off and buried in deeper levels of the unconscious. The self can be split into good and bad, with the good part of the self being idealised and introjected and the bad part projected on to an external object. One characteristic symptom that people suffering from schizophrenia report is that of hearing voices and being 'controlled' by inanimate external objects such as the television. For many people who do not suffer from this disorder this is difficult to understand. Taking a Kleinian perspective (Klein, 1952) we can see, rather simplistically, that the voices, which are often critical and punishing, represent the superego making the person feel guilty for splitting the self. Also, the voices from the television may represent the bad part of the self, which has been split off and externally projected on to an inanimate object such as the television.

As a defence mechanism, splitting and the other early defence mechanisms of the primitive ego develop and are used extensively before the defence mechanism of repression. In Freudian theory (see Chapter 3) repression is the most important defence mechanism employed by the ego to deal with id demands. In Klein's theory the early defence mechanisms are powerful and if used excessively by an individual have consequences for adult life that are difficult to undo. Getting at these primitive defence mechanisms through psychotherapy using language often proves unproductive because they were used by the ego well before language had developed in the child.

5.2.6 Evaluation of Klein's theory

Klein's theory of psychological development paints a rather negative image of humankind, in a similar way to Freud's theories. Whilst acknowledging and emphasising the importance of our relationships with others and our internal representation of them as a child, one is left feeling a little helpless as an adult. If, as Klein claims, the first six months or so of life are so important for the adult personality it is difficult to see how a person grows and develops throughout life (as with Erikson or humanistic psychology) when so much has been laid down in the two developmental positions. Klein did not subscribe to Freud's sexual dogma, but did develop the idea of the death instinct to be on a level with the life instinct. The operation of these two powerful instincts within the unconscious means that human personality is characterised by conflict and how to cope with aggressive tendencies.

Evidence for Klein's theories has not been forthcoming in the sense that her theories have generated specific hypotheses that can then be tested empirically. Mainstream experimental psychology has given little time to putting Klein's concepts to scientific scrutiny. Indeed, many psychologists find the claims of Klein to be even more difficult to accept and understand than those of Freud! If you think about it, it is very difficult to see how scientific investigations could look at the inner, mostly unconscious, psychological workings of an infant between birth and six months of age. At this age language is underdeveloped and primitive, and the infant is limited in terms of the physical movements he or she can control. Developmental psychologists have conducted experiments and recorded the behaviour of young babies, but not in an attempt to establish psychoanalytic mechanisms such as splitting the part object of a breast into good and bad!

In terms of the application of theory to therapy, Klein's concepts have been influential. She developed a form of psychoanalytic therapy with children that, whilst controversial, is used in a modified form today. Klein's approach to adult psychoanalytic therapy has also been highly influential. Initially causing rifts in the British Psychoanalytic Society, training in the Kleinian approach is still available today. Klein's theories have been modified and have evolved over the years. Her thinking influenced the development of attachment theory by John Bowlby and other psychoanalysts, such as Winnicott, more generally.

5.3 KLEIN'S INFLUENCE

Klein's shift of emphasis from ego conflicts as a result of the sex instinct in Freudian theory to the nature of relationships with significant others by the young child allowed other psychoanalysts to think in different ways about the young child. Rather than focus on the first few months of life, relationships with parents, brothers and sisters, other close family members, and peers became an important consideration in child psychology.

5.3.1 Bowlby's attachment theory

John Bowlby was trained as a psychoanalyst and was interested in the nature of the emotional relationship between the child and its primary caregiver – usually the mother. Bowlby called the emotional relationship between the child and mother an **attachment relationship** (Bowlby, 1969; 1980). This choice of words reflects Bowlby's view that as humans we need to form an attachment to somebody who will protect and care for us. Of particular interest to Bowlby were the emotional and other reactions of the child when separated from his or her primary caregiver. Bowlby observed that some children cope well, but others display crying and emotional distress, whilst others react by showing despair combined with little emotional reaction. Ainsworth *et al.* (1978) identified three types of parent–child relationships consistent with Bowlby's observations. These are secure attachments, anxious/ambivalent attachments and avoidant attachments.

Bowlby, consistent with Klein's theory of object relations, believed that these early mother–child attachment styles had long-term implications for the individual and future relationships. To quote Bowlby (1973: 204–5).

> An unwanted child is likely not only to feel unwanted by his parents but to believe that he is essentially … unwanted by anyone. Conversely, a much loved child may grow up to be not only confident of his parent's affection but confident that everyone else will find him loveable too.

Bowlby, as a psychoanalyst, thought the young child, from birth onwards, formed an unconscious representation of the relationship with the mother (or primary caregiver). This becomes an unconscious model for how to enter into and act in future relationships. Basically, as indicated in the above extract, if the child experiences love and trust in the first attachment relationship, the child as an adult will see himself or herself as lovable and trustworthy.

The past ten years has seen a great deal of interest in researching attachment style and adult relationships, especially romantic or intimate relationships. For example, Brennan and Shaver (1995) found that people are more likely to be happy with their romantic relationship if their partner has a secure attachment style. They also found that adults with secure attachment styles tend to have partners with the same style. Hazan and Shaver (1987) showed that people with avoidant attachment styles are frightened of intimacy and are reluctant to enter into long-term commitment to another person.

Bartholomew and Horowitz (1991) have developed a model, based on Bowlby's characterisation of parent–child attachments. This model is based on the person's internalised self-image and the image the person has of others. Each falls into positive and negative categories to produce a 2 × 2 matrix, as shown in Table 5.3. This demonstrates that a secure relationship is seen as the

Table 5.3 The four-category model of attachment styles in adult relationships (adapted from Bartholomew and Horowitz, 1991)

		Model of self	
		Positive	**Negative**
Model of other	**Positive**	**Secure relationships** Comfortable with high degrees of intimacy and autonomy in a relationship.	**Preoccupied relationships** Trusting of others but preoccupied with feelings of unworthiness in the relationship.
	Negative	**Dismissing of relationships** Avoids close relationships, dismissing of intimacy, does not trust others, does not become emotionally dependent.	**Fearful of relationships** Sees self as unworthy of intimacy and not trusting of others. Avoids relationships.

person having a positive image of self and other person. By contrast where there is a negative image of self and other, the person will be fearful of entering into a relationship.

All this is a long way from the original ideas and concepts of Klein, but does show how the adoption of certain Kleinian concepts by Bowlby has subsequently influenced more scientific research into adult relationships. Underlying all this is the view that the nature of early childhood attachments follows the person through to adult life.

5.3.2 Winnicott and 'the good enough mother'

Donald Winnicott (1896–1971) trained as a paediatrician and then as a child psychoanalyst. He was strongly influenced by Klein's object relations theory, but emphasised the more normal and less pathological occurrences in Klein's depressive developmental position. Winnicott (1986) also focused on the development of the infant in the context of a relationship with the mother. Klein focused on the internal, and largely unconscious, conflicts and anxieties that the young child had to deal with. In contrast, Winnicott was unable to see the baby outside of the mothering relationship. This led Winnicott to look more closely at mothering, and he coined the phrase 'the good enough mother'.

Winnicott thought the characterisation of the depressive position by Klein placed too much emphasis on pathological and abnormal processes than typically took place. He renamed this position as the **stage of concern**, to reflect the general concern of how the child develops and maintains a relationship with the mother as a whole, rather than part object. The stage of concern was seen by Winnicott as involving aspects of cognitive and emotional development that were not to do with defensiveness towards depression. The cognitive and emotional developments he said took place are to do with personality integration, personalisation and realisation. Personal integration relates also to attachment style – for example, the securely attached child will not feel frightened by not feeling 'whole' or integrated. In contrast, the insecurely attached child will experience anxieties due to feelings of not being 'whole' or integrated. Personalisation is to do with feeling your body is you, and aspects of the physical and psychological self are personalised and recognised as self. Realisation is to do with recognition of external reality and the limits it places on the self.

Winnicott once stated (1969) 'there is no such thing as a baby'. By this he meant that babies only make sense in the context of a mothering relationship. He described the good enough mother as the ordinary devoted mother who in the first few weeks of her baby's life entered a special state called 'primary maternal preoccupation'. In a sense, this means the mother is obsessed with her child at this time and develops strong empathy and loving attachment to the child. This sensitises the mother to the state and needs of her child. The behaviours and responses of Winnicott's good enough mother can be characterised as 'holding'. In a literal sense the mother holds her child securely whilst feeding, playing and cleaning. This holding extends to emotional communications from the mother. Holding on the part of the mother also serves to reduce the potentially uncontrollable anxieties of the child. For Winnicott, mother and child represent a single unit, with the child coming to realise that there is another person in the world other than him or herself. The 'not good enough mother', for Winnicott, occurs where the mother does not show empathic understanding to her child, and does not help the child come to realise a reality beyond itself.

Winnicott's influence was to emphasise the importance of the child in the context of mothering. As a result he shifted the Kleinian emphasis away from the child's understanding of the external world based on projective identification. The good enough mother is reliable and trustworthy for the child and through this learns to adjust to the challenges and demands of the external world. Winnicott has been criticised for paying too much attention to the mother and not enough to the father and significant others in the young child's development.

5.4 HEINZ KOHUT AND THE AMERICAN TRADITION

Kohut's (1971; 1977) self-theory developed from the object relations approach and places emphasis on understanding how the young child evolves from a disorganised, vague and undifferentiated image of self to a clear and confident sense of personal identity. Kohut focuses on what can go wrong, and spent much time considering and treating what he called narcissistic personality disorders. As with Bowlby and Winnicott, Kohut regarded the mother–child relationship as of fundamental importance to later development and adult functioning. Kohut put forward the view that human relationships and not instinctual drives, as with Freud and Klein, were the key to understanding adaptive and non-adaptive human functioning.

Kohut subscribed to the fundamental aspects of Freudian theory – the id, ego and superego, psychosexual stages of development, Oedipus complex and unconscious mental processes. However, these were all interpreted in the context of human relationships, especially the key influence of mother–child, parent–child interaction on the development of the self.

5.4.1 Kohut's self-psychology

Kohut's self-psychology (1971; 1977) emphasises the central role that relationships with other people play in developing a sense of self for the person. A well-developed, coherent and clear sense of self gives the person a sense of awareness of who they are and a sense of purpose to their life, as well as meaning to their behaviour and adult relationships with other people. When a person does not develop a clear sense of self he or she will show a narcissistic personality (see the next section). To encourage a well-developed sense of self Kohut states that parents need to show empathy and mirror the child's behaviour. Mirroring on the part of the parent involves appropriate responses that meet the needs of the child. Children need to have their accomplishments and achievements acknowledged, praised and accepted. For example, when a young child first says the word 'mama' parents usually show pride and mirror the child by saying 'mama' back. In a similar way, acknowledgement and praise is given when a child first crawls, walks, etc.

According to Kohut, young children treat others who care and provide for them, both physically and psychologically, as what he calls 'self-objects'. Essentially, infants treat others as extensions or parts of themselves. Through parental empathic interaction the child takes in self-objects' responses such as pride, guilt, shame, envy and love. These responses form part of the self as the child develops. Initially, the child idealises self-objects, but learns that these idealisations are incorrect and comes to have a more realistic image of his or her parents. Failure by parents to respond in appropriate, mirroring ways prevents a well-developed self from emerging.

The ideal development of the self for Kohut is marked first by the development of the nuclear self and then the autonomous self. The nuclear self emerges in the second year of life and has two poles: ambitions and ideals. The ambitions and ideals produce a creative tension for the child that

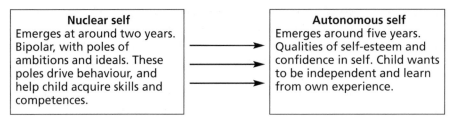

Figure 5.1 The nuclear self and autonomous self as processes for the development of a clear sense of self

furthers development and drives the person to acquire skills and abilities. Being aware of skills and abilities promotes a well-developed sense of self. This leads to the autonomous self, which emerges between the ages of four and six years. The autonomous self has the general qualities of high self-esteem and confidence in one's abilities and potential. Crucially, the autonomous self shows autonomy from other people and the need for other people to provide everything for the child. The child wants to act independently and learn by experience. This is summarised in Figure 5.1.

5.4.2 The narcissistic personality

Healthy and ideal personality development, according to Kohut, comes from the emergence of the nuclear self, followed by the autonomous self and then to the well-developed and clear sense of self. However, failure to develop an independent sense of self is characteristic of narcissism and narcissistic personality disorders. Narcissus was a character in Ancient Greek mythology who fell in love with his own reflection in a pool of water. Narcissus would talk to his reflection and became obsessively in love with himself, to the exclusion of other people. For Kohut the **narcissistic personality** is shown by an exaggerated sense of self-importance and self-involvement, but underneath this is a vulnerable and fragile sense of self-worth and low self-esteem. Kohut (1977) did not think narcissism is linked to any stage of development, but is a general aspect of personality that develops in childhood but affects the individual throughout life. Kohut regarded narcissistic disorders and the narcissistic personality as common in modern western society because of people's absorption with themselves, their own personal achievements and successes, and a generally selfish approach to life.

The narcissistic personality results from the absence of parental empathy and the shortcomings or failure of parents to mirror the child. Lack of empathy on the part of the mother may come about as a result of, for example, post-natal depression, not being overwhelmingly obsessed with the child in the first few weeks of life, or rejecting an unwanted child. Failure to empathise, claims Kohut, will lead to parents not providing sufficient acceptance of the child for what he or she is, not acknowledging successes and achievements, and not providing praise for achievements and developmental milestones. This failure or relative lack of acceptance and approval in early childhood results in the narcissistic person: an adult constantly seeking approval and admiration from other people. However, whilst this may appear to show narcissistic people as dependent on others, their low sense of self-worth and self-esteem means that they cannot accept the praise and admiration that others may offer. This may be because, at heart, such people feel unworthy of praise and will not see achievements as reflecting their own abilities. This means that the narcissistic personality does not trust other people and will not allow itself to depend upon or rely on other people.

To some extent Kohut recognised that everybody is narcissistic. However, this may best be thought of as a continuum between two extremes. At the narcissistic extreme is what Kohut called the grandiose self. The grandiose self can be traced back to very early childhood when objects and part objects are split into good and bad. The good is internalised and the bad externalised. Thus the grandiose extreme of the narcissistic personality maintains the unrealistic image of the good being the self and the bad belonging to other people. The narcissistic personality at this extreme finds it difficult to view the world and other people differently than in good and bad, black and white, terms. Narcissistic parents will perpetuate the narcissistic personality in their children.

Raskin and Hall (1979; 1981) developed a self-report questionnaire to measure narcissism; this is called the Narcissistic Personality Inventory (NPI). The NPI is a forced-choice questionnaire where two statements are presented to a person and the person has to select the statement that best describes themselves. There are 54 statement pairs, which assess four aspects of narcissism. These are superiority, leadership, self-absorption and exploitiveness/entitlement. The exploitiveness/entitlement factor has been regarded as the key one associated with psychological maladjustment. Some of the statements that are indicative of narcissism are given in Table 5.4.

Table 5.4 Statements from the Narcissistic Personality Inventory that relate to narcissism (Raskin and Hall, 1979)

Statements where agreement indicates a narcissistic personality
I really like to be the centre of attention. I have a natural talent for influencing people. I like to look at my body. I think I am a special person. Everybody likes to hear my stories. I insist on the respect that is due to me. I will never be satisfied until I get all that I deserve.

Considerable empirical research has been conducted using the NPI. For example, Raskin and Shaw (1988) found that students who scored high on the NPI (i.e. indicative of narcissism) used the self-referent words I, me and myself more in conservation with others than did students who scored low. Wink (1992) reports a longitudinal study on narcissism in women who were followed from the age of 18 to 43 years. Wink (1992) distinguished three sub-categories of narcissism: hypersensitive type, wilful type and the autonomous type. The former two Wink found were related to difficult relationships with parents, especially the mother, when a child.

5.4.3 Kohut's reinterpretation of the Oedipus complex

Kohut viewed the Oedipus complex as potentially a positive and joyful experience for the child rather than the conflict- and guilt-ridden characterisation given by Freud. You may find it useful to refer back to Chapter 3 to make sure you understand Freud's view of the Oedipus complex and the conflicts engendered for boys and girls. Kohut claims that the Oedipal conflict does not occur unless the child has developed a clear and strong sense of self. To quote Kohut: 'Unless the child sees himself as delimited, abiding, independent centre of initiative, he is unable to experience the object-instinctual desires that lead to conflicts and secondary adaptations of the Oedipal period' (Kohut, 1977: 227).

For Kohut, the Oedipal desires of the child for the opposite-sex parent are to do with assertiveness, possessiveness and affection, often sexual in nature. For the same-sex parent the desires are competitive, self-confident and assertive. How parents respond to the desires of the Oedipal child will determine the transition through the Oedipal conflict. For Kohut, the ideal responses of parents are of two sorts. First, pride and pleasure at the child's development and assertiveness. Second, a degree of hostility and counteraggressiveness towards the child's own aggression. Parents able to respond in both ways, with a balanced, tempered response, will promote self-confidence and healthy psychological development in their child.

Kohut suggests that the conflict-ridden portrayal of the Oedipal complex by Freud is more akin to a child whose parents are each narcissistic. This would mean that either or both would not be able to respond appropriately and promote confidence in the child during this critical stage of psychological development. Kohut sees healthy psychological development during the Oedipal complex as promoting the development of the self, and not typically characterised by almost unresolvable conflicts as stated by Freud.

5.4.4 Techniques of psychotherapy

Kohut's approach to psychoanalysis was not to use the technique of free association fundamental to the Freudian approach. Instead Kohut adopted a style of showing empathy and introspection with his clients. The use of empathy by the analyst helps the client to see that he or she is understood and that it is safe to reveal inner anxieties and feelings such as low self-esteem and low self-worth. Introspection, for Kohut, means to analyse in a reasoned and logical way the issues that come up in therapy. This contrasts with the interpretative approach of free association in Freudian psychoanalysis. What Kohut attempts to achieve is the empathy and mirroring of the ideal parent; in the adult this is aimed at building a stronger sense of self, and reducing narcissistic tendencies. In this therapeutic climate Kohut found that narcissistic clients developed a transference with the analyst that reflected early child–parent relationships. The narcissistic client would idealise and mirror the analyst, as had happened when a child. However, as a child the parental response was not one of empathy and mirroring. Kohut said that the analyst was to adopt this role so that the early child–mother and child–father relationships could be uncovered and worked through in a more conscious way as an adult. Kohut believed that considerable change could occur in a person away from narcissism towards high self-esteem, self-worth and a stronger sense of self.

Initially the client would find this threatening and anxiety-provoking since underlying feelings of low self-worth would be uncovered. The defensive cover-up through the use of narcissim would cease to be effective, and the person would have to learn new and more psychologically healthy ways of interacting and entering into relationships with other people.

5.4.5 Evaluation of Kohut's self-psychology theory

Kohut's self-psychology projects a positive image of humankind in which people can grow in self-confidence, self-esteem and self-worth to have a strong sense of self. The emphasis, as in the general object relations approach, on relationships with other people recognises the importance of others for our well-being. This is especially so with early child–parent relationships. There are a number of parallels in Kohut's self-psychology theory with the key themes of the humanistic approach (see Chapter 8). For example, personal growth, personal responsibility and the importance of subjective experience. Kohut believed that through his approach to psychoanalysis the self can grow and change to result in the person feeling a greater sense of achievement and fulfilment in life. In psychotherapy the analyst very much places responsibility for growth and change on the person and not the analyst.

Kohut's theory has also generated a considerable amount of empirical work, especially in relation to the narcissistic personality. This has allowed claims and hypotheses of self-psychology theory to be empirically investigated. The narcissistic personality or syndrome has gained widespread attention and is thought by many psychologists to be a defining personality characteristic of modern, western society where individual success, achievement and attention are such prominent features. Empirical research has provided a considerable degree of support for Kohut's views on narcissism. What has proved more difficult is arriving at a clear and precise definition of the well-developed, strong self, which is what Kohut thinks we should all strive to achieve.

Kohut's approach to psychotherapy has been highly influential in that he has succeeded in moving therapy away from the focus on internal, largely unconscious conflicts to a more external focus on interpersonal relationships. Human beings seem to be naturally social creatures needing supporting relationships when young to allow meaningful relationships to develop in adulthood. Kohut recognised this and built a theory and therapy around this simple model of humankind.

5.5 KERNBERG AND THE BORDERLINE PERSONALITY

Otto Kernberg (1975; 1995) regarded the mother–child relationship as all-important for an understanding of the adult personality, whether healthy and adjusted or disturbed and dysfunctional. He also adopted a more Freudian approach in relation to internal drives within the individual. Kernberg regarded aggression to be an important source of human motivation, with rage and anger as the emotions expressing this drive. Kernberg saw that people with narcissistic personalities typically expressed anger, rage and envy. In the psychoanalytic setting Kernberg criticised Kohut for not analysing the negative transferences or negative relationships that the client often demonstrated towards the analyst.

Of greater influence and importance has been Kernberg *et al.*'s (1989) work on the **borderline personality**. In general terms the borderline personality refers to people who occupy a line or exist at the border between neurotic (anxiety) and psychotic disorders. The borderline personality may at times show psychotic behaviours such as loss of contact with reality, delusions and hallucinations. At other times the person may have a good sense of reality. People with a borderline personality also show dysfunction in their interpersonal relationships. This is often characterised by destructiveness, self-destructiveness, anti-social behaviour in general, fear of being alone, and lacking insight into the consequences of these types of behaviours for other people. For Kernberg (1992) the central feature of the

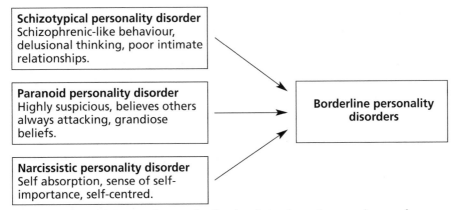

Figure 5.2 Three sub-groups of personality disorders that make up the general group of borderline personality disorders

borderline personality is the lack of a strong and continuous sense of personality identity or self. Kernberg regarded aspects of the narcissistic personality as a sub-group of the borderline personality. As shown in Figure 5.2, schizotypical and paranoid personality disorders were identified by Kernberg (1976) as two other sub groups of the borderline personality.

Borderline personality disorders often show powerful mood changes in interpersonal relationships – at the extreme this is evidenced by such a person showing intense love and care for another at one time, and strong hate and destructiveness at another time. Intimate relationships and friendships with a borderline personality are not easy, are unpredictable and difficult to sustain.

Kernberg used the primitive defence mechanism of splitting, which we saw played an important role in Melanie Klein's object relations theory (see Section 5.2.2), to explain these extreme mood changes. Borderline people oscillate between conflicting images (good and bad) of a person, and are unable to accept that one person can be both loving and rejecting at different times. They are also unable to accept that, within a loving or close friendship relationship, negative emotions will be expressed at times, but within the general context of a secure relationship. For the borderline person, a relationship is not viewed as secure, strong and continuing, hence occasional negative behaviours are grossly overreacted to.

Kernberg's approach to psychoanalytic treatment pays greater attention to the present and present behaviours, rather than past events in early childhood typical of the traditional Freudian approach. Basically, the therapist attempts to engage the client to talk about distortions of reality and how adjustments can be made to reflect reality better. This extends to the person's distorted view of the therapist. Kernberg typically found that when treating people with borderline personalities extreme mood swings were displayed. The danger for the therapist would be that the client would totally reject the therapist and never return for further therapy.

Since Kernberg saw the mother–child relationship to be of fundamental importance in determining the adult personality he regarded the foundations of the borderline personality as arising from splitting the mother into good and bad. This is normal, however, since for Kernberg the mother does not provide sufficient empathy and mirroring for the child to feel secure and integrate the split-off aspects of the mother into an integrated whole. The failure to develop a strong sense of self allows the splitting of the mother to continue and be transferred to other people in the person's life.

Bell *et al.* (1986) developed a self-report questionnaire to measure the borderline personality; it was called the Bell Object Relations Inventory (BORI). This has 90 statements that a person has to rate as true or false in relation to recent experience. Bell *et al.* (1986) found four main factors to reflect the borderline personality; these are alienation, insecure attachment, egocentricity and social incompetence. Using the BORI, Bell *et al.* (1988) showed that borderline personalities score higher on each of these four scales than people suffering from schizophrenia or depression. The factor that seems to distinguish most between borderline personalities and other psychological disorders is alienation.

In summary, Kernberg attempts to bring together elements of Freudian theory and object relations theory to explain and treat the borderline personality disorders. More recently he has extended his theoretical approach to eating disorders (Kernberg, 1995), Kernberg's work is widely respected by psychoanalysts and clinicians, and has engendered a degree of empirical research and empirical support.

5.6 EVALUATION OF THE OBJECT RELATIONS APPROACH

The object relations approach of theorists such as Melanie Klein, Donald Winnicott, John Bowlby, Heinz Kohut and Otto Kernberg has been and continues to be an important influence on present-day psychodynamic approaches to personality. Object relations addresses the imbalance of Freud's emphasis on conflicts arising as a result of the sexual instinct. For object relations theorists the emphasis is on interpersonal relationships, especially child–parent relationships and the importance of parental behaviour and their attitude to their young child. As a result of object relations theory, psychoanalysis has evolved from a theory of instincts and conflict to a theory of healthy and unhealthy personality development as a result of interpersonal interactions. Drives and conflict are not ignored by the object relations approach, but are seen to be more characteristic of unhealthy than healthy personality development. As a result a much more positive and hopeful image of humans is fostered by this approach than by Freudian psychodynamics.

The object relations approach does, however, suffer some of the same shortcomings of other psychodynamic approaches. Namely that many of the claims and ideas in the theories are untestable by scientific standards. The object relations approach makes inferences about what is going on at an unconscious level in the mind of the young child in its first year of life. It is difficult, if not impossible, to see how any direct empirical evidence for these unconscious mental processes could be gained. In another way, some of the key concepts and ideas in object relations are not clearly or well defined. This includes the 'well-developed self' of Kohut and the ideas about healthy and unhealthy personalities. The approach is also prescriptive about good and bad parenting behaviour, especially in the cases of Kohut and Kernberg. Little evidence underlies the desirability or otherwise of different parental styles in bringing up children, let alone whether certain styles are directly responsible for producing the narcissistic or borderline personality.

However, object relations theories have generated a considerable amount of empirical research, which whilst not scientifically testing some of the fundamental concepts and claims, has provided a degree of support for the approach. Psychometric measures of the narcissistic personality and the borderline personality have been developed and widely used to examine and predict the nature and type of relationship that such people enter into. The predictions and claims of the object relationships approach have received a degree of support from the use of these questionnaires. However, whether the explanations of how such personalities develop from childhood experiences is true is another matter.

Finally, the object relations approach has resulted in distinct versions of psychodynamic therapy. Each of the theorists we have considered in this chapter has produced a therapy distinctive to their approach and main concerns. Kohut's therapy has been developed to deal specifically with narcissistic personality types, and Kernberg's with the wider grouping of borderline personalities. However, little scientific research has properly evaluated the effectiveness of these types of therapies for 'curing' the individual. Indeed, the concept of cure is not really present in their writings, with therapy aimed at improving the individual's adjustment to everyday life or developing a stronger and more secure sense of self.

5.7 SUMMARY

- Object relations theory is a development of Freudian psychoanalysis that has its central interest in the relationships that people have with others. Object relations has been developed by Melanie Klein in Britain and Heinz Kohut in the USA.
- Klein proposed that in the first six months of life the young infant employs

primitive defence mechanisms of splitting, projection, introjection and projective identification. If overused these may lead to psychotic disorders, such as schizophrenia, later in life.

- Klein proposed the two developmental positions of paranoid-schizoid and depressive, which the ego uses to cope with the unconscious effects of the life and death instincts. The task of the ego in the paranoid-schizoid position is to overcome fears of disintegration by splitting part objects into good and bad. The task of the ego in the depressive position is to establish the mother, and significant others, as a whole object. A position may be returned to in later life under traumatic circumstances.

- Klein developed child analysis through interpretation of the play of young infants. She noticed that play could be symbolically violent and destructive, which led her to gain insights into the psychological effects of the death instinct. Klein shifted the Freudian focus from ego conflicts as a result of the sex instinct to looking at relationships, particularly mother–child interactions. This influenced developmental psychologists such as John Bowlby and Donald Winnicott.

- Heinz Kohut developed self-psychology theory from the object relations approach. Kohut was interested in how the child developed into an adult with a confident sense of personal identity. Kohut claimed that parents need to mirror a child's behaviour so that achievements and accomplishments are acknowledged. Kohut saw young children as seeing others as extensions of themselves, this he called 'self-objects'. The ideal development of the self goes from the nuclear self to the autonomous self.

- The narcissistic personality is characterised by a person sharing an exaggerated sense of self-importance and self-involvement, but with low self-worth and self-esteem. Narcissistic disorders are, according to Kohut, common in western society. The narcissistic personality is a result of a lack of parental empathy and a failure to mirror the child.

- Kernberg developed the idea of the borderline personality – this refers to a person who exists at the border of neuroticism and psychoticism. A borderline personality will show psychotic behaviour at times, and dysfunctionality in personal relationships. Kernberg regarded the narcissistic personality as a category of the borderline personality.

- The object relations approach is an important influence in psychodynamics, but suffers similar shortcomings to Freudian psychoanalysis. There are difficulties in investigating such theories scientifically and difficulties in knowing how to resolve different interpretations of the same behaviour by different therapists. Little empirical research has been conducted to test either claims for the theory or the effectiveness of therapy. Nevertheless the approach has been influential and has highlighted the central importance for all of us of relationships with other people.

5.8 FURTHER READING

Feist, J. and Feist, G.J. (1998) *Theories of Personality*. (4th edn), Chapter 5. McGraw-Hill. Provides good and accessible coverage of Melanie Klein's object relations theory, but is rather sketchy on the other theorists considered in this chapter.

Segal, J. (1992) *Melanie Klein*. London: Sage. Provides readable and good coverage of Klein's theories and approaches to child analysis. Also provides critical assessment of Klein's contributions.

Shaver, P.R. and Clark, C.L. (1994) The psychodynamics of adult romantic attachment. In J.M. Masling and R.F. Bornstein (eds) *Empirical Perspectives on Object Relations Theory*. Washington, DC: American Psychological Associations. Provides a good summary of the research on attachment style and romantic relationships in adults. The chapter is also useful because it gives a historical perspective to object relations and attachment.

Winnicott, D.W. (1986) *Home is Where we Start From: essays by a psychoanalyst*. New York: Norton. A useful collection of essays that provide an accessible insight into the object relations approach of Winnicott.

6 Dispositional Approaches

6.1 INTRODUCTION

Jennifer would rarely say no if invited to a party. If a friend dropped by her house without warning she would always invite them in. If a friend phoned her on her mobile she would always be pleased to hold a conversation.

From this brief description of Jennifer you quickly gain a strong impression that Jennifer likes to be around people and to talk to people. In everyday language you would probably describe Jennifer as extrovert, gregarious, talkative, friendly and welcoming. No doubt you can think of some more adjectives to describe Jennifer's behaviour. Such a description identifies dispositions or traits that Jennifer may possess. In everyday life we readily make dispositional descriptions of both ourselves and other people – sometimes such descriptions are reasonably accurate, and at other times misleading as may be the case with stereotypes (Pennington, 2000).

The dispositional or trait approach in personality is intuitively appealing because it somehow reflects how we describe, and at times judge, people in our daily lives. Psychologists have long been interested in this approach and typically use the questionnaire method (see Chapter 1) to measure dispositions. In this chapter we will look at four different, but not totally unrelated, approaches to dispositions. The early work of Gordon Allport, the highly influential factor analysis approach of Raymond Cattell, Eysenck's 'three dimensions of personality' and what are known as the 'big five personality traits', which represent current psychological thinking in this area.

6.1.1 Dispositions and traits

In personality psychology the terms dispositions and traits are used interchangeably, but what are dispositions? Dispositions may be regarded as labels we use to explain a person's behaviour across a range of situations. Dispositions are also relatively enduring aspects of personality that may change over a longer period of time (a number of years), rather than on a day-to-day basis. Put another way, we may define traits as 'internal dispositions that are relatively stable over time and across situations' (McAdams 2001: 252). Notice that this definition shows traits to be internal to a person, and stable, which means unlikely to change easily and occurring in many different situations. In more technical language dispositions are said to be cross-situationally consistent. However, we shall see at the end of this chapter that this idea has been strongly challenged.

Dispositions are also characterised as bipolar adjectives or in terms of opposites such as very talkative–very quiet, very friendly–very unfriendly, etc. Each bipolar adjective is usually conceived on a continuum ranging from one extreme to another and usually measured on five- or seven-point scales (see Chapter 2). Dispositions are usually regarded as independent but may be clustered together to provide a more general picture of somebody, as with the description of Jennifer at the start of this chapter. Finally, dispositions refer to thoughts, feelings and behaviours, and are used to characterise how one person differs from another.

6.1.2 Historical perspective

Attempts to describe people using dispositions date back to Ancient Greek times with the Greek physician Galen's idea that the body contains four 'humours' – blood, black bile, yellow bile and phlegm. Each of these humours was associated with a number of dispositions. Blood was associated with a sanguine personality – bold, confident and forceful. Black bile was associated with a melancholic type – depressive, anxious and pessimistic. Yellow bile was associated with a choleric person – restless, irritable and angry – and phlegm with a phlegmatic person – cold, aloof and apathetic. The overall temperament or personality of a person, according to Galen, was a result of how the four humours came together through some kind of balance.

Francis Galton (1822–1911) was a pioneering psychologist who studied dispositions scientifically (Galton, 1884). Galton thought that dispositions were inherited, influenced no doubt by the fact that Charles Darwin was his half-cousin. Galton thought that human characteristics, such as dispositions, were distributed in a normal or bell-shaped curve. Galton developed numerous measures of dispositions and used these measures on thousands of people to show how individual differences followed a statistical distribution (the normal curve). Hence Francis Galton is regarded as the founder of modern personality research (Rushton, 1990).

6.1.3 Inheritability

The dispositional approach to personality has attracted considerable research over the years, dating back to Galton, who investigated the extent to which dispositions are inherited or a result of experience. Galton thought genetics played a strong determining role and attempted to show this by studying eminent people in Britain in the nineteenth century. His book *Hereditary Genius* (1869) attempted to prove that genius was hereditary. There were many flaws in his research, most notably very few women were included in his study, and he failed to take account of people being born into wealth and status. Nevertheless his research interests in inheritance of dispositions have been pursued by psychologists to this day.

Table 6.1 Correlation statistics for monozygotic and dizygotic twins reared together and apart for 11 dispositions (adapted from Plomin *et al.* 1990); note that a figure close to zero indicates no similarity, a higher figure towards 1 indicates a good degree of similarity

Dispositions	Monozygotic twins		Dyzygotic twins	
	Reared apart	**Reared together**	**Reared apart**	**Reared together**
Extroversion	0.30	0.54	0.04	0.06
Neuroticism	0.25	0.41	0.28	0.24
Openness	0.43	0.51	0.23	0.14
Conscientiousness	0.15	0.41	−0.03	0.23
Agreeableness	0.19	0.47	0.10	0.11
Sociability	0.20	0.35	0.19	0.19
Activity level	0.27	0.38	0.00	0.18
Hostility	0.21	0.33	0.21	0.40
Assertiveness	0.16	0.32	−0.08	0.20
Ambitious	0.40	0.30	0.08	0.11
Responsibility	0.36	0.30	0.30	0.18

Perhaps the most highly regarded approach to attempting to unpick the influence of nature and nurture is the use of twin studies (see Chapter 2). Monozygotic and dizygotic twins reared either together or apart have been studied extensively. One study, based on data from Sweden, looked at how similar, through a measure of correlation, twins reared apart and together were on a number of dispositions (Plomin *et al.* 1990). The findings are shown in Table 6.1. As can be seen, monozygotic twins reared together show a greater degree of similarity (the correlation figure is higher or nearer 1.0) than either monozygotic twins or dizygotic twins reared either together or apart. Monozygotic twins reared together share both the same genes and the same environment. In consequence it is difficult to separate out the relative importance of each in determining dispositions in a personality. The picture that emerges from such research over this issue is that genetics plays a part, but that twin studies may overestimate its importance (Plomin *et al.* 1990).

6.2 GORDON ALLPORT

Gordon Allport is widely regarded as the founding father of the modern dispositional approach to personality. Whilst Allport developed a scheme to categorise dispositions he also recognised the uniqueness of the individual, as the following quotation from his first and highly influential book, *Personality: a psychological interpretation* (1937: 3), shows.

> The outstanding characteristic of man is his individuality. He is a unique creation of the forces of nature. Separated spatially from all other men he behaves throughout his own particular life in his own distinctive fashion.

The language may seem a little odd and the use of the masculine throughout is inappropriate these days, nevertheless this does demonstrate why Allport used an ideographic (see Chapter 1) approach to study the personality.

6.2.1 Biographical sketch

Gordon Allport was born in Ohio in the United States of America in 1897. He studied psychology and social ethics at Harvard University, graduating at the age of 22. He then took a post as a teacher of English and sociology in Istanbul, Turkey. He returned to Harvard University to complete his PhD, with the title 'An experimental study of the traits of the personality'. Shortly afterwards he travelled around Europe and whilst in Vienna visited Sigmund Freud. As a result of his conversation with Freud he felt that psychoanalysis tried to go too deep into the personality, and he did not agree with Freud's emphasis on the sexual instinct and unconscious forces (Allport, 1967).

Allport, as we have seen above, recognised the uniqueness of each person and used a type of case study approach, which he characterised as exploring the 'psychic surface' of life (Allport, 1960).

On his return from Europe Allport taught social ethics at Harvard University. He left Harvard for a short period and, on his return in 1930, established a new Department of Social Relations. Allport researched and published extensively throughout his career. He died in 1967.

6.2.2 Structure of personality

Allport distinguished between common traits and personal dispositions. Common traits are hypothetical constructs that allow comparison between people in a culture or society. Allport thought that different cultures gave emphasis to different common traits. So, for example, western cultures often encourage the common trait of competitiveness, whilst eastern cultures may give emphasis to a common trait such as sharing. Personal dispositions are traits that are characteristic of an individual and distinguish one person's personality (a cluster of personal dispositions) from that of another person. The description of Jennifer at the start of this chapter represents her personal dispositions. Within this distinction between common traits and personal dispositions it is often the case that two people possess the same trait. However, because Allport saw each person as a unique individual, the expression or behavioural enactment of a trait will differ from person to person.

Allport then said that for any one individual personal dispositions could be classified according to how broad and persuasive the trait is with respect to behavioural consistency. Think back to the description of Jennifer at the start of this chapter; here you would think that friendliness towards other people would be shown by Jennifer to many people in many different situations. For Jennifer friendliness is a trait that applies broadly and reflects consistency of behaviour. Such a trait Allport called a cardinal trait (Allport, 1937). Allport illustrated the concept of cardinal traits by reference to famous historical or fictional figures with which we associate a trait (for example, Machiavellian for the trait of manipulativeness or Christ-like for the trait of holiness).

The next level of traits Allport called central traits. These have a less pervasive influence on a person's behaviour than cardinal traits, but exert a major influence. For Allport most people possess between five and ten central traits.

Finally, traits with a minor influence on behaviour Allport called secondary traits. Such traits are peripheral and may only come into operation in specific circumstances or situations. Each person is said to have many secondary traits, but such traits are not defining, as cardinal traits, to the individuality of the person. Secondary traits, whilst of minor importance trait by trait, are often only known on closer acquaintance with a person. By contrast cardinal traits would be noticed on very brief acquaintance with a person (an interview is a good example of when a person's cardinal traits come across after only a short conversation with them).

6.2.3 Studying the person

Whilst Allport is classified as a psychologist within the dispositional approach to personality, it can also be seen from the little we have read about his concern to see people as individuals that Allport falls into the category of humanistic psychology (see Chapter 8). Since Allport regarded no two people as being exactly alike, even identical twins, and thought that the same trait operates in a unique way in different people he was not interested in the questionnaire approach. The use of questionnaires, as we shall see later in this chapter, is characteristic of most trait psychologists and represents the nomethetic approach (see Chapter 1) to personality. Allport, though, was firmly in the ideographic category and said that an individual can only be studied through intensive, detailed and long-term case studies. Hence, Allport reports many in-depth studies of people's lives rather than generalisations across groups of people (Allport, 1942).

Interviews are one method of collecting detailed information about the personal dispositions of an individual. Allport thought that personal documents were also a valuable source of information. He used personal documents such as letters, diaries and autobiographies, and gave a general definition as to what counts as a personal document: 'any self-revealing record that intentionally or unintentionally yields information regarding the structure, dynamics and functioning of the author's mental life' (Allport, 1961).

Allport approached analysis of personal documents from a strictly scientific viewpoint of understanding, prediction and control. At the same time the approach is phenomenological in that the personal dispositions are understood from the subjective perspective of the focus of the case study.

Clearly there are difficulties with the use of personal documents. For example, it may not be appropriate or correct to take them at face value; some knowledge of the motives underlying why they were written may be needed. Also, there may be ethical issues to do with access to such documents and the use of them that the author would allow. Finally, a person's level of educational achievement may need to be taken into account. This may be important because the ability and fineness of expression may differ. Taking just personal documents to provide evidence of the unique personal dispositions of an individual ignores the rich information that comes from verbal accounts from the person.

6.2.4 The growth of personality

Allport coined the term *proprium* to refer to the central experiences of self-awareness and self-knowledge as a person grows psychologically and moves forward in life. Allport wanted to avoid such terms as ego or self, which may have specific connotations (for example, the ego in Freudian psychology) or which may be catch-all words used loosely in every day language. Allport (1961) stated that the proprium has seven emerging aspects, representing the psychological growth of the person. Six of these are in childhood and one in adolescence. Adulthood is self-awareness of all these seven aspects of the proprium. These are identified and briefly described in Table 6.2.

Each of these seven aspects represents a function to the person. The first to

Table 6.2 The seven aspects of the proprium suggested by Allport (1961)

Proprium	Emergent period	Personality function
1. Bodily self	First year	Pleasures, pains and sensations of the body.
2. Self-identity	Second year	Continuity of experience, especially through language use.
3. Self-esteem	Third year	Independence and sense of achievement.
4. Self-extension	Four to six years	Possession and knowledge of 'mine'.
5. Self-image	Four to six years	Good and naughty self. Sensitive to praise and blame.
6. Self as rational coper	Six to twelve years	Realistic solutions and problem solving.
7. Propriate strivings	Adolescence	Ownership of feelings, thoughts, needs. Life goals identified.
Self-awareness	Adulthood	Awareness of self though all seven aspects coming together.

emerge is the sense of bodily self; here the person becomes aware of bodily sensations, the importance of different parts of the body, and the pleasures and pains the body can give to the person. Self-awareness of the body is the psychological function to emerge. The second function is the sense of self-identity, which comes when a child can differentiate themselves as an individual separate from other people and objects in the world. In short the child discovers a sense of 'I'.

Between the ages of two and three years the function of self-esteem emerges; here children feel pride in their achievements and are sensitive to negative criticism. High self-esteem is essential for mental well-being and achievement throughout life (Baumeister, 1993). The next aspect of the proprium to emerge is self-extension, which refers to a child extending themselves in the world to say what is theirs or what they own or possess. At the same time the function of self-image emerges, which is to do with the expectations others have of the child and how they compare with the actual behaviours and achievements of the child. Between the ages of six and twelve years the function of self as rational coper emerges. This is where the self explores the intellect to solve problems through rational and logical thought.

Those seven proprium functions produce for the adult an awareness of the self that reflects all of these functions as a totality. Allport made a distinction between psychologically mature and healthy adults, and adults who suffered mental disorders such as neuroses. For Allport the mature adult is not governed by child needs and can function fully independently. By contrast people who suffer mental disorders react in rigid and inflexible ways, reflecting behaviour as children rather than mature adult. For such people Allport saw their proprium as underdeveloped, with the personality functions associated with the seven aspects not fully emerged.

6.2.5 Evaluation of Allport

Gordon Allport is widely regarded as the founder of the dispositional approach in personality. He developed the idea of cardinal traits, which influenced psychologists such as Cattell, Eysenck, and Costa and McCrae, whom we shall be considering later in this chapter. Allport did not attempt to establish general laws or propositions about people, as later trait psychologists have done within the nomothetic tradition. By contrast Allport, throughout his career, remained faithful to an ideographic approach to understanding a person. As such his view of humankind was that because of the uniqueness and individuality of each person only detailed case studies could come anywhere close to attempting to capture this as well as the complexity of a person. In many ways this ideographic approach went against the grain of the development of psychology in the middle to latter part of the twentieth century. Only in the last decade has there been a resurgence of interest in the ideographic approach to personality (DeCarvalho, 1990). In clinical psychology case studies have always been important, but more to highlight general rules or concepts.

Allport adopted a scientific methodology in his research and did find supporting evidence for some of his ideas. He did not develop a school of followers and as a consequence many of his ideas, such as that of the proprium, were not taken up and researched more widely. His concept of the proprium was seen as controversial, but some of the ideas can readily be related to those of, for example, Erikson and his psychosocial stages of development (see Chapter 4). Whilst operating within a scientific tradition, Allport also exerted an influence on humanistic psychology (see Chapter 8) because of his focus on the uniqueness of the individual.

In terms of application his use of dispositions to understand prejudice and discrimination, in his classic text *The Nature of Prejudice* (Allport, 1954), broke new ground and remains a powerful influence in psychology in this area. Allport did not apply his work to a clinical setting, although the concepts and theory were there with the proprium should another psychologist have made the attempt.

Allport is regarded favourably in the development of psychology, especially in relation to personality.

6.3 RAYMOND CATTELL

Cattell brought sophisticated statistical techniques, together with rigorous scientific procedures, to the measurement of personality traits. The statistical technique he used is called factor analysis; this technique basically reduces a large number of relationships between different personality traits, or correlations between different traits, to a small number of clusters of traits. It is then the job of the psychologist to give a name to each of the clusters identified by factor analysis. Cattel (1965) identified 16 clusters and developed these into the 16 personality factor (16 PF) questionnaire, which we shall look at a little later. Cattell also engaged in the nature–nurture debate concerning whether traits are inherited or learned from experience. He suggested a strong genetic basis to personality.

6.3.1 Biographical sketch

Raymond Cattell was born in Staffordshire, England, in 1905. Whilst he was too young to serve in the First World War of 1914 to 1918, he was affected by the horror of it and felt that it made him take his studies more seriously (Cattell, 1974). He studied chemistry and physics at the University of London, and then undertook a PhD in psychology. He worked with Charles Spearman in London in the area of human abilities, but could not find a suitable permanent academic post to enable him to pursue his interests in personality. After working in Exeter and Leicester as a educationalist he saw that he would not get a professorship post in Britain and went to live and work in the United States of America. He moved around a number of universities, including Harvard, and during the Second World War worked for the armed forces developing personality tests. This position was affiliated to the University of Illinois, where he worked for 30 years until 1973. During this time he was Director of the Laboratory of Personality and Group Analysis. Here he developed both psychometric tests of personality, his methods of data collection, and his theoretical ideas about the inheritance and development of personality.

In 1977 he went to Hawaii and then to Honolulu as Professor of Psychology at the Forrest Institute of Professonial Psychology. He worked to spread the principles of 'Beyondism', a type of morality, to social scientists and lay people. He died in 1997 at the age of 92. In his career he published over 40 books, over 400 research articles, and was responsible for developing more than ten psychometric tests of intelligence and personality.

6.3.2 Scientific study of personality

Cattell offered the following definition of personality: 'Personality is that which permits a prediction of what a person will do in a given situation' (Cattell, 1950). Notice that this definition, as with science, is about precise prediction and related to actual behaviours a person will engage in – 'what a person will do'. Whilst dispositions or personality traits are some kind of hypothetical construct that cannot be seen or observed, behaviour, by contrast, can be measured and observed objectively. Hence, Cattell's over-riding interest in developing psychometric tests of personality and intelligence was in order to help predict better how people will behave in a range of social and work situations. He used the following simple formula to encapsulate this:

$$R = f(s, p)$$

where R is the behavioural response, which equals a function of both the situation (s) and the personality of the individual (p).

Cattell also claimed to use the 'inductive method' in his scientific approach to the study of personality. The inductive method he saw as first collecting a large amount of data or information and, second, conducting the statistical technique of factor analysis on this data and then drawing hypotheses from this analysis for subsequent testing. Note that Cattell claims not to start with theory, derive a hypothesis and then test empirically, as most would characterise science (see Chapter 1).

Since data collection represents the starting place for Cattell in his scientific approach to the study of personality we need to consider the methods he used. Cattell detailed three main sources of data collection, which he called L-data, Q-data and T-data (Cattell, 1983).

L-data refers to life data and is obtained from a range of life records of the person such as academic achievements and awards, views of parents and teachers, observations made in natural settings, and diaries. Also included would be indications of traits made by other people on questionnaires. Q-data refers to questionnaire data and includes self-ratings on personality questionnaires of various types including those developed by Cattell himself (for example, the 16 PF). T-data refers to test data and is obtained from observations of behaviour in controlled laboratory and experimental conditions.

Cattell said that these three types of data should be combined to allow an accurate and informed knowledge of personality to be obtained. However, Cattell himself gave more emphasis to data collected from questionnaires (Q-data). Relatively little research or uptake by psychologists was advanced for the other two data sources.

6.3.3 Surface and source traits

Returning to the definition of traits given by Allport at the start of the last section we can see that Cattell was concerned to be able to predict behaviour from an understanding of traits. Allport and Odbert (1936) identified over 18,000 words in the English language that are trait names. Clearly with so many there is overlap, but more importantly there is the problem of how to predict behaviour from so many. Cattell's approach was to distinguish between what he called source traits and surface traits (Cattell, 1950). Surface traits are clusters of traits that often go together – for example, sociability, talkativeness and gregariousness. Cattell reduced Allport's list of 18,000 traits to down to 4500 surface traits (as their name implies, these relate directly to behaviour and are to be seen in how people behave).

Cattell argued that if clusters of surface traits go together then there should be some underlying, more general trait to which the cluster of surface traits relate. These Cattell called source traits; such traits are smaller in number than surface traits and not readily observable. So, for example, the three surface traits given above of sociability, talkativeness and gregariousness might all be linked through the source trait of friendliness. Cattell used the three data collection approaches (L-data, Q-data and T-data) to investigate source traits. Some traits, for Cattell, also allow predictions of behaviour to be made. So whilst surface traits characterise and describe behaviour, knowledge of the source traits of a person would allow predictions to be made about their behaviour. In the next section we will look at Cattell's 16 personality factor (16 PF) questionnaire, which reflects the 16 most important source traits Cattell thought were needed to understand and measure normal traits in people. Cattell arrived at this small number of source traits from applying the factor analysis technique, referred to earlier, to a large number of surface traits.

Cattell (1965) also categorised source traits into either ability traits, temperament traits or dynamic traits. Ability traits refer to skills and qualities we possess that allow us to achieve certain goals in life – for example, Cattell regarded intelligence as an ability trait. Temperament traits refer to our approach in life and how to interact with other people – for example, moody and friendly. Dynamic traits refer to the interests and motivations of a person – for example, ambitiousness or sportiness.

Finally, Cattell distinguished between normal traits and abnormal traits. Cattell (1973) regarded normal as relating to pathology as well as abnormal traits. Abnormal traits are more to do with depressive and psychotic disorders than normal traits.

6.3.4 The 16 personality factor (16 PF) questionnaire

One of the most well-regarded and widely used personality questionnaires is the 16 PF. In Cattell's system this measures 16 major source traits, each on a bipolar scale. Table 6.3 lists these 16 factors. It is also important to note that Cattell gave these in order of importance. Hence the first factor, outgoing–reserved, is the most important of the 16 source traits. The surface traits that cluster around each pole of this first factor are:

- source trait of **reserve**   – surface traits of aloof, critical, precise, distrustful and independent
- source trait of **outgoing** – surface traits of warm-hearted, easygoing, good-natured and trustful.

By saying that the source trait of reserved–outgoing was the most important of the 16 traits Cattell meant that this trait has a broad and pervasive influence on behaviour. By contrast the last trait, relaxed–tense, accounts for less variation in behaviour; in other words its expression in behaviour, is more uniform and less varied from person to person.

Table 6.3 The 16 source personality factors suggested by Cattell (1979); note that the order of importance is from top to bottom

Cattell's 16 source personality factors		
outgoing	–	reserved
more intelligent	–	less intelligent
high ego strength	–	low ego strength
assertive	–	humble
happy-go-lucky	–	sober
conscientious	–	expedient
adventuresome	–	sly
toughminded	–	tenderminded
trusting	–	suspicious
imaginative	–	practical
shrewd	–	forthright
apprehensive	–	self-assured
experimenting	–	conservative
group-dependent	–	self-sufficient
casual	–	controlled
relaxed	–	tense

The standard form of the 16 PF consists of 187 questions in which the person completing the questionnaire has to make a choice from a number of alternatives provided. Table 6.4 gives six questions from the 16 PF designed to measure the reserved versus outgoing factor. Once a person has completed the questionnaire and obtained their scores for each of the 16 personality factors these have to be interpreted in relation to an appropriate reference group. On their own the scores obtained for each of the 16 factors do not mean a lot. Only by comparing a person's score to the average score of an appropriate reference group does it become meaningful. Average scores on each factor for numerous reference groups exist; these are also standardised by country, e.g. United States, United Kingdom. Reference groups include male or female students, and male or female workers (also by professional

Table 6.4 Items from the 16 PF designed to measure the reserved versus outgoing factor (note that those answers with a * would score for the outgoing trait)

1. I would rather work as   (a) an engineer
                              (b) a social science lecturer*

2. I could stand being a hermit   (a) true
                                   (b) false*

3. I am careful to turn up when someone expects me   (a) true
                                                       (b) false

4. I would prefer to marry someone who is   (a) a thoughtful companion
                                             (b) effective in a social group*

5. I would prefer to read a book on   (a) national social service*
                                       (b) new scientific weapons

6. I trust strangers   (a) sometimes
                        (b) practically always*

class); combined reference groups combining male/female also exist. By comparing a person's individual score to that of the average of an appropriate reference group it can be determined whether the score is within the average range for the group or lies towards one of the two extremes. When comparing each of the 16 scores to those of a reference group the score on each of the 16 personality factors is given on a scale of one to ten. The individual scores are then built up to provide a profile of the person on the 16 factors. An example is given in Figure 6.1.

6.3.5 Evaluation of Cattell

Cattell's statistical and scientific approach to personality has gained wide acceptance amongst psychologists, with the 16 PF being both highly regarded and widely used as a psychometric tool to measure personality. Whilst space does not permit a full investigation into Cattell's theories, he did produce a comprehensive theory of personality based on scientific principles. In contrast to Gordon Allport, Cattell has produced a nomothetic theory of personality but one that, as with Allport, recognises the complexity of human behaviour.

Cattell placed a strong emphasis on the role of genetics in determining personality and, more specifically, the source traits of a person. However, whilst he did acknowledge the relative importance of the environment as well, little research has been devoted, within Cattell's general theoretical framework, to investigating more precisely the contribution of each. In

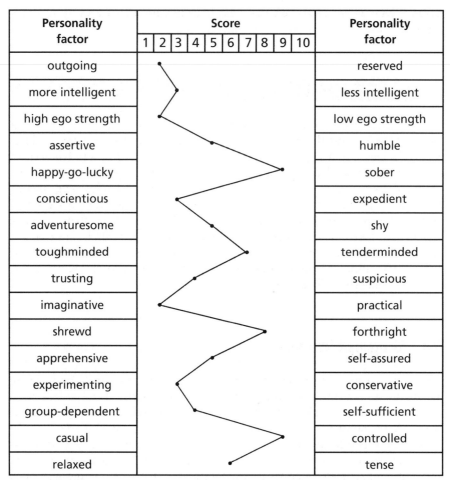

Personality factor	Score										Personality factor
	1	2	3	4	5	6	7	8	9	10	
outgoing											reserved
more intelligent											less intelligent
high ego strength											low ego strength
assertive											humble
happy-go-lucky											sober
conscientious											expedient
adventuresome											shy
toughminded											tenderminded
trusting											suspicious
imaginative											practical
shrewd											forthright
apprehensive											self-assured
experimenting											conservative
group-dependent											self-sufficient
casual											controlled
relaxed											tense

Figure 6.1 Profile of an imaginary person on the 16 PF; you may be interested to give yourself a score of between 1 and 10 on each of the 16 factors to see what kind of profile emerges

assessing the value of Cattell's work, one way is to ask what aspects have had the most impact and been taken up by other psychologists. Without doubt it is the development of the 16 PF questionnaire that has been used extensively. This questionnaire has been used by psychologists for research purposes and applied to a wide range of settings. The most notable applications, perhaps, are in the fields of atypical psychology and occupational psychology. In occupational psychology the 16 PF has been used to inform staff selection in organisations, in attempts to match personality to type of job, understand how a person works and contributes to a group, and the leadership style that a senior manager exhibits.

Generally, Cattell is favourably regarded although some of his theoretical writings have been seen as obscure and have not been followed up by other psychologists.

6.4 HANS EYSENCK

Hans Eysenck is one of the best-known British psychologists, and whilst our interest here is in his theory and measurement of personality, he wrote widely on psychology. He was particularly critical of psychoanalysis and has written a number of books detailing the scientific criticism and arguing that it should be totally rejected. Eysenck also applied techniques of learning theory, particularly operant conditioning (see Chapter 7), to developing treatment programmes for people suffering anxiety disorders such as phobias. Eysenck was also a controversial figure in psychology with his strong views on the important role hereditary had for both personality and intelligence. Eysenck, like Cattell, employed the methods and rigour of science to all the areas that he worked in, especially personality.

6.4.1 Biographical sketch

Although he was a British citizen, Hans Eysenck was born in Berlin in 1916; his father was a catholic and his mother a protestant. He lived in Nazi Germany between the First and Second World Wars and, as a teenager, became interested in politics and socialism. He left Germany for England in 1934 because he was told that he could not enter university unless he joined the SS (the Nazi secret police). He studied physics at the University of London, although he had wide interests in art, music and literature. He did not enjoy physics, however, and transferred to the study of psychology under such eminent psychologists as Sir Cyril Birt and Charles Spearman. He obtained his PhD in psychology in 1940. Because of his German origin he was not allowed to join the British forces in the Second World War. Instead he worked at a hospital treating people with anxiety, depression and other mental disorders. After that he was appointed Director of the Psychology Department at the Maudsley Hospital. In 1955 he was appointed Professor of Psychology at the University of London, where he worked until his retirement.

Eysenck was one of the most prolific psychologists, publishing over 800 journal articles and 75 books on a wide range of topics. Some of his works were written specifically for the lay academic (for example, *Sense and Nonsense in Psychology*) because he wanted to establish in the minds of the general public that psychology was and should be regarded as a respectable scientific discipline. Eysenck died in 1997 at the age of 81.

6.4.2 Three dimensions of personality

Eysenck proposed a structural, hierarchical model of personality with three main dimensions: extroversion, neuroticism and psychotism. In this section we will look at these three dimensions, then in the next section go on to consider his structural model.

Eysenck, like Cattell, was an advocate of the statistical technique called factor analysis. However, Eysenck disagreed with Cattell over the number of basic dimensions of factor of personality and initially suggested just two: extroversion–introversion and stable–unstable (the neuroticism dimension). He later added psychoticism as a third major dimension (Eysenck and Eysenck, 1985). Eysenck regarded the first two dimensions as the ones associated mainly with the normal functioning of the person. The psychoticism factor he associated more with abnormal functions such as delusional thinking, anti-social behaviour and more general psychopathic behaviour.

The **extroversion–introversion** dimension is generally concerned with an individual's interaction with other people and the stability of their behaviour over time. Extroversion refers to the tendency to seek the company of other people, to like talking to other people, and to gain pleasure and enjoyment from being with other people. Introversion is where a person is less sociable, more reserved, and is more stimulated by and finds pleasure in ideas. This dimension clearly has some affinity with Carl Jung's introversion–extroversion general attitude, and Cattell's first factor of 'outgoing–reserved' on the 16 PF. This dimension is also one of the 'big five', as we shall see in Section 6.5 of this chapter.

The stable versus unstable dimension is about the emotional behaviour of the person. People who are emotionally stable Eysenck and Rachman (1961) described as calm, even-tempered, carefree and reliable. People who are emotionally unstable are characterised as moody, touchy, anxious and restless, generally neurotic (which is another label for 'unstable').

The psychoticism dimension is different from the other two dimensions since there are not two different extremes. Rather this is conceptualised as a continuum along one dimension. At one extreme are tendencies towards anti-social behaviours, aggressiveness and egocentricity. The other end of the dimension is the relative absence of these traits indicating a high degree of self-control (whilst lack of self-control is characteristic of high psychoticism scores).

For the first two major dimensions of extroversion–introversion, and stable–unstable Eysenck associated a number of traits with each. These are shown in Figure 6.2 and mapped on to the four temperaments resulting from the four humours identified at the beginning of this chapter in Section 6.1.2.

Eysenck developed personality questionnaires to measure each of these three dimensions. Perhaps the most commonly used is the Eysenck Personality

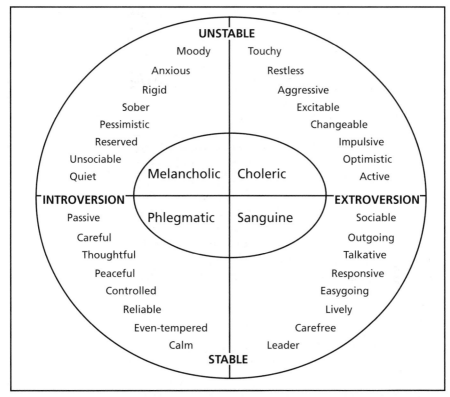

Figure 6.2 The two main dimensions of extroversion–introversion and stable–unstable proposed by Eysenck, with traits associated with each major trait; the diagram also shows how the four temperaments are related to these traits (adapted from Eysenck, 1973)

Inventory (EPI), which measures the two main dimensions shown in Figure 6.2. The EPI consists of 57 questions that require simple yes/no answers; 24 questions measure E–I (extroversion–introversion), and 24 questions S–U (stable–unstable, or neurotic). The remaining nine questions are designed to measure whether the person is presenting themselves in a more socially desirable light than is actually the case. Some examples of each type of question are given in Table 6.5.

Thus for the two main dimensions of personality a score between 1 and 24 is obtained. To understand what this means, reference is made to an appropriate comparison group, as with Cattell and the 16 PF. For large groups of people scores on each of these dimensions fall roughly into the standard bell-shaped or normal distribution.

Table 6.5 Some examples of questions used in Eysenck's EPI; note that there are opposite-worded questions on the EPI as well

Personality dimension	Examples of questions
Extroversion–Introversion	1. Do you prefer action to planning for action? 2. Do you usually take the initiative when you make new friends? 3. Would you rate yourself as lively?
Stable–unstable (neurotic)	4. Do you sometimes feel happy, sometimes depressed without any apparent reason? 5. Are you inclined to be moody? 6. Does your mind often wander when you are trying to concentrate?
Social desirability	7. Are all your habits good and wholesome ones? 8. Have you ever been late for an appointment?
Answer yes or no to each question. If you answer 'Yes' to questions 1–3 this counts as extroversion; if you answer 'yes' to questions 4–6 this counts as unstable and if you answer 'yes' to questions 7 and 8 this counts as high social desirability.	

6.4.3 Structure of personality

Eysenck proposed a hierarchical structure to personality with a trait from one of the main dimensions at the top of the hierarchy followed by levels or examples of the main trait at the next level. This is followed by habitual responses, which are clusters or types of behaviours that are associated with a trait. At the bottom of the hierarchy are the actual behaviours of a person that we can observe. This model is shown in Figure 6.3.

Hence for each of the main traits of extroversion, introversion, stable and unstable, a hierarchy, such as that shown, in Figure 6.3 can be devised (Eysenck, 1947). This hierarchical model of personality shows how the high-level or 'super' traits relate to a cluster of other traits, which finally result in behaviour. Hence, Eysenck, as with Cattell, was concerned to show how traits relate to and determine behaviour. Figure 6.4 shows the cluster of traits Eysenck (1985a) associated with extroversion and psychoticism.

Eysenck (1967) then went on to claim that the two main dimensions were largely inherited, and to offer a neurological/biological explanation of these two traits or factors to explain individual differences. With respect to the

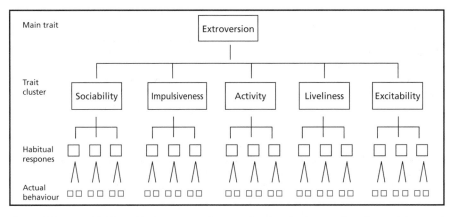

Figure 6.3 Eysenck's hierarchical structure of personality showing how main traits result in actual behaviour (after Eysenck, 1967)

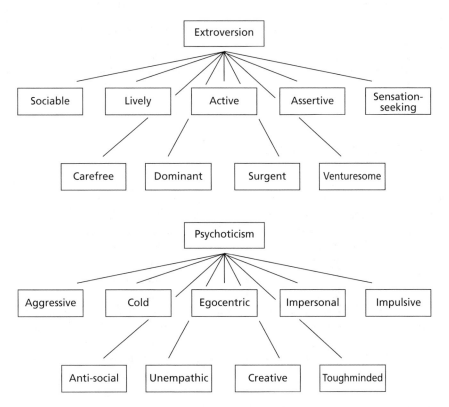

Figure 6.4 Clusters of traits associated with the main traits of extroversion and psychoticism (after Eysenck, 1985)

biological explanation, Eysenck linked individual differences in extroversion–introversion to the activity of a lower part of the brain called the reticular activating system. Put simply, this system plays a role in the arousal of the brain, especially the higher, critical areas of the brain. Eysenck claimed that extroverts basically had a relatively low level of cortical arousal, resulting from the inhibitory actions of the reticular activatory system. As a consequence extroverts, to compensate, seek high levels of stimulation in the outside world. By contrast, introverts have a high level of cortical activity resulting from the excitatory effect of the reticular activating system. Hence, introverts avoid high levels of external stimulation because there is already plenty going on inside their heads!

Research has attempted to investigate these ideas, but not at the level of brain activity itself. For example, Furnham and Bradley (1997) investigated the effect of playing music on the performance of introverts and extroverts. They argued that because music is stimulating, introverts should perform less well with music playing, than when music is not playing. The opposite was argued in the case of extroverts. Measuring performance at a music test, findings confirmed this hypothesis. Perhaps this might explain why some people prefer to work and study in silence, and others prefer to have music in the background.

The classic method for studying the inheritance of characteristics such as personality traits is to use twin studies (see Chapter 2). One study investigating the degree of similarity for introversion and extroversion in monozygotic (identical) and dizygotic (non-identical) twins was conducted by Rose *et al.* (1988) in Sweden. These researchers studied 14,000 pairs of twins and measured the degree of similarity for males and females for both personality traits. As Figure 6.5 shows, monozygotic twins for both males and females showed higher similarity for both personality traits than dyzogotic twins.

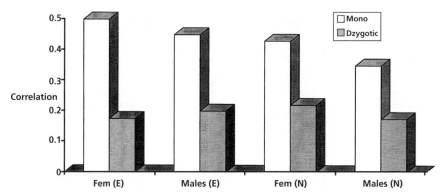

Figure 6.5 Correlations between extroversion, and male and female monoxygotic and dzygotic twins; note that higher correlation indicates a greater degree of similarity between the twins (after Rose *et al.* 1988)

6.4.4 Evaluation of Eysenck

Perhaps the greatest strength of Eysenck's work is the scientific rigour to which it was subjected. The identification of the three main personality dimensions through statistical techniques has proved to be of immense value to personality psychology and, as we shall see in the next section, relates well to present-day thinking and research in the dispositional approach. The EPI questionnaire has enjoyed a wide range of uses and applications in both normal and abnormal spheres of psychology.

Eysenck, as has already been mentioned, wrote and published on a wide range of topics in psychology. His influence in other areas, such as clinical pyschology and the treatment of behavioural disorders, has also been widely adopted. Given the focus of this chapter it has not been possible to evaluate more widely the contribution Eysenck has made to present-day psychology. His empirical research was conducted carefully and with scientific rigour; however, Eysenck did at times go beyond justified extremes to make claims about the inheritance of intelligence and personality. This often led him into controversy in the nature–nurture debate on inheritance. His ideas about the biological underpinning of extroversion and introversion have been more difficult than others to research directly. Much research has been conducted testing hypotheses derived from his ideas in this respect, but evidence for the basic biological workings has been much more difficult to establish and less forthcoming.

More widely, Eysenck has influenced the development and empirical approach of psychology, especially in Great Britain. This is largely the result of his determination to make psychology a discipline based on science, with applications of benefit to society.

6.5 THE 'BIG FIVE' PERSONALITY TRAITS

Ever since the early work of Sir Francis Galton, psychologists have searched for just a small number of dispositions or traits to describe the human personality. Galton proposed (1884) a 'lexical hypothesis', which states that the differences between people affect how they interact with one another and that these differences are coded in words. A key and small number of words are used frequently and reflect how we understand other people. Allport, as we have seen, attempted to reduce nearly 18,000 words in the English language used to describe people to a small number. Cattell suggested 16 personality factors, and Eysenck just three factors. Thurstone, back in 1934, suggested that just five factors were adequate to characterise the important aspects of human personality.

Goldberg (1981) reviewed a large number of studies and research, including his own, on the dispositional approach to personality. He argued that the literature reported a small, but consistent, number of personality factors – five. These were soon to become known as the 'big five' dimensions of personality.

6.5.1 The big five and the five factor model

Digman (1990) claimed that there had been a significant amount of literature over the past 50 years which had suggested that there were five main factors of personality. However, this had largely been ignored until the 1980s. Psychologists now seem to agree that there are five factors, but do not consistently agree on what they are. The most commonly cited five factors, and those that have attracted an enormous amount of research over the past 20 years, are: neuroticism, extroversion, openness, agreeableness and conscientiousness. (Neuroticism and extroversion are similar to the factors suggested by Eysenck that we looked at in the previous section).

The openness factor at one end of the scale concerns generally being open to experience–including the traits of creative, daring, independent and artistic. At the other end of the scale–closed minded–adjectives such as conventional, unadventurous, conforming and unartistic apply. The agreeableness at one end of scale includes the traits good-natured, helpful trusting and lenient; at the other end of the scale, the general factor is called 'antagonism' and includes the traits of irritable, uncooperative, suspicious and critical. The fifth of the big five is conscientiousness, which includes the traits careful, self-reliant, scrupulous and knowledgeable. At the other end of the scale – undirectedness – are the traits of carelessness, helpfulness, laxness and ignorance.

These big five factors of personality simply provide a description, based on studies of language use, of the main personality traits that are commonly used to describe people. The five factors were also arrived at through the statistical technique of factor analysis. As such these five factors make no assumption about the existence of traits in the human personality, nor do they offer any explanation of how they have come about or any theory of personality. The five factor model, largely developed by Costa and McCrae (1985; McCrae and Costa, 1989; 1990), provides both a measure of personality using these five main factors and offers a theoretical framework that attempts to explain how we acquire these factors and how they result in behaviour.

6.5.2 The five factor model of personality

Costa and McCrae developed a questionnaire to measure these five factors; they also developed a theoretical framework in an attempt to explain human personality. In this section we will consider the theoretical framework, and in the next section the questionnaire, called the NEO-PI-R, they devised and which is extensively used in psychological research.

The theoretical framework is organised around four principles. First, that the structure of personality can be described adequately in terms of the five factors. However, each factor consists of a number of specific traits (six for each according to Costa and McCrae). These specific traits are measured by the NEO-PI-R, and for each set of traits associated with one of the five factors can be combined to give an overall score for that factor.

Second, the scores a person obtains on each of the five main factors will be stable over time and relate to internal mechanisms of the brain. This latter claim is similar to Eysencks' claim about the biological underpinning of extroversion and introversion. In the case of the five factor model a neurological mechanism in relation to each of these five factors is yet to be described and identified.

Third, the particular way in which these five factors are present in any one individual reflects inheritance and a genetic basis. Costa and McCrae follow in the tradition of psychologists such as Eysenck and Cattell in asserting a strong biological and genetic basis to personality. Evidence in support of this claim comes largely from twin studies. The evidence is not without criticism, however.

Fourth, and finally, the five factors relate to causal mechanisms such that how each factor is represented in the individual will be consistent with their actual behaviour. Again, as we have seen with other trait psychologists, there is a strong requirement to link personality traits to observable behaviour. Costa and McCrae approach these matters with some degree of caution, since they say that:

> . . . there must be some neurophysiological or hormonal basis for personality, but it is unlikely that we will ever find a single region of the brain that controls neuroticism, or a neurotransmitter that accounts for extroversion, or a gene for openness. (McCrae and Costa, 1990)

So whilst quite strong general claims are made about the causal influence of traits on behaviour, neuropsychological bases of the traits and the role of genetics, little research has been conducted to look specifically at them. This is a weakness of the five factor model, and renders it more a description of personality than a theory.

6.5.3 Measuring the five factors: the NEO-PI-R

Originally Costa and McCrae developed a personality questionnaire to assess just three factors – Neuroticism, Extroversion and Openness – hence the label NEO ('PI' standards for Personality Inventory). They revised this questionnaire to include the factors of agreeableness and conscientiousness – and it was then called the NEO-PI-R (R stands for Revised). The questionnaire actually consists of six sub-scales for each of the main factors, totalling 30 sub-scales in all. These are shown in Table 6.6. Each sub-scale consists of up to ten items. Each has to be answered on a five-point scale from 'strongly agree' to 'strongly disagree'. Some examples of items are:

- I really like most people I meet
- I often crave excitement
- sometimes I feel completely worthless.

A score is calculated for each of the 30 sub-scales. The six sub-scales for each factor provide a profile, and then a total score for the factor is calculated. The 60-item short form of this questionnaire exists (NEO-FFI), which provides a measure of the five factors. As with the 16 PF, scores on each of the 30 sub-scales are profiled, with the profile form indicating very low, low, average, high and very high score bands.

In the manual detailing the NEO-PI-R (Costa and McCrae, 1992) a number of case studies are provided in which ratings are given by both the person under consideration and one or two others that know the person well (spouse, friend, work colleague). Figure 6.6 provides a profile of the five factors of an imaginary person together with scores on the agreeableness sub-scales.

Table 6.6 The five factors of the NEO-PI-R, together with the six sub-scales for each factor (Costa and McCrae, 1992)

Neuroticism	Extroversion	Openness	Agreeableness	Conscientiousness
Anxiety	Warmth	Fantasy	Trust	Competence
Angry hostility	Gregariousness	Aesthetics	Straightforwardness	Order
Depression	Assertiveness	Feelings	Altruism	Dutifulness
Self-consciousness	Activity	Actions	Compliance	Achievement-striving
Impulsiveness	Excitement-seeking	Ideas	Modesty	Self-descriptive
Vulnerability	Positive emotions	Values	Tendermindedness	Deliberation

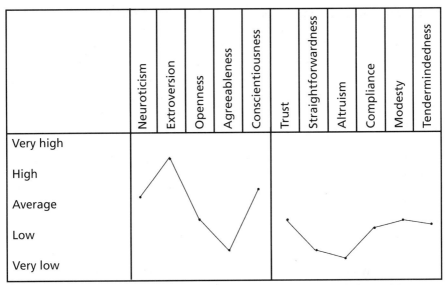

Figure 6.6 Profile of an imaginary person for the five factors, and the six sub-scales of the agreeableness factor (after Costa and McCrae, 1992)

In relation to the five factors, this person has an average score on neuroticism and openness, a high score on conscientiousness, a very low score on agreeableness, and a very high score on extroversion. Now look at the agreeableness profile for the five sub-factors. On three – straightforwardness, altruism and compliance–scores are very low. On the other three sub-scales – trust, modesty and tendermindedness–scores are low. Costa and McCrae (1992) provide the following commentary on this profile:

> People who score in this range are antagonistic, and tend to be rude or even brusque when dealing with others. They are generally suspicious of other people and sceptical of others' ideas and opinions. They can be callous in their feelings. Their attitudes are usually tough-minded in most situations. They prefer competition to co-operation and express hostile feelings with little hesitation. People might describe them as stubborn, critical, manipulative and selfish. (1992: 25)

The NEO-PI-R is a highly regarded and extensively used personality questionnaire. In what follows we shall take a brief look at cross-cultural research and applications of the inventory.

6.5.4 Cross-cultural research

Evidence from cross-cultural research has shown that these five factors are applicable across a wide range of cultures. For example, Digman (1990) found support for the generality of the five factors in Israel, Germany and Japan. McCrae and Costa (1997) have shown that very similar clusters of personality factors to the big five are to be found in six nations using different languages – Germany, Portugal, Israel, China, Korea and Japan. However, Cheung *et al.* (1998) produced evidence from studies in China for an additional factor to the big five measured by the NEO-PI-R. This they called the 'Chinese tradition', reflecting a cultural approach and way of life different to that in western cultures. It may be that other cultures will show a cultural factor that differs from culture to culture, in addition to the five factors measured by the NEO-PI-R.

McCrae and Costa (1997) argue that because research evidence shows the five factors to be important across a diverse range of cultures and languages then this set of dispositions may be universal. However, some caution is needed here since, for example, whilst the five factors may be present across cultures they may play a different role in other cultures. Church (1987) conducted a series of experiments on Filipino personality and attempted to identify traits central to the Filipino culture. Of central importance is the concept of 'pakikisama'. Translated, this means 'going along with or conceding to the ingroup'. This may mean that the 'agreeableness' factor is of greater importance than the other few in the Filipino culture. Fargas and Bond (1985) provided further support for this when comparing Australians with Hong Kong Chinese people. The latter group saw agreeableness as more important than did the former group.

In general, it does seem that those cultures that place greater emphasis on what is called 'collectivism' (concern and care for the good of others and society) rather than 'individualism' (greater focus on individual achievements, reflective of western societies), may need a sixth factor or a modification of the agreeableness factor.

Some psychologists have argued that the evidence supporting the universality of the five factors across cultures and languages points to an evolutionary and genetic basis for the structure of personality (Buss, 1991). This supports the theoretical framework of the five factor model we considered earlier, in Section 6.5.2.

6.5.5 Applications of the five factor model

Research into the five factors has enjoyed a wide range of applications. We will look at two here: job performance and job satisfaction; and personality disorder and its treatment.

In relation to job performance the factors of conscientiousness and agreeableness appear to be predictors of success at a job. Barrick and Mount

(1991) found that high scores on these two factors showed people to be more successful at their jobs than those who scored low on these factors. An interesting and unusual study was concluded with lorry drivers by Hogan and Hogan (1995). The found that a good lorry driver scored higher on conscientiousness and emotional stability, and lower on sociability and impulsiveness than a poor lorry driver. Emotional stability and conscientiousness would, then, seem to be important characteristics for the safe driving of large lorries on our roads!

Tokar and Subick (1997) measured the job satisfaction of adults employed in a variety of occupations and related this to their scores on the NEO-PI-R. They found that above-average scores on extroversion and low scores on neuroticism were key predictors of job satisfaction.

In a clinical setting Funder and Sneed (1993) showed that extroverts may benefit more and contribute better in a group therapy situation. By contrast, introverts may benefit more from one-to-one types of therapeutic treatment.

With respect to disorder of personality, Trill and Sher (1994) provided evidence suggesting that the following factors were associated with specific disorders as shown below.

Substance abuse disorder:	high neuroticism, low extroversion, high openness, low conscientiousness
Anxiety disorders:	high neuroticism, low extroversion, high openness, low agreeableness
Depression:	high neuroticism, low extroversion, high openness, high conscientiousness

To generalise, it would seem from this research that clinical disorders such as anxiety, depression and substance abuse show a pattern of high neuroticism, low extroversion and low conscientiousness.

Studies on teenagers and young adults have shown scores to be higher in neuroticism and extroversion, and lower on agreeableness and conscientiousness than for older adults (Costa and McCrae, 1994). If you think back to the psychosocial stages of development proposed by Erikson (see Chapter 4), this personality profile does fit with the fifth stage of identity crisis. The turbulence and difficulties that teenagers often go through in attempting to establish their role and identity as an adult may be well reflected in the above personality profile. Research by Costa and McCrae (1994) has shown that from about the age of 30 the personality profile of an individual as measured by the NEO-PI-R remains relatively stable.

6.5.6 Evaluation of the five factor approach

The past 20 years have seen a explosion of research on the five factors and the five factor model. The appeal of a small number of key traits to characterise human personality is very strong. However, there is not good agreement over what the five factors should be and whether five is the correct number. Pervin (1994) has argued that psychologists have too readily adopted the idea of five factors. Cattell has stated that five factors are too few; whilst Eysenck, as we have seen, suggested that three main factors are sufficient to describe personality.

Another criticism is that the five factors offer only a description of personality without explaining how the traits are represented *inside* the person (McAdams, 1994). We have seen, in Section 6.5.2, that whilst a theoretical framework about the neurological and biological aspects of the five factors has been suggested, little research has been conducted. Hence, the general view of this framework is that evidence, at present, neither supports nor refutes the claims made.

The questionnaires developed by Costa and McCrae are well constructed and regarded by psychometricians as well researched and conforming to required criteria of reliability and validity. The questionnaires have enjoyed wide applications as we have seen in relation to job performance and clinical settings.

The idea that five personality traits or dispositions can provide a good characterisation of people across a wide range of cultures is well established. However, there are serious and important criticisms of the dispositional approach in general that cast doubt on the validity of the approach as a whole.

6.6 EVALUATION OF THE DISPOSITIONAL APPROACH

Whilst the dispositional or trait approach to personality may have intuitive appeal and reflect our common-sense view of personality a number of serious criticisms have been made by other psychologists. The most important and serious was made by a personality psychologist called Walter Mischel in a book called *Personality and Assessment*, published in 1968. In what follows we will look at Mischel's critique and then consider other criticisms made of the dispositional approach.

6.6.1 Mischel's critique

We have seen in looking at different trait psychologists that a concern of all of them has been to link traits with actual behaviour. Traits are seen as some kind of mental structure that can be used both to predict behaviour and understand why people behave in the specific ways that they do. So if someone, for example, possesses an extrovert trait then we would expect that person to behave in an extrovert way (talkative, sociable, like going to parties, like being with people, etc.). This is what is meant by the term cross-situational consistency, i.e. an extrovert person will behave in an extrovert way across a wide range of different social situations.

Mischel challenged the idea of traits resulting in consistent behaviour across different social situations, and stated that behaviour is much more situationally specific and situationally determined than allowed for by the dispositional approach. This viewpoint was not new in psychology, and had been made by behaviourists such as Watson back in 1924. However, Mischel's criticism was more powerful since in his book he reviewed psychological research as a range of different dispositions (such as honesty, aggression, rigidity and attitudes to authority) and found the correlation between dispositions and behaviour to be quite low. He also found that the same person did not display the same type of behaviour across a range of different situations.

Based on this extensive and thorough review of the research literature on dispositions Mischel went as far as to suggest that traits do not exist at all. This corresponds with, and is reinforced by, research in social psychology where a general tendency is found for people to ignore situational facts when explaining the causes of behaviour. This has been called the **fundamental attribution error** (Ross, 1977); supporting research also shows that people overemphasise the importance of traits when explaining the behaviour of other people.

If we accept Mischel's damaging criticism about the dispositional approach what are we to make of all this effort by psychologists? One way to look at it is to return to Galton's original idea about the role of language. Traits may be seen as more to do with the way we describe our own and other people's behaviour and less to do with a scientific psychological explanation. In terms of research and theory going forward in psychology, Mischel stimulated a deep and long-lasting discussion on the role of traits (the person) and the situation in predicting behaviour. This became known as the person–situation debate, and has resulted in a compromise position whereby the person and the situation are seen to interact to result in behaviour. We will look in more detail at this interactionist position in Chapter 9.

6.6.2 Other criticisms

One criticism, made especially by behaviourists (see Chapter 7) is that traits are not observable, and that only behaviour can be observed. Since this is the case, dispositions are hypothetical constructs seen to exist in some way in the mind and with some biological foundation. Direct evidence has not been found to support these claims, and you may argue that the vast number of dispositions or traits that psychologists have looked at supports the idea that they are more to do with how we describe people than actual psychological phenomena as conceptualised by trait theorists.

Another criticism has been to do with the use of the statistical technique of factor analysis to determine a small number of 'super' or key dispositions. Without going into the technical aspects of factor analysis, the problem is that whilst the technique will cluster a number of different traits together it is up to the psychologist to apply a label to the cluster. In some ways this is part of the problem of which five traits should be in the big five. Different psychologists may come up with different names for the big five depending on how they see the cluster of traits produced by factor analysis.

Finally, the dispositional approach is characterised as one producing numerous questionnaires to assess or measure personality. The question arises as to whether such questionnaires actually measure the dispositions they claim to measure, or whether the scores reflect how people respond to personality questionnaires. Because most use one or another type of self-rating scale, the psychologist has to assume that the person is answering honestly and openly. But this may not necessarily be the case and the responses people give could reflect a range of underlying motives. One of the most commonly recognised is that of social desirability – the wish to present yourself in a more socially desirable light than is actually the case. Some questionnaires, as we have seen with Eysenck's, build in questions to check if a person is answering in such a way. If they are then the validity of all their responses comes into question.

On a more positive note, the dispositional approach has been highly influential, especially in developing personality tests. Such tests, of which there are very many, have enjoyed widespread application in clinical areas and organisational psychology especially.

6.7 SUMMARY

- Dispositions or traits are internal dispositions that are relatively stable over time and across situations. Dispositions are regarded as predictive of behaviour. Dispositions have most commonly been conceptualised as bipolar adjectives such as introversion–extroversion. Interest in describing behaviour using dispositions dates back to Ancient Greek times and Galen's theory of the four humours. Early psychologists such as Galton and Allport pioneered the dispositional approach in psychology.

- Allport distinguished between common traits (hypothetical constructs) and personal dispositions (traits characteristic of an individual). Allport also made a distinction between cardinal, central and secondary traits to reflect the relative importance of different traits. Allport was concerned to emphasise the uniqueness of the person and adopted an ideographic approach. His concept of the proprium as the central experiences and self-knowledge of the person reflects this approach. Allport is regarded as the founding father of the modern dispositional approach in psychology.

- Raymond Cattell adopted a nomothetic approach, bringing scientific rigour and statistical techniques to personality psychology. Cattell used the inductive method of research and collected data using L-data, Q-data and T-data techniques. Cattell distinguished between source traits and surface traits; surface traits relate directly to behaviour whilst source traits are more general underlying traits. Cattell developed the 16 personality factor (16 PF) questionnaire, reflecting 16 source traits. The 16 PF is highly regarded and has been widely used in psychology.

- Hans Eysenck suggested there to be three dimensions of personality: extroversion–introversion, neuroticism–stable and psychoticism. Eysenck developed the EPI (Eysenck Personality Inventory) to measure these three dimensions. He claimed that inheritance had an important part to play in personality and that biological brain mechanisms could be identified to explain differences in personality between people.

- Five factors have emerged in the dispositional approach, these are: neuroticism, extroversion, openness, agreeableness and conscientiousness. Costa and MCrae developed the five factor model of personality and the NEO-PI-R as a way of assessing people on these factors. The NEO-PI-R consists of six sub-scales for each of the five main factors. The five factor model and associated questionnaire has enjoyed a wide range of applications, especially in clinical and organisational settings.

- The dispositional approach was seriously challenged by Mischel who, on the basis of a review of research, claimed that cross-situational consistency for traits was low. The present position acknowledges an interaction of personality and the situation to determine behaviour. Other criticisms of the dispositional approach include use of statistical techniques and response bias when people complete questionnaires.

6.8 FURTHER READING

Allport, G.W. (1961) *Pattern and Growth in Personality.* New York: Holt, Rhinehart and Winston. Provides an account of Allport's theory of personality, concept of traits and the proprium. Allport did not change his ideas radically after this publication.

Rykman, R.M. (2000) *Theories of Personality* (7th edn), Chapter 8, 272–300. United Kingdom: Wadworth Learning. Provides a good overall account of Allport's work, offering both more breadth and depth than could be achieved in this chapter.

Cattell, R.B. (1965) *The Scientific Analysis of Personality.* Baltimore, MD: Penguin. Introductory text written by Cattell for the lay reader. Some of Cattell's work is highly technical and statistical. This short text avoids this and provides a more accessible introduction to his theory of personality.

Rykman, R.M. (2000) *Theories of Personality* (7th edn), Chapter 9, 300–49. United Kingdom: Wadworth Learning. Good introductory chapter, which covers the main aspects of Cattell's work without being too technical.

Eysenck, H.J. and Eysenck, M.W. (1985) *Personality and Individual Differences: a natural science approach.* New York: Plenium Press. Provides a reasonably up-to-date account of Eysenck's views of personality and its biological basis.

Monte, C.F. (1999) *Beneath the Mask: an introduction to theories of personality* (6th edn), Chapter 17, 871–930. London: Harcourt Brace College Publishers. Thorough and detailed chapter that extends the breadth and depth of what has been covered here.

McAdams, D.P. (2001) *The Person: an integrated introduction to personality psychology* (3rd edn), Chapter 6, 302–63. Good, detailed account of the 'big five' factors of personality.

John, O.P. (1990) The 'big five' factor taxonomy: dimensions of personality in the natural language and in questionnaires. In C.A. Pervin (ed.) *Handbook of Personality: theory and research*, 66–100. New York: Guildford. Good summary of research and the main issues around the five factor model. Also includes an interesting historical account of the research leading up to the 'big five'.

7 Social Learning and Social Cognitive Approaches

- Introduction
- Bandura's cognitive social learning theory
- Rotter's social learning theory
- Loss of control and reactions to failure
- Evaluation of the social learning and social cognitive approaches
- Summary
- Further reading

7.1 INTRODUCTION

> The behaviourist asks: why don't we make what we can observe the real field of psychology? ... Now what can we observe? We can observe behaviour – what the organism say or does. (Watson, 1925)

The behaviourist approach in psychology attempts to formulate laws and principles about the way in which observable behaviour is learned and shaped by a person's environment. The above quotation, by J.B. Watson the founder of behaviourism, captures well the view that psychology should focus only on that which is observable – that is, behaviour. In part this view came about as a reaction to the complicated and unobservable mental processes suggested by psychologists such as Freud (see Chapter 3) and Jung (see Chapter 4). There was also a reaction to the introspectionist approach to psychology, established by Wilhelm Wundt in Germany in the late 1800s, which attempted to analyse mental events and feelings. Radical behaviourists, such as Watson and Skinner, attempted to apply the rigours of science to the study of people.

Whilst different types of behaviourism, as we shall see in this chapter, have developed all adhere to three important guiding themes. First, only that which can be observed – behaviour – can be studied by scientific psychology. This means that thoughts, feelings and consciousness are outside what can be observed and therefore cannot be the object of study of scientific psychology. Second, environmental forces provide stimuli, which shape behaviour and determine a response. The role of genetics and inheritance, as a consequence, is very much sidelined. Third, the environment shapes and determines behaviour through learning, and the learning takes place through reinforcement and punishment of behaviour.

J.B. Watson and B.F. Skinner adopted a radical behaviourist tradition, which both excluded mental events as an object of study for psychology and stated they had no role to play in explaining human, or other animal for that matter, behaviour. The emphasis of this chapter is on social learning and social cognitive approaches within a behaviourist tradition. Psychologists such as Albert Bandura and Julian Rotter included mental events and regarded them as necessary for explaining behaviour. They also thought that an understanding of the social situation was necessary. In this chapter we will look in some detail at the work of these two important psychologists. We will also consider more recent theory and research on learned helplessness, and cognition and emotion.

7.1.1 Watson's radical behaviourism

Give me a dozen healthy infants, well formed, and my own specification to bring them up in and I'll guarantee to take any one at random and train him to become any type of specialist I might select – doctor, lawyer, artist, merchant-chief and yes, even beggarman and thief, regardless of his talents, penchants, abilities, vocations and [the] race of his ancestors! (Watson, 1925)

In this clear statement Watson is saying that we can ignore dispositions, inheritance and unconscious forces, and need only look to environmental forces and learning to 'create' a personality.

Watson largely based his approach to learning on the work of Ivan Pavlov and classical conditioning. Ivan Pavlov, a famous Russian physiologist, conducted his now famous experiments with hungry dogs and conditioned them to salivate to a neutral stimulus, such as a bell, instead of food. In traditional classical conditioning, which is concerned with learning by association, an unconditioned stimulus (UCS), such as food, will cause a dog to salivate (the unconditioned response – UCR). This is a biologically governed reflex action. What Pavlov did was to ring a bell a fraction of a second before presenting the UCS of food to the dog. This pairing of the UCS with another stimulus (called the conditioned stimulus – CS) was carried out on a number of occasions. Pavlov then removed the UCS and found that the dog salivated at the sound of the bell only. The conditioned stimulus of the bell therefore elicited the conditioned response of salivation. Notice in this account that there is no recourse to internal events, such as the dog expecting

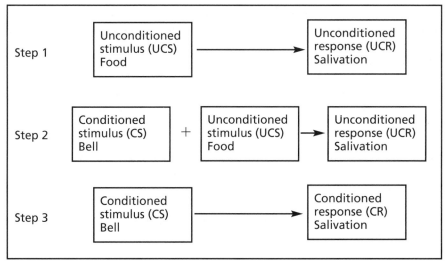

Figure 7.1 The process of classical conditioning: Step 1 – a UCS (food) elicits a UCR (salivation); Step 2 – a UCS (food) is paired with a CS (bell) and salivation occurs; Step 3 – the CS alone produces the CR of salivation

food to be presented shortly after hearing the sound of the bell. This classical conditioning of Pavlov is represented in Figure 7.1.

Pavlov also found that if the bell is presented to the dog many times without pairing it with food the salivation behaviour ceases or is extinguished. To maintain the learned association between the bell and food pairings are needed at times to elicit the salivation response of the dog. Food is said to be a reinforcement to maintaining the UCS producing the UCR of salivation.

Watson and Raynor (1920) adopted these ideas of classical conditioning in the famous case of 'Little Albert'. They wanted to condition fear of a white rat in Albert, who was 11 months old. Accordingly, over a number of occasions they placed a white rat in front of Albert so that he could see it and at the same time made a very loud noise. The noise was so loud and sudden that Albert showed a fear response, such as crying. After seven pairings of the white rat with the loud noise the rat was removed and Albert showed the fear response to just the loud noise. This is represented in Figure 7.2.

Watson and Raynor (1920) demonstrated that emotional reactions can result from classical conditioning. The experiment conducted on Little Albert could be regarded as unethical by present-day standards of psychological research. Many psychologists were greatly influenced by the ways in which classical conditioning can be applied to human behaviour (including Eysenck, 1985). Watson also extended the principles of classical conditioning to abnormal behaviour (Watson, 1924).

Garcia and Koelling (1966) noted that some associations were learned

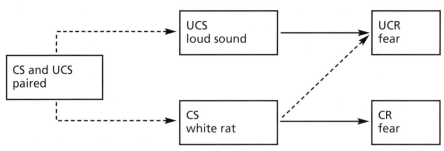

Figure 7.2 Watson and Raynor's (1920) use of classical conditioning to condition a fear response from 'Little Albert' upon seeing a rat

more rapidly than others. For example, rats quickly associate taste with later illness, but do not associate auditory or visual clues with later illness. From this they proposed that animals, including humans, are more biologically prepared to learn certain associations and not others. As a result a modern view of classical conditioning is that people are 'information seekers using logical and perceptual relations among events along with their own preconceptions, to form a sophisticated representation of the world' (Rescorla, 1988). This characterisation of classical conditioning shows there to be an irreducible cognitive or mental element, which refutes a lot of Watson's radical behaviourism position.

7.1.2 Skinner's operant conditioning

Classical conditioning is based on pairing a stimulus known to naturally produce a response (UCS → UCR) with another stimulus (CS) that does not on its own produce such a response. As such, classical conditioning makes use of reflex behaviour. By contrast, operant conditioning involves learning through the consequences of behaviours. Only when a behaviour is emitted is it rewarded (or reinforced) so as to increase the likelihood of it occurring in the future, or punished to decrease the future likelihood of occurrence.

Thorndike (1911) laid the foundations for the development of operant conditioning in his investigation of trial and error learning. Thorndike would put a cat in a puzzle box and, in order to escape, the cat had to pull a piece of string, which would then open the door. The reward was some food, which was placed outside the puzzle box. Once the cat had pulled the string once and escaped it quickly learned to pull the string very soon after being placed in the box. These observations led Thorndike to formulate the law of effect, which states that 'a response which leads to a satisfying state of affairs is strengthened, whereas responses that are less satisfying are weakened and will occur less frequently' (Monte, 1999: 798).

B.F. Skinner developed this approach but substituted Thorndike's more mentalistic terms of 'satisfying' and 'less satisfying' with reinforcement and punishment respectively. Skinner (1974) did not deny that mental events (thoughts and feelings) existed; his prime interest, however, was to study the environmental conditions that result in observable behaviour. As commonly stated, Skinner did not wish to enter the 'black box' of the mind in his scientific approach to psychology. Skinner (1938) coined the phrase 'operant conditioning' to reflect his view that the person or, more generally, organism has to operate on the environment to receive a reinforcement or punishment. Operant behaviour is also called instrumental behaviour because the person is instrumental in producing the desired effect.

Skinner used his famous 'Skinner box' to investigate operant conditioning. The set-up is quite simple: the box contains a bar or lever which, when pressed, delivers a pellet of food. Skinner would put a hungry rat in the box, initially the rat would explore the box but since pressing a bar or lever was not initially in the rat's repertoire of behaviour the experimenter has first to 'shape' the behaviour of the rat. Basically, this would be done by giving the rat a pellet of food from the feeder next to the bar if the rat came close to the bar. The next step of shaping the behaviour of the rat to press the bar would be to require the rat to be touching the bar to get a pellet of food. The final step would be for the rat to actually press the bar to get food.

In this set-up, food acts as a positive reinforcer and as such strengthens the bar-pressing response or behaviour of the rat. The rat quickly learns to press the bar to get food. Another type of reinforcer is called negative reinforcement; here a response is likely to be repeated in the future when the behaviour removes or provides escape from an unpleasant (usually painful) stimulus. The standard set-up for investigating negative reinforcement is a shuttlebox where one side contains metal bars on the floor, which can be electrified, and the other side an area where this painful stimulus is absent. A rat is put in the side with the metal bars in the floor, then the floor is electrified. To escape the rat has to press a lever to open a door to gain access to the other side of the box.

Reinforcers can be delivered according to a schedule, either ratio or interval. An interval schedule is where a pellet of food, for example, is delivered to the rat in the Skinner box after a certain time interval (regardless of how many times the rat presses the lever (the time interval may be fixed or variable). The ratio schedule is where a reinforcer (food) is given after so many presses of the lever (this may also be fixed or variable). It is found that a behaviour is more likely to be repeated in the future from either a variable ratio or variable interval schedule. For example, gambling using slot machines may prove addictive because the machines are programmed to pay off (reinforcement) on a variable-ratio schedule. A worker in a factory who is paid according to the number of items produced is being paid (reinforcer) according to a fixed-ratio schedule (for example, £10 for every ten items produced).

Skinner claimed that the principles of operant conditioning could explain and help change human behaviour without recourse to mental events. For example, Freud's concept of repression (see Chapter 2) as unconscious forgetting by the ego is formulated by Skinner as behaviour avoidance. Behaviours that cause anxiety will be avoided (punished), whilst behaviours not resulting in anxiety will be repeated (negative reinforcement). Armed with operant conditioning Skinner sought to explain all human behaviour according to its principles.

7.1.3 Implications of radical behaviourism for human personality

Radical behaviourists, whilst formulating laws about human behaviour, such as the law of effect, regarded each person as experiencing a unique history of reinforcement and punishment schedules of behaviour. Each person is unique because of this but at any point behaviour can be changed by changing the reinforcements or punishments in the environment. Skinner (1974) regarded personality as a repertoire of behaviour imparted by a set of contingencies. For Skinner personality is a set of behaviours that are unique to the individual and whereby the individual learns throughout life which contingencies produce reward or reinforcement and which produce pain or punishment. The person learns to discriminate between those stimuli and situations that produce reward and those that produce punishment or, in mentalisation terms, pleasure and pain respectively. In this sense operant conditioning, particularly through the work of Skinner, does not regard the individual as a passive organism at the mercy of environmental schedules of reinforcement and punishment. Instead people are seen to have self-control over their environment by actively being engaged in selecting and changing environmental forces to suit the person.

Whilst it is common to regard Freud and Skinner as being at two extremes, Skinner (1974) did think that Freud provided insights into human behaviour. For example, ego defence mechanisms Skinner recast into behaviours designed to attempt to avoid punishment or escape pain (negative reinforcers). So for scientific psychology there is no need to refer to inner mental events, such as the unconscious, to predict, change and control personality.

Radical behaviourists also do not subscribe to 'stage theories' of development, such as Freud's psychosexual stages or Erkson's eight lifespan psychosocial stages. Behaviour patterns and habits develop over the life of the individual as a result of reinforcement schedules and punishment. There are no major stage changes with radical behaviourism, but a building of behavioural repertoires resulting from experience and interaction with the environment.

7.1.4 Evaluation of radical behaviourism

Radical behaviourism is regarded as both deterministic and reductionist in its approach to explaining human behaviour. Deterministic because of its claim that all behaviour is a result of environmental reinforcement schedules and punishment. At the extreme this implies that we have little, if any, control over our behaviour and how we may grow and change throughout life. This contrasts markedly with the humanistic view (see Chapter 8) of human beings as possessing freewill and being in control of who they are and how they grow and change. As we saw above, Skinner did think that people could have some control over the environmental schedules they experience. However, this level of control still puts Skinner's operant conditioning at the deterministic end of the continuum.

Radical behaviourism is regarded as reductionist since all behaviour is reduced to reinforcement schedules and stimulus–response associations. Again, in contrast to humanistic psychologists who regard the whole person as of central importance, the radical behaviourist position seems to take something away from what we think it is to be a person.

Much of the research in the radical behaviourist tradition has been conducted using animals such as rats and pigeons. Basing laws and principle of human behaviour on such research means that we have to assume that humans are really no different from other animals. This ability to generalise from animals to humans is questionable, and certainly rejected by humanistic psychologists. These psychologists regard self-consciousness and self-awareness as features that set us apart from other animals. As such, mental or inner events have to be taken into account, they say, in any psychology of the person.

Radical behaviourism also encounters a problem with personal responsibility, upon which society and law is based. This is a problem since if our behaviour is determined by environmental forces largely beyond our control then how are we to say a person is responsible (has control over, can choose to do or not do) for their behavioural acts. Society sets great store by the concept of personal responsibility and controlling our behaviour. Potentially radical behaviourism undermines this.

However, on a more positive note radical behaviourism has produced therapies that effectively treat anxiety disorders such as phobias and other fears. These are known as behaviour modification techniques and operate to eliminate undesired or anti-social behaviour by changing the environment in which the behaviour occurs (Skinner, 1988).

General dissatisfaction with the radical behaviourist position developed because of its apparent denial of mental processes, and if not denial then putting them outside the scope of scientific psychology. Experimental evidence showed that in human beings conditioning of behaviour was often related to whether or not the person was aware he or she was being reinforced (Dulaney, 1962; Farber, 1963). Indeed, Murray and Jacobson (1978) suggested that very little human learning takes place outside of the awareness or consciousness of the person. Farber (1973) showed that people can choose whether or not a reinforcer is actually reinforcing.

As a result of dissatisfaction with the image of humankind projected by radical behaviourism, together with evidence suggesting that the study of mental events cannot be ignored, behaviourists included the study of mental processes (cognition) and regarded these as essential to explain human behaviour. It is to this we now turn.

7.2 BANDURA'S COGNITIVE SOCIAL LEARNING THEORY

The prospects for survival would be slim indeed if one could only learn from the consequences of trial and error. One does not teach children to swim, adolescents to drive automobiles, and novice medical students to perform surgery by leaving them to discover the requisite behaviour from the consequences of their successes and failures. (Bandura, 1986: 20)

The above quotation highlights a fundamental problem with operant conditioning explanations of behaviour: that account needs to be taken of the capacity of humans both to think and to plan how to behave. The quotation also, indirectly, refers to an important distinction that Bandura and Walters 1963) made between what people do (their actual behaviour) and what people learn about behaving. This distinction can be seen to be one between acquisition of behaviours (learning) and the performance of behaviours. Rewards and punishments may determine what people will do, but are not necessarily needed to explain what people learn.

The social-cognitive learning theory of Bandura (1977b) takes account of how people think (their cognitions) and the social context to explain when and how people will behave.

7.2.1 Biographical sketch

Albert Bandura was born in 1925 in a small farming area of Alberta, Canada. His parents were of Polish descent, and he was one of six children, last born into a family of five sisters. Bandura studied psychology for his degree at the University of British Columbia. He selected the University of Iowa to study and research for his PhD largely because of the Department of Psychology's tradition in learning theory. Following this he qualified as a clinical psychologist in 1953. After a year practising as a clinical psychologist he took up a post at Stanford University in the United States of America. At Stanford he collaborated with Richard Walters, his first doctoral student, and worked in the area of delinquency and aggression. This started him on the path of developing social learning theory, with particular emphasis on observational learning and the role of cognitions in determining behaviour. Bandura's social learning theory, with its application to clinical treatment, has become one of the most influential theories of learning, taking over from Skinner's operant conditioning approach.

Bandura has published numerous highly influential books, and many journal articles. His achievements and contribution to psychology have been widely recognised. He was elected president of the American Psychological Association in 1974 and has received many honours and awards during his career. In 1972 he received the Distinguished Scientific Contribution Award from the American Psychological Association, and in 1980 won the Distinguished Contribution Award from the International Society for Research on Aggression. He is currently Professor of Social Science in Psychology at Stanford University.

7.2.2 Concepts and principles

Bandura's social cognitive theory of learning is built upon three basic assumptions. First, human personality and human behaviour are to be seen as products of learning, although biology may play some role in personality. Second, whilst we can and do learn from direct experience (in the sense of operant conditioning) the most important influences in our behaviour come from observations we make of others behaving in social situations. Third, and finally, language and other forms of symbolism allow people to turn experience into internal thoughts that guide future behaviour. People are self-conscious and reflective and able to plan behaviour. To quote Bandura (1991: 248): 'People form beliefs about what they can do, they anticipate the likely consequences of prospective actions, they set goals for themselves and they otherwise plan courses of action that are likely to produce desired outcomes.' What Bandura is saying here is that because of our capacity for reflective self-consciousness we decide what behaviour to perform in a particular social situation and anticipate the consequences, normally reinforcements or rewards, in advance of actually behaving in a certain way. Hence within Bandura's approach account is taken of a person's environment, a person's cognitions and actual behaviour. Bandura called the interaction of these three elements reciprocal determinism (Bandura, 1978).

Reciprocal determinism means, for Bandura, that each of the three

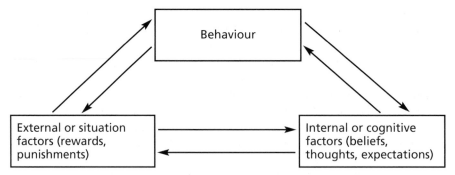

Figure 7.3 Bandura's reciprocal determinism model in which the three elements interact and influence each other in determining behaviour

elements of the environment, the person and behaviour interact with each other and influence each other. This is shown in Figure 7.3. An example may help clarify Bandura's ideas. Imagine that someone you do not like very much asks you to visit an art exhibition with him. Whilst you enjoy going to art exhibitions this one has an expensive entrance fee and you do not have the money to pay. This person offers to pay your entrance fee. You then go to the exhibition and find that you enjoy both the art display and company of this person. At the end of the day you reflect upon the experience and change your mind about not liking the person very much, and think you would enjoy visiting another exhibition with him in the future. In this imaginary episode having the entrance fee paid is an external factor (a reward in this case), and the behaviour of going to the exhibition has changed your cognitions or expectancies about this person for the future, and hence your behaviour towards this person in the future. All three elements of the concept of reciprocal determinism have been in interaction.

The relative influence of these three interacting elements will vary from person to person, and situation to situation. The use of 'determinism' in the phrase reciprocal determinism should not be taken to mean that behaviour is determined by the environmental, as with operant conditioning. Rather that behaviour is determined by previous behavioural experience, cognitions and external or environmental factors. Bandura (1989) does not subscribe to either a strong deterministic or freewill position (see Chapter 1), but recognises that personality and behaviour result from both influences.

7.2.3 Observational learning

As we have seen, Bandura made an important distinction between the learning of a behaviour and the actual performance of the behaviour. What determines whether a person will perform the behaviour he or she has learned will depend on perceived rewards of behaving in that way and, importantly, the belief a person has that successful performance of the behaviour will lead to the desired outcomes or rewards. This is encapsulated in Bandura's (1977a) concept of self-efficacy. Here we will consider observational learning in more detail and use the next section to look at self-efficacy.

Bandura argues that a great deal of learning takes place from watching or observing other people behave, and that behaviour often results from imitating what a person has observed another do. This sounds simple, but is more complicated than at first appears. Bandura (1977b) viewed observational learning as a four-stage process. Stage 1 concerns attentional processes involved in observing the model (this is the word Bandura uses to describe the person being observed). Certain features of the model may attract greater attention from the observer than other features. For example, attractiveness, status, respected friend, well-known pop star are just some features of the model that may draw the attention of the observer. The observer must be motivated to observe. Stage 2 is retention processes; here the behaviour has to be encoded using language and visual or other kinds of imagery. Stage 3 is the motor reproduction processes, which are to do with the ability of the observer to perform such a behaviour. Stage 4 is the final stage and relates to the motivational processes of the observer. Not only must the person be able to perform the behaviour he or she must also want to imitate the observed behaviour. This is where rewards and punishments play a major role. If the person expects to receive a reward for performing the behaviour then he or

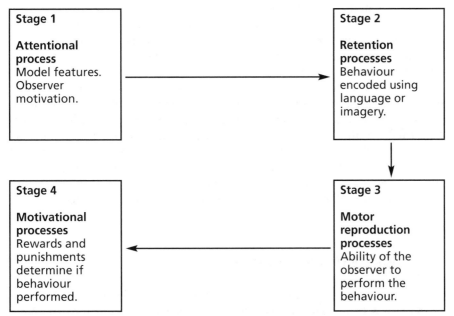

Figure 7.4 The four-stage process of observational learning suggested by Bandura (1977b)

she is likely to perform that behaviour, assuming it is appropriate to the particular social situation. Figure 7.4 summarises this four-stage process of observational learning.

The next question that has to be addressed is what determines whether or not a person expects to be rewarded (or punished for that matter) for performing or imitating a previously observed behaviour of another person. Bandura states that when we observe another person behaving we also observe and learn the consequences for that person. So that if, for example, a person in the street picks up a wallet that someone else has inadvertently dropped and returns it to the other person, the observer is likely to see the wallet-returning behaviour praised and even rewarded. Hence, the observer learns that imitating such behaviour in the future is likely to lead to rewards. Take another example: suppose you are waiting at a pedestrian crossing for the 'green man' to show so as to allow you to cross safely. Whilst waiting somebody else attempts to cross the road whilst the 'red man' is showing. This person narrowly escapes being hit by a passing car. As the observer you should see the outcome of the behaviour as negative (punishment) and having learned the behaviour by observation you are unlikely to imitate it in the future. Bandura called observational learning where the outcome was rewarding vicarious reinforcement. Strictly speaking, vicarious reinforcement increases the chances that the observer will imitate the model because the observer has learned that the consequences for the model of a particular behaviour were rewarding. Vicarious punishment, by contrast, reduces the likelihood that the observer will imitate the model because the observer has seen negative or undesirable consequences of the behaviour. It is also important to note that what counts as rewarding or punishing for the observer is very much to do with the perceptions or cognitions of the observer.

7.2.4 Observational learning and aggression

As we saw in the biographical sketch of Bandura, he received a distinguished award for his work on the study of aggression. Bandura has conducted many studies applying the principles of observational learning, modelling and vicarious reinforcement to the study of aggression, particularly in relation to violence in the media (most notably on television) and the potential harmful effects on observers (viewers).

Bandura *et al.* (1961) demonstrated how aggressive behaviour is imitated by children, between the ages of four and seven years, by observation of aggressive models. This is the famous and often-cited experiment in which children in the experimental condition watched an adult behave aggressively to a life-size inflatable doll, called a Bobo doll. The model sat on the doll, hit it and struck it with a hammer. Children in other conditions watched an adult behave non-aggressively to the Bobo doll, or were put in a control condition where they did not see the model and doll at all. After observing the model and the Bobo doll, children were individually put into a room containing a Bobo doll and other toys. Children who had watched an adult behave aggressively to the doll imitated the aggressive behaviour. By contrast, children who had watched an adult behave non-aggressively to the Bobo doll showed little aggression to the doll, as did those children in the control condition.

Bandura *et al.* (1963) followed up this study by investigating the effect of showing children either a live model behaving aggressively to the doll, or a film showing the adult behaving aggressively to the doll, or a fantasy film in which the adult dressed as a black cat and behaved aggressively to the doll. Bandura and his colleagues found, surprisingly, very little difference across these three conditions in the level or type of aggressive behaviour shown by the children of the Bobo doll subsequent to observation. The types of aggressive behaviours shown by the children were similar to those performed by the adult.

From these and numerous other studies Bandura has concluded that frequent exposure to violence and aggression on the television may well result in children imitating the violent behaviour they have seen. This may be especially the case when aggression and violence is seen to result in rewards for the model rather than punishments. Research has been extended to look at video games and material on the internet; however, evidence is mixed about the cause and effect between television violence and aggressive behaviour (Comstock and Strasburger, 1990; Russell, 1992).

7.2.5 Self-efficacy

Bandura (1989) defined self-efficacy as 'people's beliefs about their capabilities to exercise control over events which effect their lives'. Self-efficacy is to be seen as a continuum from high to low. A person with a high level of self-efficacy believes they can exercise control over events in their lives. By contrast a person with low self-efficiency will regard themselves as unable to behave in ways that will achieve the desired outcomes for them. Efficacy, then, refers to the confidence a person has in his or her ability to perform a certain behaviour. Bandura distinguishes between efficacy as the confidence and ability to perform the behaviour, and outcome expectations that are to do with the likely consequences (rewards or punishments) of performing the behaviour. An example may clarify this distinction. Imagine that you have an interview for a job. You are confident that you can give a good account of yourself at interview, respond well to the questions posed and generally present yourself as a well-qualified candidate for the job. In terms of self-efficacy you have high levels of confidence in your ability to perform well at interview. However, your outcome expectations for being offered the job may be low because you know that there is another candidate who is more experienced and has already been doing the job in an 'acting up' role.

Self-efficacy results from past achievements, from comparison with other people and from social influences (for example, other people having the belief that we can perform a certain behaviour well). Skills at a behaviour, such as driving a car, come from experience of hours of driving, but being a good, careful driver is a result of both skill and our belief that we can drive a car safely and well. Bandura (1977b) regards self-efficacy as a key aspect of personality that affects all aspects of our lives. In particular, self-efficacy has been applied in the field of health psychology to great effect. For example, a person wishing to give up smoking is much more likely to be successful if the person thinks he or she can give up smoking and behaves in ways that help them to cope with the difficulties.

Laboratory	Typical demands	Role of high self-efficacy
Infancy	Learning that behaviour has consequences.	Links actions to outcomes. Learning self-efficacy fundamental.
Early childhood	Learning strengths and weaknesses. Self-comparisons with others, e.g. siblings.	Attention to models to observe behaviour. View mastering by others as good rather than threat.
School age	Knowledge and problem-solving skills, peer-pressure comparisons.	Explore new ideas, interests. Not inhibited.
Adolescence	Transition to adulthood. Changes of puberty and associated demands.	Able to manage and cope with demands and changes. Achieve transition of adulthood.
Adulthood	Career, relationships, family.	Enabling adult to be successful in career, sustain relationship, bring up children.
Old age	Physical and psychological decline. Retirement.	See accumulated wisdom of life experiences. Seek new challenges.

Table 7.1 Bandura's (1977b) developmental perspective on self-efficacy and the importance of a high level of self-efficacy to meet the challenges of life

Bandura (1977b) has also suggested that self-efficacy may develop and change over the lifespan of the individual. He has linked this developmental approach to the mastery of certain skills at different times in life. For example, in infancy the child masters the idea that behaviours have effects (good or bad, rewarding or punishing); also that behaviours may have unintended and intended effects. For adolescents, high levels of self-efficacy help the successful transition from teenager to adult, and to cope with the changes and demands placed upon them. In old age, high self-efficacy may cause a person to seek new challenges, and the benefits of knowledge and experience over their life. Table 7.1 summarises the development approach of Bandura (1977b).

7.2.6 Evaluation of Bandura

Bandura's social-cognitive learning theory applies the scientific methods of experiment, careful observation and hypothesis testing to the study of people. One of the main criticisms of operant conditioning is that the empirical research is based largely on animals such as rats and pigeons. By conducting research using people Bandura has been able to apply his theory to contemporary issues such as the effects of media violence on behaviour, self-efficacy and health psychology, and the development of treatment therapies for people suffering mental disorders.

A huge amount of empirical research has been conducted within the umbrella of Bandura's theory – for example, between 1990 and 1996 around 1400 journal articles on self-efficacy alone were published. This large empirical base for Bandura's theory means that confidence is gained in its effectiveness in applied areas of psychology.

Including both cognitive and social aspects in a theory of learning has meant that the problems encountered by radical behaviourists could be solved. The approach also acknowledges what makes intuitive sense as well – that how people think and what they believe they can do affects behaviour and how well a behaviour is performed. Additionally the approach demonstrates the important influences that other people have on our lives, how we think and what we do.

On a more critical note, Bandura's theory does neglect to articulate and detail the role of biology and inheritance in areas such as aggression. Empirically, much of the early research investigating imitation of aggression in laboratories, with adults behaving aggressively to a Bobo doll does seem highly artificial. However, more recent research has placed greater emphasis on realism or the ecological validity (see Chapter 1) of empirical studies.

Overall, Bandura has made an important and substantial contribution to understanding human behaviour. The theory and associated research reflect a careful scientific approach to the study of personality.

7.3 ROTTER'S SOCIAL LEARNING THEORY

Rotter, like Bandura, is another social learning theorist who thought radical behaviourism too narrow and inadequate to explain human behaviour. Bandura, as we have seen, focused on observational learning and self-efficacy to predict behaviour. Rotter also focuses on cognitive factors, but those of perceptions, expectancies and values.

Rotter was influenced by the ideas of Alfred Adler; in particular the idea that human behaviour is very much goal-directed, i.e. consciously aimed at achieving specific objectives or outcomes. Rotter was also influenced by Lewin's (1938) field theory, which sees human behaviour resulting from multiple causes and a result of the interrelatedness of many factors. Generally speaking, Rotter's social learning theory deals with inner conscious mental processes to a greater extent than Bandura.

7.3.1 Biographical sketch

Julian Rotter was born in Brooklyn, New York, in 1916, the son of immigrant parents (his father was from Austria and his mother from Lithuania). Rotter found growing up in Brooklyn rough and soon became streetwise. As a teenager he read books by Freud and Adler, and wanted to study psychology at university. However, he thought that job prospects were better as a chemist and studied chemistry, with minor studies in psychology, at Brooklyn College and graduated in 1937. He went to graduate school at the University of Iowa and obtained a PhD in psychology in 1941.

During the Second World War Rotter served in the US Army as a psychologist, advising on the selection of officers. After the war he went to Ohio State University where he developed his social learning theory of personality, described in his book *Social Learning and Clinical Psychology* (1954). He moved to the University of Connecticut in 1963 as Professor of Psychology and Director of the Clinical Psychology Teaching Programme. His theoretical ideas were applied to treatment techniques in clinical psychology. In 1989 Rotter was awarded the American Psychological Association Distinguished Scientist Award. He is currently Emeritus Professor of Psychology at the University of Connecticut and has developed interests in interpersonal trust. Rotter has been a major influence in contemporary social learning theory.

7.3.2 Concepts and principles

Rotter's social learning theory is built upon five assumptions (Rotter, 1982). First, human behaviour is a result of interactions between the environment and the person, such that whether something is rewarding or reinforcing depends on the cognitions of the person. Second, human personality is learned through experience, and can be changed or altered throughout life. Third, personality is relatively stable and has a basic unity. Fourth, behaviour is goal-directed and, finally, people anticipate events in deciding how to behave.

How people perceive reinforcement or rewards is of major importance in Rotter's theory, this will be dealt with more fully in the next section. Basically, Rotter states that the effectiveness of reinforcement depends on internal, cognitive factors. People have a subjective expectation of the outcome of behaving in a certain way, and the subjective expectation is in terms of the likely reinforcement that will follow the behaviour. For example, imagine that you have been asked to go out to a nightclub with a group of friends. You think about the nightclub they suggest going to and you think about spending an evening with this small group of people. The nightclub plays the music you like to dance to and you enjoy being with your friends. Hence, your subjective expectation informing your agreeing to go out is that you will have a good time. You expect the night out to be rewarding or reinforcing, so you will take up the invitation.

Rotter's concern is to produce a theory that will predict human behaviour, and he introduces four major concepts that he claims are required for prediction. These are behaviour potential, expectancy, reinforcement value and the psychological situation (Rotter and Hochreich, 1975).

Behaviour potential is the likelihood that a particular behaviour will occur in a particular situation. The individual makes a subjective interpretation or assessment of the situation he or she is in and what behaviours are available to the person in that situation. The likelihood of performing any particular behaviour is determined by the perceived reward or reinforcement the person thinks will follow the behaviour. The behaviour potential, the likelihood of a particular behaviour occurring, is a function of both expectancy and reinforcement value.

Rotter and Hochreich (1975) define expectancy as 'the probability held by the individual that a particular reinforcement will occur as a function of a specific behaviour on his part in a specific situation or situations' (1975: 96). The belief that if you behave in a certain way reinforcement will follow can vary from 0 to 100 per cent. In a sense, the individual makes a probability estimate of the likelihood of a reward following a behaviour. In our nightclub example, the assessment of the reward following the 'going-out behaviour' may be 70 per cent. You may have thought of some negatives that have reduced the expectancy from 100 per cent: for example, one of your friends sometimes gets very drunk and spoils the evening at the end. Expectancy is influenced by previous reinforcement experience, and generalisation from other similar rewarding situations. Expectancies can be generalised or specific. Generalised expectancies come from previous experiences of reinforcement in similar situations; specific expectancies are those specific to one situation.

Reinforcement value is the preference a person has for one reinforcement over another, and is defined by Rotter and Hochreich (1975) as 'the degree of preference for any reinforcement to occur if the possibilities of their occurring were all equal' (1975: 97). Each person differs with respect to reinforcement value and finds reinforcement of different values in different situations. Think again about our nightclub example: suppose instead of your friends asking you out to a nightclub they had given you the choice of a nightclub, a night in the pub or going to watch a film. You had the choice and chose to go to the pub. In Rotter's theory this means that going to the pub, as opposed to the other two options, has higher reinforcement value to you. Reinforcement value comes from past experience where past reinforcement from situations is associated with the present situations or behavioural options presented to you.

The psychological situation is the social situation as it is seen from the person's perspective. Rotter places special emphasis on how the person perceives and interprets the situation, so that different people may have different perceptions of the same social situation. To continue with our nightclub example, you chose to go to the pub when offered three options by

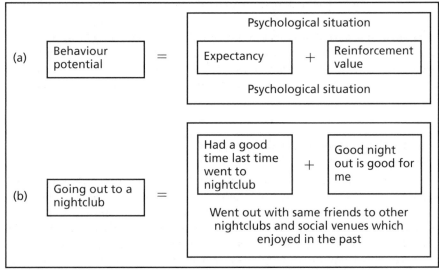

Figure 7.5 Rotter's social learning theory, showing how behaviour potential is a function of expectancy, reinforcement value and the psychological situation; an example is shown in (b)

your friends. One of these friends may hold a negative perception of going to the pub, particularly the one you have chosen. So whilst you may be enjoying yourself in the pub your friend may not, but will stay there in loyalty to you and not wanting to spoil your evening.

If we put these four concepts together, behaviour potential, expectancy, reinforcement value and the psychological situation behaviour is predicted as shown in Figure 7.5.

Finally, Rotter introduces two more broader concepts in his social learning theory: freedom of movement and minimal goal level (Rotter *et al.* 1972). Freedom of movement is the person's overall expectation that behaving in a certain way will lead to reward. If the expectation of reward is high, then the freedom of movement is said to be high. If the expectation of reward is low, the freedom of movement is low. Basically, if you do not have much expectation of reward you are unlikely to engage in the behaviour, thus your choice is more restricted or determined for you.

Minimal goal level is the idea that a person has a minimal level of reinforcement that he or she is prepared to settle for. Rotter regards individuals as setting minimal goals in most situations. For example, your choice of going to the pub was not attractive to one of your friends. However, being with other friends may have meant the level of reinforcement was just above that person's minimal goal level. If one of the others in the group was a person this friend had just had a row with, then this might have pushed the level of reinforcement expectation below the minimal goal level. As a consequence your friend may have made some excuse and at the last minute cried off from going to the pub with you.

As you can see, Rotter developed a comprehensive theory to predict human behaviour. You will recall that Bandura distinguished between learning a behaviour and performing the behaviour. Rotter's social learning theory is more focused on performance, rather than how we come to learn the behaviour in the first place. However, his development of the idea of interna–external control of reinforcement does redress this to same extent.

7.3.3 Internal–external control of reinforcement

How people perceive rewards or reinforcement, together with past experiences, is at the heart of Rotter's social learning theory. The most important generalised expectancy for Rotter is the perception people have over whether or not they have control over receiving reinforcement from the behaviours they choose to make. Rotter (1966) distinguished between two extremes of a continuum: people who perceive rewards or reinforcements as dependent and directly related to their behaviour, and people who do not perceive rewards or reinforcements to relate to or follow from how they behave. In this latter case Rotter characterised such people as perceiving rewards beyond their control. Rotter (1966) called this internal–external control of reinforcement. People who have a high level of internal control of reinforcement believe that rewards are under their control. Such people perceive and believe there to be a strong relationship between what they do

---

For each item, read the two statements and circle the one (a or b) that you agree with or think applies to you.

<u>a</u>   Many of the unhappy things in people's lives are partly due to bad luck.
b   People's misfortunes result from the mistakes they make.

a   One of the major reasons why we have wars is because people don't take enough interest in politics.
<u>b</u>   There will always be wars, no matter how hard people try to prevent them.

a   In the long run people get the respect they deserve in this world.
<u>b</u>   Unfortunately , an individual's worth often passes unrecognised no matter how hard he tries.

a   The idea that teachers are unfair to students is nonsense.
<u>b</u>   Most students don't realise the extent to which their grades are influenced by accidental happenings.

<u>a</u>   Without the right breaks one cannot be an effective leader.
b   Capable people who fail to become leaders have not taken advantage of their opportunities.

<u>a</u>   No matter how hard you try some people just don't like you.
b   People who can't get others to like them don't understand how to get along with others.

<u>a</u>   I have often found that what is going to happen will happen.
b   Trusting to fate has never turned out as well for me as making a decision to take a definite course of action.

a   In the case of the well-prepared student there is rarely, if ever, such a thing as an unfair test.
<u>b</u>   Many times exam questions tend to be so unrelated to coursework that studying is really useless.

a   Becoming a success is a matter of hard work; luck has little or nothing to do with it.
<u>b</u>   Getting a good job depends mainly on being in the right place at the right time.

a   The average citizen can have an influence in government decisions.
<u>b</u>   This world is run by the few people in power, and there is not much the little guy can do about it.

To score add up the items you have circled and that are underlined. The higher your score the more external you are, the lower the score the more internal (on a scale of 1–10).

Table 7.2 Items from the Internal–External Locus of Control Scale developed by Rotter (1966) (their behaviour) and the consequences of those actions (rewards or punishments). Those with internal control are more likely to take responsibility for their actions, but at the extreme may overstate just how much rewards are under their control.

At the other extreme are those Rotter classifies as having a perception of external control. Such people see little relationship between what they do and rewards. The occurrence of reinforcement for externals is often seen to be as a result of fate, luck or from other people. With such perceptions, externals approach new situations with low expectation of success, and are locked into a vicious circle because previous experience of rewards does not increase the feelings of personal control for the future.

Rotter's concept of locus of control needs to be distinguished from Bandura's concept of self-efficacy (see earlier in this chapter). Self-efficacy is to do with the belief that you are able to perform certain behaviours. By contrast locus of control is to do with whether you believe your behaviour is related to outcomes (such as rewards). Both concepts are about perceived competence and mastering, but approach these from different directions.

Rotter (1966) developed a measurement instrument to assess a person's locus of control and the extent to which a person might be internal or external. The Internal–External Locus of Control Scale consists of 29 forced-choice statements; 23 pairs of statements contribute to an internal or external score and six pairs of statements are filler items that are included in order to disguise the purpose of the personality questionnaire. Table 7.2 shows ten items from those that measure internal–external control of reinforcement.

Rotter does not prescribe a cut-off score that separates internals from externals, however, norms or averages, for different groups of people have been developed. For example, high-school students show an average of 8.6, where a low score indicates internal locus of control (Rotter, 1966). The I–E scale has been widely used across a broad range of research areas.

7.3.4 Research on locus of control

Over the lifespan of a person internal control tends to increase with age. As children move into adolescence locus of control moves towards internal, from an initially more external position. In middle age through to old age the move towards internal control stabilises and generally sees little change over the second half of a person's life (Lefcourt, 1976). Parenting styles and their effects on locus of control in children and adolescents have also been investigated. Parental practices where the use of discipline is consistent, support is given to the child and independence is encouraged, tend to result in the child developing a sense of internal control. By contrast, where parents tend to be overprotective and controlling towards the child, and discipline is inconsistent, the child tends to develop external locus of control (de Mann *et al.* 1992).

In terms of academic performance and achievement it has been found that internal locus of control is associated with higher levels of performance (Kalechstein and Nowicki, 1997). Furthermore, internals are more likely to complete their course of study at college or university (Mooney, *et al.* 1991). One explanation may be that internals see a stronger relationship between the amount of effort and work they put in and the marks and grades achieved through assessments. Externals may not work so hard and not achieve so much since they tend not to see a direct relationship between work and effort, and academic outcomes. Moving on to careers and success at a job, internals have been shown to be more satisfied with their jobs, report less stress, and perceive autonomy and control in their job. In general, internals have been shown to be more successful in a career than externals (Kapalka and Lachenmeger, 1988).

On a more intimate level in personal relationships, especially romantic relationships, internals have been found to have fewer romantic relationships than externals, and are less likely to hold idealistic views of love than externals (Dion and Dion, 1973). Internals are more likely to disagree with each of the three following statements than externals.

1. There is only one real love for a person.
2. True love lasts forever.
3. True love leads to almost perfect happiness.

The internal–external locus of control scale has also been used to look at physical and psychological health. In relation to physical health, internals tend to be concerned to look after their health, are more physically fit and exercise more, and cope better with illness (Wallston and Wallston, 1981). In relation to psychological or mental health, the general finding is that internals are more healthy and experience fewer mental disorders (Cooper *et al.* 1995). Drug addicts score more highly on external locus of control and report not feeling able to control aggressive behaviour (DeMoya, 1997).

From the research areas we have looked at above, and the findings, you can see that internals tend to come out well and externals seem to possess many negative characteristics and behaviours. In many ways this should not be surprising since control over ourselves and our environment is a key element of successful adaptation on the part of the individual. By contrast, externals are more associated with maladaptiveness. However, there are negative characteristics that have been found to be associated with internals. For example, at the extreme internals may become compulsive or obsessive in their need for control and concern for excessive levels of order in their lives. Also internals may be what we call 'control freaks' in that they have a need to control everything and everybody (Berrenberg, 1987). Finally, internals tend to experience higher levels of guilt and shame than externals (Phares, 1978); this may become maladaptive if such feelings become very strong and overwhelming.

The general view is that scoring at the extreme either as an internal or external is not healthy and may not be adaptive or help the individual cope with life (Wang and Sproule, 1984). At times it may be more healthy to take an external position especially when situations really are beyond our control.

Rotter developed the Internal–External Locus of Control Scale in 1966 and it has enjoyed widespread application and generated valuable research findings for getting on for 40 years. Clearly a testament to its value and worth.

7.3.5 Interpersonal trust

Rotter (1980) developed another generalised expectancy, one that he called interpersonal trust, into another scale of measurement. Rotter (1980) defines interpersonal trust as 'a generalised expectancy held by an individual that the word, promise, oral or written statement of another individual or group can be relied upon'. This reminds one of Erikson's first psychosocial stage of development concerning basic trust or mistrust in the world by the infant (see Chapter 4). The Interpersonal Trust Scale asks people to score 25 items on a rating scale, using statements such as those below.

- In dealing with strangers one is better off to be cautious until they have provided evidence that they are trustworthy.
- Most publicly elected officials are really sincere in their campaign promises.

Rotter (1980) has conducted a considerable amount of research using this scale. He regards high levels of interpersonal trust as a basic requirement of an effectively functioning society. He has found that people who score highly on interpersonal trust are less likely to lie or cheat, more likely to give others a second chance, and more likely to respect the rights of other people. High scores were found to show no difference to low scores on intelligence or gullibility.

7.3.6 Evaluation of Rotter

The great strength of Rotter's work is that his theory of social learning, particularly the concept of generalised expectancies, paved the way for the development of scales to measure two different generalised expectancies. This has allowed research in a wide range of fields and applications to be conducted. Rotter's original interest in clinical psychology has also allowed theoretical and empirical research to be applied to treatment therapies (as we shall see in Section 7.4.1). Nevertheless a number of well-founded criticisms have been made.

The Internal–External Locus of Control Scale, although widely used, has been criticised because it only measures general expectancies and not specific expectancies. This has led some researchers to develop new scales to measure specific behaviours – for example, related to health (Wallston and Wallston, 1981) and adjustment in elderly people (Reid and Zeigler, 1981). Another criticism of the scale is that it confuses perception of control over personal outcomes with control over political entities such as governments (Mirels, 1970). The problem here is that whilst a person may have control over personal outcomes control over governments and what they do is not directly within the control of an individual. Theoretical questions have been raised about the concept of locus of control. Here the problem is that a link between behaviour and outcome is not always obvious. Furthermore, skill as an internal perception and luck as related to how an external may perceive things represent two different general concepts. Skill is a stable feature whilst luck or chance is variable. The question then is whether the I–E scale confounds locus with stability.

Rotter has concerned himself with how the person, social situation and society come together and interact. The internal locus of control and high interpersonal trust types of people have, according to Rotter, the very qualities required for a society to run smoothly with people living together in a high degree of harmony. In view of this, Rotter's approach does offer a highly responsible attempt by a psychologist to engage in broader debates on how people contribute to, and ought to think and behave in society.

7.4 LOSS OF CONTROL AND REACTIONS TO FAILURE

Bandura's concept of self-efficacy and Rotter's concept of locus of control both deal with how people perceive themselves in relation to their ability to perform a behaviour or link behaviour to outcomes (rewards). Low self-efficacy and high external locus of control may come together to result in a person thinking and feeling that he or she is helpless in many situations. Furthermore, the reactions to failure of such people may perpetuate such thoughts and prevent a person learning and be willing to try harder in the future. In what follows we will briefly look at work on learned helplessness (Seligman, 1975; 1992) and implicit self-judgement concepts (Diveck, 1975; 1996).

7.4.1 Learned helplessness

Seligman (1975) developed a theory of depression based on the idea of learned helplessness. When the implicit belief is held by a person that they have no control over reinforcement in their lives and that how they choose to behave has no influence over outcomes then that person feels helpless. With this basic proposition Seligman (1975) produced a three-stage theory stating two consequences of learned helplessness. The first consequence is that the person will believe and come to expect behaviour and outcomes to be independent and unrelated in the future. Second, such an expectation means that future learning, motivation and emotions will be adversely affected. Seligman (1975) identified common features of learned helpless and depression, as shown in Table 7.3.

These ideas of learned helplessness were reformulated by Abramson *et al.* (1978) to take account of how people attribute causes to behaviour. This draws on the concepts of the attributional approach in social psychology (see Pennington, 2000, for an introduction to this area). In this reformulation of learned helplessness what is of interest is how a person attributes causes to the lack of control. If a person attributes the lack of control to an internal cause (i.e. something to do with the person rather than the situation) and regards the cause as stable (unlikely to change) and global (reflects how the person is at many things) then the person will fell helpless in future situations. If the lack of control is seen as external (in the situation), unstable (likely to change) and specific (not applicable across a range of situations) the person will not feel helpless in the future situations. To highlight this, consider a student who has just broken up with his girlfriend. If the student attributes the cause of the break-up as his fault (internal) – 'I can never keep a relationship and that's how it is with friendships as well' (global), 'and that's how it will always be' (stable) – this would be learned helplessness and may

Learned helplessness	Depression
Symptoms include passivity, lack of aggression, weight loss and appetite loss. Stress. Difficulties with learning.	**Symptoms** include passivity, aggression formed towards self, weight and appetite loss. Negative cognitive set.
Cause: learning that behaving and reinforcement are not related.	**Cause:** belief that responding is useless.
Treatment: exposure to responses that produce reinforcement.	**Treatment:** produce belief that responding does result in reinforcement.

Table 7.3 Some common features between learned helplessness and depression (adapted from Seligman, 1975)

result in depression. If on the other hand the student made the following attributions: 'she was very difficult to talk to' (external), 'I have not had problems with talking to a girlfriend before' (specific), 'and I do not see this as a future problem' (unstable), then the student will not feel helpless for the future.

This attributional approach to learned helplessness has resulted in a questionnaire being developed that measures a person's attribution style (Seligman *et al.* 1974). This measures how a person makes attributions to events, and often informs therapeutic treatments for people suffering from depression. More recently the concept of attributional style has been broadened to one of 'optimism–pessimism' and applied more broadly to general well-being and not just to depression (Peterson, 1993).

7.4.2 Implicit self-judgement

Diveck (1975; 1991) tried to understand and explain why some people respond to failure by becoming helpless, whilst others respond positively and make efforts to do better in the future. Diveck focused her work on children, and using ideas from learned helplessness developed the two categories of 'helpless children' and 'mastery-oriented children'. Helpless children, according to Diveck, perceive their failure to be due to lack of ability, whilst mastery-oriented children perceive their failure as due to lack of effort. Diveck (1975) provided coaching and tutoring for helpless children and tried to get them to view failures as the result of lack of effort. After tutoring these children did show improvement in performance on tasks that they had initially failed.

Diveck and Leggett (1988) found that helpless children differed from mastery-oriented children in their implicit ideas about intelligence and personality. Helpless children tend to think that intelligence and personality are fixed traits and ones they cannot control or change. This Diveck and Leggett (1988) labelled an implicit 'entity theory'. By contrast, mastery-oriented children tend to think of intelligence and personality as traits but ones that can be developed and changed. This the psychologists labelled 'incremental theory'. Children who are categorised as 'incremental theorists' try to increase and develop their abilities and skills by seeking out opportunities to learn new things. Henderson and Diveck (1990) conducted a longitudinal study on children, looking at their achievements at school over a number of years. They found that entity theorist children who were initially low achievers at school, remained so at later points in their school career. In contrast, incremental theorist children who were low achievers initially showed dramatic increases in achievement later in their school career. Disturbingly, the researchers also found that entity theorist children who were initially high achievers at school became low achievers later in their time in school.

The implicit self-judgements that people make about their abilities as fixed (entity theorists) or changeable (incremental theorists) may have far-reaching consequences throughout life, especially in relation to success or failure at work and in a career as an adult. Finally, it may seem from the above that an incrementalal theorist view of your own abilities is more adaptive and will serve the person better than an entity theorist self-perception. As a general rule this may be the case; however, at times, circumstances require an individual to make a realistic appraisal of their strengths, weaknesses and limitations.

7.5 EVALUATION OF THE SOCIAL LEARNING AND SOCIAL COGNITIVE APPROACHES

Social learning theorists such as Bandura and Rotter have had an enormous impact on psychology over the past 40 years or so. The modification of the radical behaviourist position of Watson and Skinner, to include cognitions (perceptions, beliefs, thoughts and feelings), has allowed the richness of our intuitive sense of what it is to be human to be researched. The greatest strength of these social-cognitive approaches is how theory has generated empirical research based ultimately on objective observation of human behaviour. This empirical research has then been applied to assess the effectiveness of therapeutic treatments for mental disorders based on these approaches. This contrasts with psychoanalytic (see Chapter 3) and humanistic approaches (see Chapter 8), which, generally speaking, have not generated a strong empirical research base and have concepts that are difficult to conduct empirical research on.

The social-cognitive approach, as well as the traditional behaviourist approach, have been applied to the understanding and treatment of mental disorders, in particular those of depression and anxiety disorders. The use of treatment programmes based on theory supported by empirical research has also allowed assessments to be made of the effectiveness of treatments such as behaviour modification programmes. In addition, the therapies based on behaviourists' approaches have been attractive to psychologists since training is relatively short compared to the years needed for psychoanalysis. They have also been attractive because treatments of people are relatively quick and, up to a point, effective.

On a more critical note the social cognitive learning theories tend to ignore or downplay the role of biological and hereditary factors. Indeed, the extreme radical behaviourist position is that all we learn comes from experience. These approaches fail to take account of the vast amount of research conducted by psychologists, often through twin studies, to try to establish the role of inheritance in abilities such as intelligence and in personality traits and dispositions. Finally, the view of humanity that emerges from social learning approaches is rather narrow since whilst some account of cognition is taken, wider aspects of the person, such as consciousness and emotions, are not really considered much at all.

Overall, the social cognitive learning approaches, despite some shortcomings, have provided theory, empirical research and a range of practical applications that have benefited people.

7.6 SUMMARY

- Radical behaviourists, such as Watson and Skinner, applied scientific methods to the study of behaviour. Since only behaviour can be observed objectively, radical behaviourists regarded this as the sole object of study and did not take mental processes into account. Watson's radical position was based on Pavlov's classical conditioning. Skinner based his work on operant conditioning. The roles of reinforcement and punishment are to determine future behavioural responses. Radical behaviourism is regarded as deterministic and rejects the idea that people have freewill. General dissatisfaction with this radical position developed because mental processes were shown to be needed to explain learning and performance of behaviour.
- Bandura's cognitive social learning approach is based on the concept of reciprocal determinism, which means that the environment, person (cognitions) and behaviour interact. Learning occurs from observation of models, and what determines whether or not a person will perform a learned behaviour are the perceived rewards for doing so. Observational learning, where the outcome is rewarding, is called vicarious reinforcement; where the outcome is negative, it is called vicarious punishment. Self-efficacy is the belief that a person can exercise control over their lives and their ability to perform certain behaviours.
- Rotter's social learning theory focuses on cognitive factors such as perceptions, expectancies and values to predict behaviour. Rotter claims four concepts are required to predict how a person will behave in a particular situation; these are behaviour potential, expectancy, reinforcement value and the psychological situation. These operate in the context of perceived freedom of movement and minimal goal level for reinforcement. Internal–external locus of control is a generalised expectancy to do with whether or not people believe they have control over reinforcement from their behaviours. Internals believe rewards to be under their control; externals perceive little or no relationship between what they

do and rewards. Another generalised expectancy Rotter has investigated is that of interpersonal trust. Both of these generalised expectancies have attracted a great deal of empirical research.

- Research on loss of control and reaction to failure has focused on the concepts of learned helplessness and implicit self-judgement. Learned helplessness has been developed within an attributional approach to look at how people attribute causes to their behaviour. Implicit self-judgement, through the work of Diveck, has researched 'helpless' and 'mastery-oriented' children through the self-perceptions of implicit entity theorists and implicit incremental theorists.

- The social learning and social-cognitive approaches, as modifications of the radical behaviourist view, have been highly influential in psychology. The use of theory and empirical research has resulted in valuable applications to therapeutic treatments of certain mental disorders.

7.7 FURTHER READING

Skinner, B.F. (1974) *About Behaviourism*. New York; Knopf. Presents the behaviourist position clearly, and also identifies and responds to 20 commonly held beliefs about behaviourism, which Skinner argues are incorrect.

Monte, C.F. (1999) *Beneath the Mask: an introduction to theories of personality* (6th edn), Chapter 16, 778–836. London: Harcourt Brace College Publishers. Provides a good account of Watson and Skinner's radical behaviourist position and the transition to including cognitions.

Bandura, A. (1977) Behaviour theory and models of man, *American Psychologist*. **29**, 859–09. An accessible and relatively short account of Bandura's concept of personality and the key aspects of his social-cognitive learning approach.

Rykman, R.M. (2000) *Theories of Personality* (7th edn), Chapter 17, 596–626. United Kingdom: Wadsworth. Useful chapter that provides more detail than has been given in this chapter.

Rotter, J. and Hochreich, D. (1975) *Personality*. Glenview, IL: Scott Foresman. Probably still the best introduction to Rotter's social learning theory, but obviously not up to date on research and more recent developments.

Rykman, R.M. (2000) *Theories of Personality* (7th edn), Chapter 16, 519–62. Provides a good expansion of what has been covered here on Rotter's theory and research. Some useful sections on applications to education and society.

8 Humanistic Approaches to Personality

- Introduction
- Abraham Maslow
- Carl Rogers
- George Kelly
- Evaluation of the humanistic approach to personality
- Summary
- Further reading

8.1 INTRODUCTION

Think back over the past week or so and try to identify an experience that you found pleasant, satisfying and fulfilling. Also think of a experience that you found unpleasant, dissatisfying and unfulfilling. Whilst these two experiences, whatever they are to do with, seem on the surface to be opposite to each other; in what ways could they be considered to be alike? A number of suggestions come to mind. First, to state the obvious, they are both unique experiences to you, and whilst you can try to describe and explain them to other people, no one else can have exactly the same experience as you. Second, as a result of these experiences, it is likely that you will learn certain things about life and, as a consequence, grow and change as a person. Third, you may be able to exercise personal choice over whether similar experiences could be repeated in the future. This little exercise, getting you to focus on your own personal experiences, is essentially what the humanistic approach to personality is all about. In this chapter we will consider the theories, concepts and ideas of three people who had an important influence on humanistic psychology: Abraham Maslow, Carl Rogers and George Kelly. Whilst each of these personality theorists offers a different perspective of the person, they all emphasise the positive, creative and experimental aspects of what it is to be human. Before looking at each in some detail, consideration will be given to the historical origins and key themes of the humanistic approach.

8.1.1 Historical development of humanistic psychology

Whilst humanistic psychology only became an important influence in psychology in the 1950s its roots date back nearly 200 years. These roots come from a type of philosophy called **existential philosophy**. Existential philosophy developed in Europe in the nineteenth and twentieth centuries through such famous philosophers as Frederick Nietzsche, Søren Kierkegaard and Jean-Paul Sartre. Existential philosophers asked very fundamental questions about what it is to be human, such as: 'What is the meaning of life?', 'What is unique about human beings and human experience?' and 'What role does freewill play in my life?' These are questions aimed at the subjective experience of what it is to be human.

Kierkegaard wrote extensively about the tensions and dilemmas people face in trying to balance individual freedom with personal responsibility. Existential philosophers assume people have freedom of choice over what they do. However, behaving in certain ways may be anti-social, selfish or upsetting to other people. At the same time each person lives in a social and societal context, and because of this has a responsibility to other people and to behaving in ways acceptable to others and, more widely, to society. For existential philosophers such as Kierkegaard, the burden of freedom and the pain of responsibility results in anxiety. This is compounded by the knowledge each of us has that we will die, cease to exist and cease to have experiences at some point in the future. These considerations result in people searching for meaning in their life.

These questions and themes about human existence and human experience influenced european psychiatrists such as Ludwig Binswanger and Victor Frankl during the 1940s and 1950s. For example, Victor Frankl (1955; 1958) wrote about his experiences as a prisoner in a German concentration camp during the Second World War. From his experiences and his understanding of other prisoners, gained from talking to them, Frankl suggested that the most important defining characteristic of what it is to be human is 'will to meaning'. People, according to Frankl, have to find meaning in their lives, even in such extreme conditions as living in a concentration camp as a prisoner. Frankl observed that some prisoners lost all meaning to their lives, and were unable to find any meaning to life in such extreme conditions. Often such people lost the will to live and gave up trying to survive.

Existential psychology was developed by Rollo May in the United States of America in the 1940s and 1950s. May (1953; 1969) was a psychotherapist who approached his clients by trying to understand people as living in a world of here-and-now experiences and personal responsibility. May attempted to get people to live in the present whilst recognising the inevitability of their death. Whilst May's general approach was influential in the development of humanistic psychology, it was criticised for being anti-theoretical and lacking guidelines for conducting psychotherapy. To some extent, humanistic psychology does address these shortcomings.

8.1.2 Key themes of the humanistic approach

From what has been said so far in this chapter a number of key themes have recurred. This can be formalised to say that five key themes characterise and define the humanistic approach. These are: freewill, personal responsibility, subjective experience, the 'here and now', and personal growth. We will look at each of these briefly to provide a general context for the consideration of Maslow, Rogers and Kelly.

Freewill is a key theme since it represents a rejection of the behaviourist and psychoanalytic approaches, which subscribe to a determinist view of human behaviour. In many ways this is one of the reasons for the humanistic approach being called the 'third force' in psychology (the other two forces being the behaviourist and psychoanalytic approaches). The humanistic approach recognises that people have freedom to choose what they think, say and do; however, how freewill is exercised reflects the social and societal context in which a person lives. Psychotherapy based on a humanistic approach encourages people to understand how freewill may be constrained but also how a person may restrict what he or she thinks they can and cannot do.

Personal responsibility is tied up with freewill in that if we are free to choose then we must also take full responsibility for what we say and do. Taking personal responsibility for our actions may be frightening at times and people may try to avoid personal responsibility by saying 'I have to do this' and 'I have to do that'. By using the term 'have to' the implication is that a person is somehow compelled to do something or has their behaviour determined by external forces. Within reason there are not that many actions or behaviours we *have to* do in life. This is the humanistic view.

Subjective experience is another key theme since humanistic psychologists value and emphasise the importance of each person's unique experiences. Psychotherapy from a humanistic perspective does not offer a person advice or tell them what to do. Instead the purpose of humanistic therapy is to assist the person in understanding themselves better and making choices themselves.

The **'here and now'** reflects the importance placed on subjective experience and gives emphasis to creating a greater focus on the present, here and now experiences rather than dwelling on the past or thinking too much about the future. Humanistic psychologists such as Fritz Perls (1969) claimed that because people live too much in the past or future they miss a great deal of the richness of here and now experiences. Missing this means that much of what it is to be human is also missed.

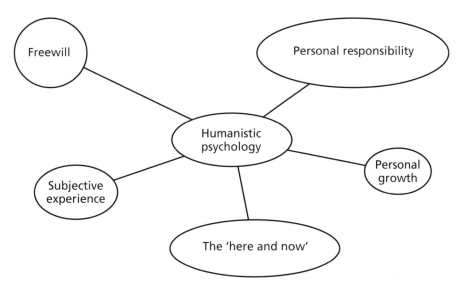

Figure 8.1 The five key themes of the humanistic approach to psychology

Personal growth takes us back to the good and bad experiences you were asked to identify at the start of this chapter. Different terms have been coined to reflect the continual psychological growth that humanistic psychologists emphasise. Terms such as 'self-actualisation' and 'fully functioning individual' reflect a never-ending striving for change, development and fulfilment that characterises human beings. For humanistic psychologists everybody searches for fulfilment, and what is fulfilling may be very different from person to person. These key themes of humanistic psychology are shown in Figure 8.1.

8.2 ABRAHAM MASLOW

Abraham Maslow is often regarded as the person who both popularised and influenced the development of the third force in psychology. Perhaps more than any other humanistic psychologist Maslow's theories and ideas have enjoyed application outside psychotherapy in areas such as organisational behaviour and the psychology of work. Most books on human motivation and motivation in the workplace recognise the importance of Maslow's hierarchy of needs (see Section 8.2.2) and his ideas about the satisfaction of needs on the path to self-actualisation.

8.2.1 Biographical sketch

Abraham Maslow was born on 1 April, 1908 in New York. He was the first-born of seven children, and by accounts not close to either his mother or father, who were Russian–Jewish immigrants. It seems that he was angry and disliked his mother, both as a child and an adult, because of her overpowering religious beliefs and practices, which she tried to impose on him. As a result he did not become a religious person, although disturbed by anti-Semitism as a child and adult.

As a child and teenager Maslow appeared to be lonely, shy and socially introverted. He spent much of his time in libraries reading books. He regarded himself as unattractive, felt inferior and often suffered from depressive episodes. Initially he studied law to please his parents, but this held little interest for him and he went on to study psychology, obtaining his PhD under the supervision of Harlow (who had conducted influential studies on attachment in monkeys). Maslow was influenced by the work of a behaviourist called Thorndike (see Chapter 7) and the ideas of inferiority of Alfred Adler (see Chapter 4).

Maslow had initial interests in behaviourism and psychoanalysis but with the birth of his daughter and the advent of the Second World War became disenchanted with these approaches in psychology. For Maslow behaviourism, in which he had worked for many years, could not account for human experiences so he set about developing a psychology that could. The negativity of war caused Maslow to focus on the optimistic, positive and creative side of people rather than the pessimistic and destructive tendencies.

Maslow's period of fame and influence as a humanistic psychologist came when he was at Brandeis University in Massachusetts. During this 14-year period he received many honours, and was elected president of the American Psychological Association for 1967–68. Even with success, fame and honours Maslow remained shy with people and was terrified of speaking in public. He died in 1970 having suffered poor health for many years.

8.2.2 Motivation and the hierarchy of needs

Maslow's (1970) theory of human motivation rests on the assumption that people seek fulfilment and change through personal growth. This contrasts with the psychoanalytic approach, which characterises people as seeking to avoid conflict and achieve a state of psychological balance (see Chapter 3). It also contrasts with the behaviourist approach, which states that our behaviours are determined by the reinforcement of stimulus–response associations. Maslow characterised people as 'wanting animals', meaning that they are always seeking and desiring something. As one desire is satisfied or fulfilled then another comes along to take its place. On the path to continuous personal growth the person seeks happiness, satisfaction and fulfilment. These are the key characteristics of what Maslow calls **self-actualisation**.

Maslow (1970) makes a distinction between motivation and what he called meta-motivation. Motivation is concerned with meeting the needs of a person that result from deficiencies and the need for survival. These include needs for safety, food and general regard from other people. In contrast to these deficiency needs, which the person is motivated to fulfil and satisfy, are growth needs. Meta-motivation is concerned with personal growth needs that push or drive a person to self-actualisation. It is important to recognise this distinction between needs that stem from a lack or deficiency and the growth needs of self-fulfilment. Maslow saw motivation stemming from deficiency needs as taking priority over growth needs. However, this may not always be the case since artists and religious people, for example, may attempt to ignore deficiency needs when creating a work of art or seeking religious enlightenment. Buddhist monks, for example, train themselves to ignore the deficiency needs of being with other people when they go on 'retreats' to meditate, which may last a year or two at a time. Obviously, some psychological needs, such as for food and water, can only be ignored for a certain amount of time.

Maslow (1970) conceptualised these needs into a **hierarchy of needs**, in which there are five basic types of need. These are physiological needs, safety needs, belonging and love needs, self-esteem needs and self-actualisation needs. These are shown in Figure 8.2. The figure also shows that as each need is satisfied the person will go on to attempt to satisfy the next higher need in the hierarchy. Some people – for example, those in extreme poverty – may spend most or all of their time and effort trying to fulfil the basic needs. People who suffer from very low self-esteem and high levels of anxiety may spend most of their time and effort trying to satisfy the deficiency needs of self-esteem.

Physiological needs are strong basic needs that relate directly to the survival of the individual. They included the need for food, water, oxygen and sleep. *Safety needs* include needs for security, protection and stability, and freedom from fear (or threat). These needs are particularly important for children and adults that suffer from neurotic and anxiety disorders. Safety needs make themselves known when the future is uncertain or unpredictable – for example, during war or when a person loses his or her job. People who dwell too much on the uncertainties of life may seek to compensate by hoarding food or clothes so that bad times are provided for. *Belonging and love needs* reflect the view that people are social animals and need others around them as colleagues, friends and people to love and be loved by in return. In western society many people, if not most, have their physiological

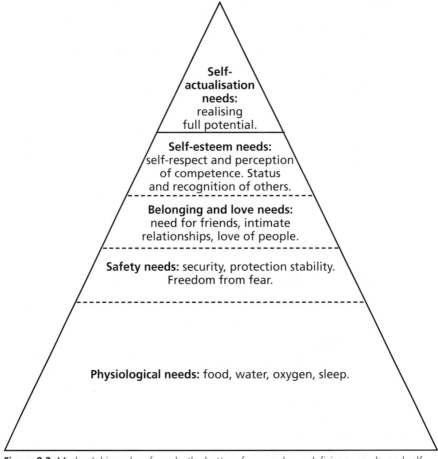

Figure 8.2 Maslow's hierarchy of needs; the bottom four needs are deficiency needs, and self-actualisation is the only growth need

and safety needs fulfilled, with the consequence that the deficiency need of friendship and love motivates the person. If these needs are not met a person may face loneliness and alienation from the society and culture in which they live. Maslow distinguished between two kinds of love with these needs; these are D-love and B-love. D-love is based on deficiency and needs to be satisfied – that is, each person needs to love others (partner, children, parents, etc.) and be loved in return. In contrast, B-love is not a deficiency but love for the 'being of another person' – that is, you love somebody for what they are; this reflects a growth need.

Self-esteem needs are to do with self-respect and respect from other people. In a sense there are two different needs here – the need to perceive oneself as competent and able to achieve goals set. The other need reflects the need to be admired and respected, and as such is to do with status and recognition.

These interrelate with each other since low self-esteem may result in a person rejecting respect from others. Conversely, recognition and respect from others helps to maintain and raise a person's self-esteem.

Self-actualisation needs are about realising your full potential, but this growth need, according to Maslow, emerges only when all the other four deficiency needs have been satisfied. We will consider this growth need in more detail in the next section.

Maslow's hierarchy of needs does oversimplify human needs and behaviour, as Maslow himself recognised. Maslow did not say that a deficiency need had to be fully satisfied before a person was motivated to satisfy a higher need. Also, human behaviour usually results from an attempt to satisfy needs at a number of levels at the same time. Only in extreme conditions of poverty and starvation will a person be solely motivated by physiological needs.

8.2.3 Maslow's research on self-actualisers

Maslow (1970) conducted extensive, but not very rigorous, research on people he categorised as self-actualisers. Maslow defined self-actualisers as people who are 'fulfilling themselves and doing the best that they are capable of' (1970). Quite how one is able objectively to judge whether or not a person is doing the best they are capable of is not obvious. In attempting to tackle this problem Maslow offered preconditions for a person to be able to self-actualise. The three main ones are: no restraints on what you can do, little or no distraction from deficiency needs, and an ability to know yourself very well. Maslow then identified friends and colleagues he regarded as self-actualisers and studied their personality, characteristics, abilities and patterns of behaviour. Maslow's selection of people as self-actualisers was not carried out in relation to strict, objective criteria, but based largely on his own subjective judgements. Clearly, this does represent a shortcoming in his research and the value of findings in terms of generalisability. Nevertheless, this pioneering research by Maslow did result in him suggesting that there are ten characteristics that set self-actualisers apart from non-self-actualisers. These are given in Table 8.1.

Maslow also gave a general characterisation to self-actualisers as people who often have 'peak experiences'. Peak experiences are feelings of ecstasy, intensely felt, and cause a transcendence of reality for a time. Some people may regard a peak experience as deeply religious, mystical and of great significance in their life. Maslow thought that self-actualisers are much more likely to have peak experiences than non-self-actualisers. For Maslow, most peak experiences happen spontaneously – for example, a person may have a peak experience watching a sunset, gazing at the stars or as a result of a great

Table 8.1 Ten characteristics that Maslow (1970) identified with self-actualisation

Characteristic	Explanation
Accurate perceptions	Correct and realistic understanding of reality. Able to tolerate uncertainty and ambiguity.
Accepting of others	Accepts own strengths and shortcomings, and those of other people. Not threatened by others.
Spontaneous and simple	Straightforward, but often unconventional. High ethical and rural standards.
Problem-centred	Oriented to tasks and challenges in the world rather than dealing with their own problems.
Autonomous	Able to be independent of the social context and culture in which they live. Self-contained.
Creative	Able to think in new ways and produce original ideas, works of art, etc.
Sense of humour	Spontaneous sense of humour that does not get a laugh at someone else's expense.
Democratic	Friendly and considerate of other people regardless of sex, race colour, age, etc.
Detached	Similar to autonomous, but able to put aside own feelings and emotions.
Private	Has a need to spend time in solitude, reflection and privacy.

achievement. Maslow attempted to describe what people felt during a peak experience; feelings included those of wholeness, humility and awe, overlaid by feelings of freewill and personal responsibility. Generally, during a peak experience a person experiences no wants, deficiencies or needs. Peak experiences, for Maslow, are very special to a person and will have an important influence on their life.

Maslow focused on healthy people in his research and spent little time studying people with psychological disorders or those who were overwhelmed with meeting the basic physiological and security needs in their life. As a result he may have underrated and missed higher needs and growth needs that all people may strive for. For example, earlier in this chapter we considered Victor Frankl's claim that everybody searches for meaning in life. This happens even in the extreme circumstances of starvation and insecurity such as those Frankl experienced in a German concentration camp.

8.2.4 Measuring self-actualisation

The idea of self-actualisation proposed by Maslow gained widespread acceptance amongst humanistic psychologists as one of the key defining features of what it is to be human. In an attempt to put the measurement of self-actualisation on a more scientific footing Shostrum (1963; 1974) developed a standardised personality inventory called the Personal Orientation Inventory (POI). This is a comprehensive measure of self-actualisation measuring both the values and behaviour of people. This self-report questionnaire consists of 150 forced-choice items (forced-choice questionnaires are where two statements are presented and the person completing the questionnaire has to indicate which statement most closely reflects themselves). Table 8.2 provides some examples from the POI.

The POI has two major sub-scales; one is time competence–time incompetence, and the other is self-oriented–other oriented. The time competence scale measures how effectively people use their time, and a high score indicates a person is living in the here and now. Self-actualisers score

Table 8.2 Sample items from Shostrum's (1963; 1974) Personal Orientation Inventory

Sample items from Shostrum's Personal Orientation Inventory

Time competence scale
1. (a) I strive always to predict what will happen in the future.
   (b) I do not feel it necessary always to predict what will happen in the future.*
 	
2. (a) I prefer to save good things for future use.
   (b) I prefer to use goods things now.*
 	
3. (a) I worry about the future.
   (b) I do not worry about the future.*

Self-oriented scale
4. (a) My moral values are dictated by society.
   (b) My moral values are self-determined.*
 	
5. (a) I feel guilty when I am selfish.
   (b) I do not feel guilty when I am selfish.*
 	
6. (a) I am bound by the principles of fairness.
   (b) I am not absolutely bound by the principles of fairness.*
 	
7. (a) I feel I must always tell the truth.
   (b) I do not always tell the truth.*

Select one of the two statements. The starred (*) statement scores towards high self-actualisation.

high on this scale and relate past and future to present experiences. On the second scale self-actualisers tend to score as self-oriented whilst recognising the need to be sensitive to other people's needs and desires. Both scales combine to provide a measure of the extent (low to high) to which a person self-actualises in their life.

Jones and Crandall (1986) produced a short version of the POI called the Short Index of Self-Actualisation (SISA). The SISA consists of 15 statements to which a person makes a response on a six-point Likert-type scale (see Chapter 2). Because of its ease of use and speed of completion the SISA has been widely used in psychological research.

Research using one of these two measures has reported that people with low self-actualisation scores experience poor interpersonal relationships (Sheffield *et al.* 1995). Creative thinking has been shown to correlate with self-actualisation (Runco *et al.* 1991). High self-actualisation scores correlate negatively with anxiety (Richard and Jex, 1991). And Rowan *et al.* (1995) found that high self-actualisation in men, but not women, related to marital satisfaction.

Shostrum (1963) got Maslow himself to complete the POI; it was found that he scored in the direction of high self-actualisation, but not as high as people known to be self-actualisers. The main drawback with both the POI and the SISA is that people who know about humanistic psychology and the concept of self-actualisation are able to fake the outcome of the questionnaire. This reflects a social desirability on the part of individuals to want to be seen in a more positive light than is actually the case.

8.2.5 Evaluation of Maslow's approach

Maslow's theory of motivation and the hierarchy of needs has been highly influential both within humanistic psychology and more generally across psychology. It has been widely used in organisational and work psychology to help understand what motivates people to work. Whilst people work for financial reward, other motives are also involved that represent the satisfaction of needs at higher levels in Maslow's hierarchy. Maslow's ideas have strong intuitive appeal to both psychologists and lay people. The fact that Maslow himself produced little evidence of scientific value to support his theory seems not to have adversely affected the influence and importance it has in psychology.

The concept of self-actualisation has also enjoyed widespread acceptance and been employed in therapeutic and counselling settings to promote personal growth, and to help people explore themselves and the boundaries of what they can achieve. Self-actualisation as a concept has also been applied to abnormal behaviour to help understand what Maslow (1971) called the

Jonah complex. The Jonah complex is characterised as fear of success and fear of being one's best. This results, claims Maslow, in people avoiding success, and is often found in neurotic people.

On a more critical note, Maslow's theories have often been accused of being a 'middle-class' doctrine generated by comfortably provided-for psychologists in the United States of America. Maslow has also been criticised for paying too much attention to healthy people and not having enough insight into people who suffer psychological disorders. In addition the theory has been criticised for not being a theory of personality but a method of psychological adjustment to the world in which we live. This seems unfair since Freudian theory (see Chapter 3) may also be seen as a theory of good and poor adjustment to life.

Maslow has been a major influence on humanistic psychology and its development. His focus on experience and the higher adjustments of people has served to help define what it means to be a person.

8.3 CARL ROGERS

Carl Rogers, along with Abraham Maslow, greatly influenced the development and application of humanistic psychology. It was Rogers, rather than Maslow, who pioneered humanistic psychotherapy with its **person-centred** approach (Rogers, 1951). Rogers also developed a group psychotherapy approach called encounter groups (Rogers, 1970). Rogers was also keenly aware of social issues in the United States of America, and attempted to show how humanistic psychology could help improve education (Rogers, 1969) and contribute to achieving world peace (Rogers, 1982). Rogers' general view of human personality was optimistic in that he believed that each and every person could achieve fulfilment and happiness in their life.

8.3.1 Biographical sketch

Carl Rogers was born in 1902 in a suburb of Chicago. He was the fourth of six children and his parents were well-educated, conservative middle-class protestants. At the age of 12 his parents moved to a farm, and for a while he became interested in agriculture. When he went to the University of Wisconsin he studied agriculture, but after a year switched to study religion and train as a minister. To do this he moved to New York. Whilst studying religion he developed an interest in psychology and found that his commitment to a religious life waned. Rogers switched again and became a qualified clinical psychologist in 1931. In 1939 he was made director of the Rochester Guidance Centre. Throughout his academic career he maintained an active involvement in psychotherapy and counselling. In 1957 he was appointed as Professor of Psychology and Psychiatry at the University of Wisconsin, and in 1963 moved to California to found the Center for Studies of the Person. Rogers died in 1987 following surgery for a broken hip.

Rogers received many honours and accolades for his work in humanistic psychology. For example, he was president of the American Psychological Association (APA) in 1946/47. In 1956 he received the first Distinguished Scientific Contribution Award from the APA. A number of his books have been and continue to be widely read, these include *Client-Centred Therapy* (1951), and *On Becoming a Person* (1961). Carl Rogers became a very influential figure not just as a humanistic psychologist, but over the general development of psychology and the move away from behaviourism and Freudian psychoanalysis.

8.3.2 The fully functioning person

Common with other humanistic psychologists, such as Maslow, Rogers believed that self-actualisation offers the potential for all people to change and grow. People who are able to self-actualise Rogers described as **fully functioning persons** (Rogers, 1961). Broadly, to be fully functioning means to be in touch with the here and now, and open to the constant flow of experience. Rogers identified five main characteristics of a fully functioning person. First, such a person is open to experience; this means that emotions (whether positive or negative) are accepted rather than denied. Also, the person is not defensive and attempts to experience life to the fullest. Second, such people are characterised by existential living: this means being in touch with different experiences as they occur and avoiding imposing preconceptions or judging matters prematurely. Third, such people trust their feelings and gut instincts, and go with what they feel is right. Rather than spend too much time analysing and thinking logically about something; such people trust their intuitions. Fourth, creativity plays an important role in their lives, and they are not averse to taking risks at times. Fifth, fully functioning people lead richer and more fulfilled lives than other people. This involves happiness and pleasure, but also the willingness to take risks, experience failure and face challenges rather than running away from them.

Rogers did not see the fully functioning person as a personality type, although he did, as we have seen, offer key attributes of such people. If you think about the five key characteristics described above you will realise that they are all processes and ways of functioning in life. Fully functioning people, for Rogers, are well-adjusted, well-balanced and interesting people to be around. Often such people are influential in society, business and socially, being high achievers in one or more of these arenas.

8.3.3 Self-worth and positive regard

Our feelings of self-worth are determined both by what we believe we are capable of and able to achieve, and what other people think of us and how they interact with us. Self-worth is influenced most by significant others in our lives; this includes parents, brothers and sisters, friends, teachers or others we hold in high regard. How other people evaluate us in turn affects how we evaluate ourselves. Feelings of self-worth exist on a continuum from very high to very low. For Rogers (1959), a person who has high self-worth is likely to be prepared to face challenges, accept failure and unhappiness at times, and be more open with other people. From this you can see feelings of high self-worth go together with a fully functioning person. Feelings of low self-worth have the opposite effect.

Feelings of self-worth develop in childhood and, according to Rogers, result from a child's interaction with his or her parents and significant others. Rogers characterises the young child as having two basic needs: positive regard from others and positive self-regard (or self-worth). Positive regard from other people is to do with how other people evaluate and interact with the child. Rogers distinguished between unconditional positive regard and conditional positive regard. **Unconditional positive regard** is the ideal way in which others should interact with us. Here the parents accept and love their child for what he or she is. When the child does something wrong the parents make the child feel loved and wanted even though it is being told off. Positive regard is not withdrawn when the child does something the parents do not approve of. For the child this means that denial of parts of themselves does not take place and the child feels free to try out new things, even though this may lead to disapproval at times. **Conditional positive regard** is, however, the more common form of interaction between parent and child. Here positive regard to the child is conditional or depends upon the child behaving in ways the parents approve of. The child is not truly valued and loved as a person in his or her own right, but valued and loved to the extent that behaviour is approved of by parents. Conditional positive regard results in the child denying their own shortcomings and their own emotions. Their feelings of self-worth are tied up with what the parents will approve of. As adults this results in seeking approval from others and acting in ways others will like and approve of. For Rogers this type of interaction with other people represents a denial of the person. Clearly, this will not foster the development of a fully functioning person, as summarised in Figure 8.3.

Unconditional positive regard

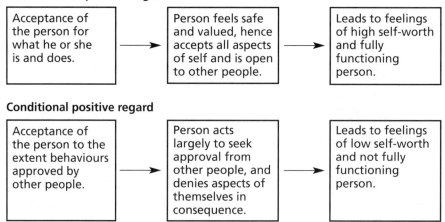

| Acceptance of the person for what he or she is and does. | → | Person feels safe and valued, hence accepts all aspects of self and is open to other people. | → | Leads to feelings of high self-worth and fully functioning person. |

Conditional positive regard

| Acceptance of the person to the extent behaviours approved by other people. | → | Person acts largely to seek approval from other people, and denies aspects of themselves in consequence. | → | Leads to feelings of low self-worth and not fully functioning person. |

Figure 8.3 Unconditional and conditional positive regard and the likely consequences of each

8.3.4 Congruence and incongruence

How we think of ourselves, our self-concept, is made up of a number of components. These include self-worth, which we have already considered, and our ideal self, which is how we think we should be. Rogers also introduced the idea of the **organismic self** which is all aspects of ourself and aspects that we may or may not be fully aware of. The organismic self also includes any feelings, desires or wishes that the person ignores or denies partly as a consequence of experiences of conditional positive regard. For some people their self-concept, ideal self and organismic self may all be closely aligned. For Rogers such a state of affairs represents congruence for the person. However, when there is a great difference between the self-concept and ideal self, and/or the self-concept and the organismic self a state of **incongruence** exists. Where a person is in a state of congruence that person is free from inner tension and anxiety, and is regarded as psychologically well adjusted. Where a person is in a state of incongruence tension, anxiety and poor psychological adjustment will result. People in a state of incongruence are seen by Rogers as denying and distorting aspects of themselves – their experiences, acceptance of emotions and willingness to be themselves. Incongruence may result in maladjustment and psychological suffering for some people; at the extreme this may result in an inability to cope with life generally. Figure 8.4 provides a diagrammatic representation of congruence and incongruence.

Rogers regarded most people to be in a state of incongruence to a certain extent, and whilst achieving congruence may be seen as a goal it is difficult to achieve in real life. Nevertheless, the concept of incongruence allowed Rogers

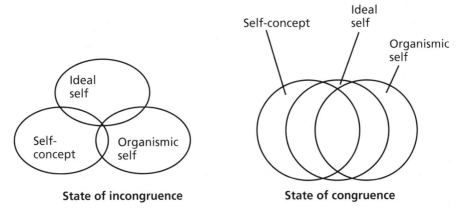

Figure 8.4 Congruence and incongruence in relation to ideal self, self-concept and organismic self

to understand which particular aspects of the person were like this and which aspects congruent. One of the aims of Rogers' approach to psychotherapy (see Section 8.3.6) is to encourage a person to tackle areas of incongruence in their life and try to make changes to achieve congruence.

8.3.5 Studying personal change: the Q-sort technique

In attempting scientifically to study the self-concept Rogers made use of an assessment technique called the Q-sort (Stephenson, 1953). The Q-sort technique provides a measure of the discrepancy or incongruence between the self-concept and ideal self. The Q-sort technique uses a set of 100 cards, each containing a statement or words that can be used to describe the self. Some examples are given in Table 8.3. For each card the person is asked to place it on a seven-point scale ranging from 'not like me' (1) to 'most like me' (7). The person does this twice, once for how they think they actually are (their self-concept), and once for how they would like to be (their ideal self). The Q-sort technique can also be used to understand how others perceive you by asking another person to place each of the 100 cards on a similar seven-point scale in which the other person offers his or her perception of you.

Rogers used the findings from the Q-sort technique to identify specific areas of congruence and incongruence between a person's self-concept and ideal self. The areas of incongruence are those that Rogers would focus on in psychotherapy and assist the person to change. Rogers would also use the Q-sort technique to assess change over time in a person as a result of humanistic psychotherapy. In this way Rogers was able to make a scientific evaluation of the effectiveness of his approach to psychotherapy.

Table 8.3 Examples of statements on cards used in the Q-sort technique; each card is sorted on to one point of the seven-point scale; this can be done for actual self, ideal self and how another person perceives you

Examples of statements on the Q-sort cards	
I make strong demands on myself I often feel humiliated I doubt my sexual powers I am warm towards others I am responsible for my troubles I am a responsible person I am disorganised I tend to be on my guard with friendly people I find it difficult to control my aggression I usually feel driven to work hard	I feel apathetic I am optimistic I am sexually attractive I am shy I am liked by most people who know me I am impulsive I am ambitious I can usually make my mind up and stick to it I am afraid of a full-fledged disagreement with another person I try not to think about my problems

1	2	3	4	5	6	7
Least like me	Somewhat unlike me	A little unlike me	Neither like me nor unlike me	A little like me	Somewhat like me	Most like me

8.3.6 Rogers' approach to psychotherapy

Rogers developed two approaches to psychotherapy; the first is called client-centred, person-centred or non-directive therapy for one-to-one sessions. The second, and later one, developed for small groups, he called encounter group therapy. Both approaches are aimed at producing fully functioning people by enhancing self-worth through unconditional positive regard, and changing incongruences into congruences.

Rogers stated that the humanistic therapist should show three attitudes when interacting with a client in therapy. These are empathy, acceptance and genuineness. Empathy is the attempt to understand and experience how another person feels and thinks. To emphathise with another person the therapist must try to put him or herself in the other person's shoes. Acceptance of another person means giving unconditional positive regard and accepting the other person for what they are. This helps to create greater congruence in the person. Finally, genuineness is where the therapist is open, aware of the therapeutic relationship and not attempting to manipulate the client or other person in any way. Rogers believed that if a therapist or counsellor adopted these attitudes with a client changes would occur in a positive and healthy direction.

Rogers did not use techniques such as free association or dream analysis. His instruction to a client would simply be to ask them to talk about what they wanted to talk about. However, there would be an emphasis on present experiences rather than undue dwelling on the past, as with Freudian psychoanalysis.

Later in his career Rogers became more interested in group counselling and developed an approach where he facilitated a group of people to express feelings and explore problems in their lives. This approach he labelled **encounter groups**. People in encounter groups explore their own thoughts and feelings in relation to how they are perceived by others in the group. Encounter groups were very popular in the 1960s and 1970s, and may be regarded as the forerunners of the more widely used self-help groups that exist today.

Both forms of psychotherapy, individual and group, have had a defining influence on the development of counselling, which is so popular and effectively used these days.

8.3.7 Evaluation of Rogers' approach

Rogers and Skinner (see Chapters 8 and 7 respectively) took part in a series of three debates in the late 1950s and early 1960s, discussing issues to do with human freedom and control (Rogers and Skinner, 1956). Skinner, coming from a radical behaviourist point of view, argued that people do not have freewill and are externally controlled in what they do. Rogers, consistent with a humanistic perspective, argued the opposite. Whilst the debate remains very much unresolved and alive in modern psychology today, Rogers changed psychology and changed how people are to be thought of as human beings. The influence of Rogers has been profound and enduring – providing an optimistic and positive view of human nature.

Whilst Rogers employed scientific techniques such as the Q-sort, the essential subjectivity of his theorising and his focus of personal experience have made it difficult to conduct scientific research on his approach. However, Rogers' careful and more scientific study of the effectiveness of person-centred therapy has enabled evidence to be produced and evaluated about how people benefit. In therapeutic terms, it may be that the three attitudes of the therapist and the emphasis on listening to what other people say may be one of his lasting and more important contributions (Cain, 1990).

Finally, Rogers' concepts and person-centred approach have been criticised for being culture-bound and a direct reflection of American culture (Geller, 1982; Marin, 1975). For example, the view that the healthy person is one who self-actualises may not be so important or relevant in non-western cultures where group achievement is more important. Others have argued that the collective good depends upon each individual feeling fulfilment (Das, 1989).

8.4 GEORGE KELLY

George Kelly (1955) developed an approach to personality called **personal construct theory**. This is concerned with how people think about their world, and how it is constructed in their mind. As such Kelly emphasises cognitive and conscious thought processes much more than other humanistic psychologists. Kelly's personal construct theory is much more concerned with how our experiences of the world lead to how we perceive and structure the world mentally. Kelly characterised people as intuitive or informal scientists; by this he meant that people, just like scientists, generate and test hypotheses about the world. This is because people desire and need to make sense of the world in which they live and, just like scientists, attempt to predict and control future events and behaviours. How each person represents or constructs the word will lead to greater or lesser degrees of predictability and control, depending on the level of complexity and the use of experience to change our perceptions.

8.4.1 Biographical sketch

George Kelly was born in 1905 on a farm near the town of Perth in Kansas, USA. His father was a Presbyterian minister and both parents practised fundamentalist religion, not allowing dancing, drinking and card playing. As an only child Kelly was loved devotedly by his parents. He graduated from college in 1926 having studied physics and mathematics, and planned to pursue a career in engineering. However, whilst at college he became interested in social problems and pursued a higher degree in sociology at the University of Kansas. By his own admission (Kelly, 1969), his first experience of academic psychology left him unimpressed – he could not make sense of the technicalities of behaviourism, and thought Freud wrote a load of nonsense! In 1929 he went to the University of Edinburgh to study education, and with a growing interest in psychology returned to America to obtain a PhD in psychology at the University of Iowa. Kelly qualified as a clinical psychologist and spent ten years at Kansas State College working with poor and destitute people who were victims of the great economic depression of the 1930s. His observations and experiences from this work were of great importance in the development of personal construct theory. Kelly did not commit himself to any one broad approach in psychology.

Following service in the navy as an aviation psychologist during the Second World War, he continued to work as a clinical psychologist. He moved to Ohio State University, where he stayed for 20 years, and developed his theory of personal constructs during this time. Kelly published his first and most important book, called *The Psychology of Personal Constructs*, in 1955. He did not publish extensively, but did spend summers on lecture tours at universities throughout America. George Kelly died in 1967.

Kelly's work has been more influential and long-lasting in Britain than in the United States of America. The British psychologists Donald Bannister and Fay Fransella (Bannister, 1977; Bannister and Fransella, 1971) opened the Centre for Personal Construct Psychology in London. This centre has taken forward the original work of Kelly and trains clinicians in the theory and practice of personal construct psychology.

8.4.2 Personal construct psychology

Kelly thought that all people are motivated to make sense of the world in which they live and, through understanding, strive towards prediction and control. Our social world is better understood and more orderly if we are able to predict what other people will do, how they will behave. Our physical and social worlds are less threatening and can be used to improve our lives if we are able to control events. In achieving this Kelly stated that we all develop cognitive structures to interpret and predict events, which he called **personal constructs**. For Kelly, everybody has a unique set of personal constructs, developed from experience. These personal constructs serve as hypotheses about the world and other people. Kelly regarded these personal constructs as being bipolar: that is, objects and people are attributed characteristics in an either/or fashion. For example, personal constructs that you might apply to your best friend could be:

friendly – unfriendly	reserved – outgoing
intelligent – unintelligent	masculine – feminine

To achieve a degree of predictability Kelly claimed that we engage in a process called template matching. Templates are similar to hypotheses in that a template is applied to a person, say your best friend, with the above constructs. If your friend behaves in ways consistent with your constructs or general template then it is retained. If their behaviour is not consistent then the template is modified and adjusted to incorporate the inconsistencies in the earlier template.

Different people may use different personal constructs to describe the same person. For example, you might use the constructs of friendly, outgoing, intelligent and masculine to describe your best friend. In contrast, somebody else might use different constructs such as sociable, sensitive, thoughtful and daring to describe the same person. Each of you will have a different template made up of component personal constructs of the same person, your friend. Indeed, both templates may adequately match this person since each of you uses different constructs. At times the constructs may not match the person, and you may have a more predictive set of constructs than somebody else.

Whilst we each order our constructs differently Kelly stated that some are more important than others for interpreting and predicting our world. The more important constructs Kelly called superordinate constructs, and the less important ones subordinate constructs. It is important to remember that a superordinate construct for one person may be a subordinate construct for another person. Superordinate and subordinate constructs can be organised in one of two ways as shown in Figure 8.5. With (a) you would first decide if the person was friendly or unfriendly; if friendly you would then go on to decide if the person was reserved or outgoing. With (a) you would not deem it appropriate to decide if a person was reserved or outgoing if your decision over the superordinate construct was that the person is unfriendly. In contrast, with (b) the subordinate construct of reserved or outgoing would be applied to both friendly and unfriendly.

Kelly produced a formal theory of personal constructs and made the fundamental assertion that a person's life and behaviour is guided by how he

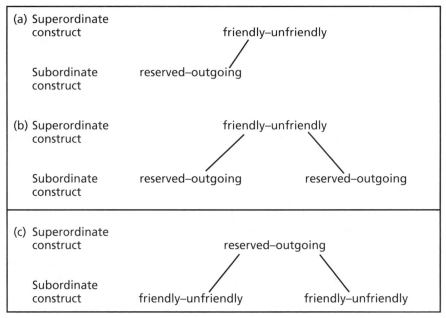

Figure 8.5 Superordinate and subordinate construct arrangements (note with (c) that a superordinate construct may be a subordinate construct for another person)

or she constructs the world. A person's construction of their world is constantly changing as a result of experience and adjustments to their templates. Kelly coined the phrase *constructive alternativism* to reflect that everyone has a different perception of reality and that each may be equally valid.

8.4.3 Role Construct Repertory Test

In order to understand in detail how a person constructs their world Kelly invented the Role Construct Repertory Test, commonly known as the **Rep Test**. The Rep Test seeks to provide an account or picture of how a person constructs his or her world by applying bipolar constructs to a range of other people of significance in the person's life. To ensure that it is the person's construct that is obtained the person has to produce his or her own bipolar constructs, but in a systematic way. Working through a hypothetical example will clarify the Rep Test.

To conduct a Rep Test a standard Repertory Grid, or Rep Grid, is used as shown in Figure 8.6. Imagine that a person has been asked to consider, and identify where appropriate, eight different people in his or her life: themselves, mother, father, brother or sister, best friend, intimate partner, a rejected person and a threatening person. Each of these people, by name, would be entered into one of the vertical columns of the grid, as shown in Figure 8.6. Each horizontal row shows three circles under different people. The task now is to think about these three people and think about a bipolar construct that categorises two as similar and one different. In our example in Figure 8.6, the person has identified themselves and their best friend as sociable and the threatening person as not sociable. The next step is for the person to consider each of the remaining five people and decide whether they are sociable or not sociable. A tick is placed if sociable is considered appropriate and the grid left blank if not sociable is thought to apply. This procedure is then repeated for a number of constructs (in our example in Figure 8.6 seven other constructs are given). Note that for each construct a different set of three people have to be considered and a decision made on how two are thought to be alike and one different. This bipolar construct is then applied to the other five people being considered in this Rep Test.

A typical Rep Grid may contain 20 different people and the same number of different bipolar constructs. To complete such a grid is both time consuming and requires careful thought on the part of the person in initially deciding how two people are alike and one different, and then which of the qualities the remaining people possess in relation to the bipolar construct.

Analysis of a completed Rep Test can also be quite complex. First, an analysis of the range and type of personal constructs produced is made. For

Self	Mother	Father	Brother or Sister	Best friend	Intimate partner	Rejected person	Threatening person	Bipolar construct
⊗	√			⊗	√	O		social – not sociable
√		O	√		⊗	√	⊗	healthy – unhealthy
	⊗	√	√	⊗		O		religious – not religious
⊗			⊗	√	√		O	outgoing – reserved
√	⊗	⊗	√	√	O			honest – dishonest
√	O	√		⊗	⊗	√		considerate – inconsiderate
O		√	⊗	√	√		⊗	conventional – unconventional
	√	⊗	⊗		√	O		quiet – loud

Key ⊗ Seen as alike on the first bipolar construct adjective ☑ Possesses first bipolar adjective
‎   O Seen as different, second bipolar adjective applies ☐ Possesses second bipolar adjective

Figure 8.6 Simplified examples of a completed Rep Grid

example, are there a limited number of themes or are the constructs wide-ranging? Do some of the constructs overlap or do they mostly seem independent of each other? The next type of analysis involves looking for patterns between related constructs and a sub-set of the people used in the grid. In Figure 8.6 our imaginary example shows the person's best friend and intimate partner to be perceived as sociable, outgoing, considerate and conventional. In contrast, the threatening person and father are both seen as not sociable and reserved, whilst the rejected person and mother are both seen as reserved and unconventional.

More detailed analysis is usually made by clinicians trained in the use of the Rep Test. However, experience of the clinician and subjectivity do enter

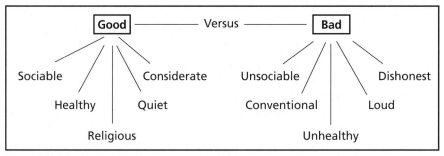

Figure 8.7 Bringing together personal constructs into an overarching construct

into interpretations of the repertory grid. Analysis, based on mathematical procedures, attempts to bring together a range of personal constructs under an overarching and more simple system. This is shown in Figure 8.7 for the constructs used in the example shown in Figure 8.6.

8.4.4 Applications of personal construct theory

Personal construct theory and the Rep Test have been used in a number of applied areas of research including health and illness (both physical and psychological), depression, grief and loss, marital and intimate relationships, attitudes and beliefs, organisational psychology and education (Fransella and Thomas, 1988; Hammond and Romney, 1995).

Bannister and Salmon (1966) compared the personal constructs used by people suffering from schizophrenia to those of psychologically well people. Using the Rep Test it was found that the personal constructs used by schizophrenics were less interrelated and showed greater inconsistency than those of healthy people. The consequences of such a profile of personal constructs for people suffering from schizophrenia is that they perceive the world in which they live to be unpredictable and have a disorganised construction of reality. The particular profile of constructions that a schizophrenic shows may then be used as the basis for a treatment programme to adjust and change constructs. Change would be to foster greater prediction and coherence in perception of the world for the person.

The Rep Test has been used to explore the complexity or simplicity of a person's personal constructs and to look at change in a person over time (Crockett, 1982). It has been found that people who show a greater level of complexity in differences and similarities perceived are better able to predict how other people will behave.

Personal constructs have also been investigated to see if any patterns emerge in the relationships we develop with other people. Two main findings have emerged. First, people with similar personal constructs and similar perceptions of the world are more likely to be friends than where personal constructs are different (Duck and Allison, 1978). Other research has shown that people will get along with each other when they have different personal constructs, but where each understands the other's constructs (Kelly, 1970).

Neimeger and Hall (1988) investigated how married women's personal constructs related to marital satisfaction. Three groups of married women were given the Rep Test, these groups were women satisfied with their marriage, dissatisfied with their marriage, and women who experienced abuse within their marriage. The general findings were that women who were satisfied with their marriage were in relationships that respected their identity, self-image and personal constructs. In contrast, unhappily married women were in relationships that threatened their personal contructs and where their identity was not respected. Such analysis can be used to help make a marriage more satisfying, and identify the particular areas to be changed.

8.4.5 Evaluation of Kelly's approach

Whilst Kelly's personal construct theory can be seen to be within the humanistic approach to personality, his influence has been greater with cognitive personality theorists such as Bandura and Rotter (see Chapter 7). This in turn has influenced more recent personality theorists who seek to look for differences between people in terms of cognitive structures and processes rather than traits (Mischel, 1979; Cantor and Mischel, 1979). This approach to personality looks at cognitive structures such as schemas and prototypes to identify differences between people (see Chapter 8).

Since Kelly operated as a clinical psychologist for much of his academic life, it is not surprising that personal construct theory has been developed in the context of psychotherapy. Kelly regarded his approach to people with psychological disorders as one of 'reconstruction' rather than therapy. He saw his role as helping the person to change and rebuild their personal constructs. One technique Kelly commonly used was that of role-playing. Here the client was asked to role-play the person they were having difficulty with – for example, their boss at work. Kelly advocated this since it helps the person understand the personal constructs of another and hence allows changes to be made so that the difficult person may be dealt with more effectively.

More critically, Kelly has been accused of focusing too much on cognitive aspects of the person and ignoring the emotional side of life. Kelly's personal construct theory takes a relatively narrow view of personality with its insistence on putting everything into bipolar personal constructs. Kelly also ignores early childhood influences resulting from conflict, and the psychoanalytic approach of unconscious mental processes.

Personal construct theory has been based on an empirical approach, mainly through the use of the Rep Test. There are two general shortcomings with this research, however. First, most is based on 'paper and pencil' tasks, which are then subjected to correlational analysis. This type of analysis does not allow for cause and effect to be established. Second, the Rep Test produces a description of personal constructs; the interpretation of the range and patterns of constructs is more subjective and open to different interpretations by different people. This holds even if two people are trained in the Rep Test procedures and interpretations.

Personal construct theory has enjoyed a greater take-up in Great Britain than in the USA, perhaps because of the establishment of the Centre for Personal Construct Psychology in London by Bannister and Fransella.

Through this Centre personal construct theory has enjoyed wide and valuable applications in fields such as occupational psychology, clinical psychology and counselling psychology. It has also been applied to the management, leadership and health arenas.

8.5 EVALUATION OF THE HUMANISTIC APPROACH TO PERSONALITY

The humanistic approach to personality has four main strengths that, together, have contributed to its success in psychology over the past 50 years. Originally developed as the third force in psychology, humanistic psychology is now well accepted but often does not feature strongly in mainstream psychology departments in universities. The first strength is its important influences, and application to psychotherapy and counselling. The humanistic focus on subjective experience and the here and now has proved more successful in helping people cope with and adjust to daily problems of living than, say, the psychoanalytic approach. Humanistic psychology tries to get people to recognise how they think and structure their perception of reality. The second strength is the application that the humanistic approach has enjoyed outside psychology. Application has been made to areas such as employers and organisations wishing to foster greater job satisfaction with employees by looking to fulfil Maslow's higher needs. Application has also been made to education and child rearing/parenting styles. The third strength is the common-sense and intuitive appeal the humanistic approach has offered. It has shown how it is relevant to people's everyday lives. Finally, the works of humanistic psychologists have been widely read by lay people and have offered informal help and advice enabling them to tackle problems for themselves and, more generally, how to understand the meaning of their lives.

From a more critical perspective a number of shortcomings and problems with the humanistic approach have been identified. For experimental, scientific psychology there is a problem with claiming people have freewill in choosing what to do and how to behave. Science is about prediction and control; freewill flies in the face of this and potentially undermines the idea that psychology can scientifically study human thought and behaviour. Maslow recognised this issue and acknowledged that people do not have complete freedom to choose and that, in some aspects of their lives, behaviour is determined.

Another shortcoming with the humanistic approach is that some of the key and fundamental concepts are vaguely and poorly defined. These include the concepts of self-actualisation, personal growth and the healthy personality. This leads to another criticism: that the approach is a reflection of western, middle-class society and has little relevance for different cultures and people who live in poverty. Much of the focus of humanistic psychology is on the individual and his or her achievements. Eastern cultures typically focus more on the collective and the good of the group rather than the individual.

Whilst dealing with subjectivity and personal experience this strength can also be seen as a weakness. Almost by definition subjectivity and personal experience cannot be studied scientifically. Indeed to do so loses the value of regarding them as important. Finally, whilst the humanistic approach uses an empirical approach at times and produces empirical evidence in support of theory and concepts, such evidence does not stand up to rigorous scientific scrutiny. As a consequence fundamentally important concepts like self-actualisation are poorly defined and hence difficult to research scientifically.

Having said all this, most psychologists would acknowledge that the strengths outweigh the shortcomings and that the humanistic approach offers a valuable understanding of human experience that other approaches fail to provide.

8.6 SUMMARY

- Humanistic psychology developed from existential philosophy; this type of philosophy asked questions about the meaning of life and human experience. Humanistic psychology is characterised by four key themes: freewill, personal responsibility, subjective experience and personal growth. These themes set it apart from psychoanalysis and behaviourism, and justify the humanistic approach being called the 'third force' in psychology.
- Abraham Maslow produced a theory of human motivation proposing that people have to fulfil a hierarchy of deficiency needs before being able to approach the growth need of self-actualisation. Deficiency needs include physiological needs, safety needs, belonging and love needs, and self-esteem needs. The concept of self-actualisation refers to the growth need Maslow said existed in all of us to realise our full potential. Maslow conducted research on healthy people who were self-actualisers to determine their characteristics. Shostrum developed the Personal Orientation Inventory (POI) to measure self-actualisation and peak experiences.
- Carl Rogers developed a person-centred approach in humanistic psychology. Key to this approach is the importance of the self-worth of the individual and how this is fostered by unconditional positive regard. Conditional positive regard is where favourable treatment by others results from behaving in accordance with the wishes of other people. Congruence is where a person's ideal self is highly similar to their actual self. Incongruence is where a person's self-concept and organismic self and ideal self are all different. Rogers developed a form of psychotherapy called client-centred therapy; he also originated encounter groups.

- George Kelly developed personal construct theory in which he regarded each individual as constructing their own unique perception of reality. Kelly regarded people as intuitive or informal scientists in which they create hypotheses about the world and use experience to test these hypotheses. Personal constructs fall into one of two categories: superordinate or subordinate. Superordinate constructs are the most important, with subordinate constructs falling beneath them. The Role Repertory Test, or Rep Test, is an empirical procedure Kelly developed to understand and describe a person's constructs. Personal construct theory has enjoyed a wide range of applications to health and illness, psychological disorders and relationships.
- The strengths of humanistic psychology are its application to psychotherapy and counselling, and to job satisfaction, education and child rearing, as well as the relevance the approach has to people's everyday life. Weaknesses of the approach include poorly defined key concepts, the scientific problems of studying subjective experience and the general lack of a strong empirical base to support theories and concepts.

8.7 FURTHER READING

Rykman, R.M. (2000) *Theories of Personality*. (7th edn), Chapters 11, 12, 13 and 14. Wadsworth: Thompson Learning. Provides in each of these four chapters a more detailed account and appraisal of Kelly, Rogers and Maslow, as well as the humanistic approach of Rollo May, which has only been considered briefly in this chapter.

Maslow, A.H. (1970) *Motivation and Personality*. (2nd edn). New York: Harper & Row. Maslow's classic account of his hierarchy of needs, study of psychologically healthy people and self-actualisation.

Rogers, C.R. (1961) *On Becoming a Person*. Boston: Houghton-Mifflin. Probably the best of Rogers' books to read. Provides his account of key concepts, person-centred therapy, and the use and application of the Q-sort technique.

Kelly, G.A. (1970) A brief introduction to personal construct theory. In D. Bannister (ed.) *Perspectives in Personal Construct Theory*. London: Academic Press. A short account of personal construct theory. Provides a readable account, which is more detailed than the information given in the present chapter.

Csikszentmihalyi, M. (1990) Flow: The Psychology of Optimal Experience. New York: Harper Perennial. A modern account of humanistic psychology applied to the author's theory of personal happiness. Easy to read and thought-provoking in relation to our lives in the modern world.

9 Other Approaches to Personality

- Introduction
- Person–situation interaction
- Self-schemas: a cognitive approach to personality
- Personality: the study of lives
- Psychobiography
- Summary
- Further reading

9.1 INTRODUCTION

In this chapter we will consider four different approaches to personality: person–situation interaction, self-schemas, Murray's personality approach, and psychobiography. Each of these approaches is quite different and they have been chosen because each represents important current trends and research themes in personality psychology. Much of what we have looked at in previous chapters has attempted to find common personality characteristics or explanations for people. This is especially true of the dispositional and learning theory approaches. In contrast, two of the sections in this chapter offer quite a different perspective by attempting to look in detail, and in a systematic, psychological way, at the life of an individual. Whilst, Freud's case studies for example, did this to some extent, Freud did not attempt to look at the complete life of a person within its historical and cultural context. Personality and psychobiography do represent very different ways of analysing and interpreting individual personality. They bring fresh and new insights that other approaches miss because of a lack of focus on the individual.

First, we will turn to the debate about the person and the situation as determinants of behaviour, which was considered briefly in Chapter 6.

9.2 PERSON–SITUATION INTERACTION

The dispositional approach, as we saw in Chapter 6, makes the assumption that personality traits are of prime importance in determining how a person will behave in a range of different situations. Hence, if a person scores high on the trait of conscientiousness as a result of completing a personality inventory, we would expect that person to be conscientious at work, at home, with friends and in a range of other social situations. Walter Mischel (1968), in his book *Personality and Assessment*, challenged this assumption and as a result of reviewing evidence stated that 'behavioural consistencies have not been demonstrated and the concept of personality traits as broad dispositions is thus untenable' (1968: 146). What Mischel was saying was that behaviour is a result of situational factors rather than personality traits. This is now, for obvious reasons, seen as an extreme and untenable view to adopt since, taken to its logical conclusion, the concept of personality and personal responsibility is rejected. In the 30 or so years since the publication of Mischel's book personality psychologists have looked seriously at how the situation or psychological features of the situation may interact with personality traits to explain behaviour. In what follows we shall consider the ideas behind this theory and the research that has been conducted in this area.

9.2.1 Stability of personality traits

The stability of personality traits may be thought of in two ways: stability over time and stability across situations. It is the latter that the person–situation debate is primarily concerned with. Here we will give brief consideration to each.

Stability over time, or longitudinal stability, is concerned with the extent to which the personality traits of an individual endure over long periods of time. McCrae and Costa (1990) concluded from an empirical study that after the age of about 30 years personality changes very little. This research used the NEO-PI-R (see Chapter 6) self-rating questionnaire for the 'big five' personality traits. McCrae and Costa (1990) also asked husbands and wives, as appropriate, of the people filling in the questionnaire to give ratings. The self-ratings of both groups confirmed the view of trait stability after the age of about 30 years. This does not mean that personality cannot and does not change over time, but that the tendency is towards stability. This may be especially the case when a person's life is fairly stable too (stable in terms of work, marriage, friendships and interests/hobbies). In such cases there are powerful external factors acting to keep personality traits stable.

Cross-situational stability is more difficult to determine and provide clear-cut evidence for and against. Ideally, one would like objectively to observe how a person behaves in all different situations so that good evidence for and against cross-situational consistency or stability can be obtained. Just looking at a small or limited number of situations in which a person behaves will not be enough. Personality questions, such as the 16 PF and NEO-PI-R (see Chapter 6) do ask people how they think they would have behaved in a wide range of situations. However, what people think or say they will do can often be quite different to how they behave when actually presented with the situation.

Another factor that needs to be taken into account when considering the extent to which we should expect people to behave consistently across situations is to do with the strength of a personality trait that an individual possesses. For example, the measure of introversion–extroversion obtained from Eysenck's personality questionnaire (see Chapter 6, Section 6.4) is on a 24-point scale where 0 is an extreme introversion score and 24 an extreme extroversion score. Norms for different populations (for example, males, females, students) show an average of around 14. This means that most people act in extrovert ways on some occasions and introvert ways on other occasions. This idea can readily be generalised to other self-report personality questionnaires measuring other personality traits. From this you can see that we would expect only the minority of people who score at one extreme or the other to behave consistently over a wide range of different situations. From this we might infer that cross-situational consistency should not be expected of most people, and in order to understand why people behave as they do we need to consider how the person or personality *interacts* with the situation to produce behaviour.

9.2.2 The interaction of the person and the situation

The person–situation debate as initially characterised by Mischel (1968) was ill-founded because it tended to polarise positions as *either* personality or situational factors for predicting and explaining behaviour. Over the intervening years Mischel has worked from an interactionist perspective in an attempt to understand when dispositions are of more importance and when situations are of more importance in determining behaviour. As a result the interactionist view of Mischel (1999) is that both have to be taken into consideration and neither one on its own is sufficient to predict or explain behaviour. A study by Ware and John (1995) highlights this interactionist approach.

Ware and John (1995) measured the punctuality of students at Berkeley University turning up for lectures over a number of days. The lectures either took place early in the morning (at 8 am) or late in the afternoon (at 5 pm).

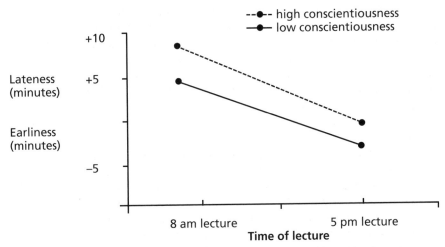

Figure 9.1 Punctuality of high and low conscientious students at an early and late lecture (adapted from Ware and John, 1995)

The same students were asked to complete the NEO-PI-R questionnaire two weeks before measures of their punctuality for lectures were taken. Of particular interest to Ware and John were scores on the trait of conscientious. Students were divided into two groups – high and low conscientiousness – and their punctuality (early or lateness) for lectures analysed. The results are show in Figure 9.1.

As can be seen, the results showed that, overall, high conscientiousness students were more punctual than those scoring low on this trait. But notice also that both groups were less punctual for the 8 am lecture than the 5 pm lecture. These findings demonstrate how personality trait and situation (time of lecture) interact to produce different behaviour. The situational factor may be conceptualised as to do with ease of being punctual. Both groups found the 8 am lecture less easy to be on time for, even though the high conscientiousness students were more punctual than the lower-scoring students.

9.2.3 Psychological features of situations

Wright and Mischel (1988) developed the ideas of and have investigated the psychological features of situations, and how different people interpret and perceive similar situations. They have developed this idea in order better to understand when situations are likely to be more powerful determinants of behaviour and when personality traits are most influental. The concept of 'response freedom' has been central to understanding the psychological features of a situation. To understand this, consider two different situations. First, imagine that you are standing on a pavement waiting to cross the road at a pedestrian crossing that has traffic signals. Second, imagine that you are at another pelican crossing, but this time at a road that is very quiet and there is not a car in sight. In the first situation your freedom to respond is highly limited – unless you want to get run over. The vast majority of people will wait for the green man sign to show before crossing. In the second situation, you are likely to cross the road regardless of the traffic lights because there is little danger of being run down by a car. In the first situation response freedom is limited and the situation determines how you behave. In the second situation, you have greater response freedom – to cross now or wait for the green man sign to show.

To generalise, where there is a high degree of freedom of response personality traits will exert a strong influence on behaviour. Where there is a low degree of freedom of response situational factors will dominate. Notice in the second situation a person with a very law-abiding personality may wait until the green man shows even though the road is clear (as may someone of an extremely anxious disposition).

Wright and Mischel (1987) have attempted to classify situations as 'diagnostic' in relation to different personality traits, and have put forward a competency-demand hypothesis. This states that situations that place high competency demands on cognitive, self-control and social skills will result in behaviours reflecting the particular personality traits of an individual. For example, response to a stressful situation which makes high competency demands may be one of aggression or withdrawal depending on the traits of the person. Shoda et al. (1993) demonstrated that situations that made similar competency demands on an individual resulted in cross-situational consistency of behaviour. Situations making different levels of competency demands produced much lower levels of cross-situational consistency.

9.2.4 Evaluation

Attempting to explain and predict behaviour by considering the ways in which personality traits and situations interact has allowed personality psychologists to assess the relative contribution of each. Understanding situations in terms of psychological features, response freedom and competency demands has provided specific ways for knowing when personality traits are and are not important. This approach has allowed traits to remain as one of the main ways of understanding and conceptualising personality. Clearly, taking a person–situation interactionist approach does characterise well the complexity of human behaviour.

9.3 SELF-SCHEMAS: A COGNITIVE APPROACH TO PERSONALITY

The cognitive approach to personality examines different ways in which people process information about themselves, others and the world around them. There have been a number of theoretical frameworks for understanding personality that have taken people's cognitions as of central importance. For example, Kurt Lewin's *Field Theory* (1951) is concerned with how each person organises and represents their 'life space'. George Kelly (1955) developed personal construct theory, where a practical approach is taken to establish how a person constructs their world.

In this section we shall look at a more recent cognitive approach to personality based around Markus's concept of self-schema (Markus, 1977; Markus and Kitayama, 1994).

9.3.1 The schema concept

A schema is any abstract knowledge structure that is represented mentally. Fiske and Taylor (1984) define a schema as 'a cognitive structure that represents one's general knowledge about a given concept or concept domain'. It is possible to have a schema about nearly all aspects of life – schemas about politicians, work, leisure and enjoyment, other people – especially those important in our lives, and ourselves, for example. Generally, schemas simplify the complex world in which we live, and are used to understand new situations or interpret new information. Schemas develop at a very early age, and whilst are simple in the young child, become more complex, greater in number and more interrelated as we grow and develop throughout our lives. As a person grows older new schemas may be developed, or existing ones may become more complex or even divide into a number of separate schemas. Schemas, therefore, are of central importance in cognitive psychology and developmental psychology alike.

9.3.2 Self-schemas

Self-schemas (Markus, 1977) represent organised knowledge that we have about ourselves. Different people have different schemas depending on what is important to them. Hence, for example, if you are a fitness fanatic and go to the gym every day for a workout, a schema to do with health and fitness will be central to your self-schema and perhaps exist as a separate schema. By contrast, if you like to spend a lot of your spare time gardening you will develop elaborate schemas for flowers and vegetables. Someone may be both a fitness fanatic and a keen gardener, and in consequence will possess both schemas within the array of schemas of the self. The self-schema gives emphasis to those aspects of the self that are significant to the person. Self-schemas may be so central to the self that they almost define what the person is about – gender, work and relationship schemas often fall into this category. Other self-schemas are important because of everyday experience, but are not so self-defining. The third category of self-schemas are those occurring in our lives, but not seen as relevant to the self. This category is illustrated in Figure 9.2.

The self-schema serves at least three important functions for the individual. First, information and experience is remembered better when it fits into an existing schema. Second, information about the self is easier to organise and categorise. Third, when presented with a new situation or experience the self-schema will help to interpret and understand new information. A major finding in research on self-schemas is that individuals process information more quickly when a particular schema is relevant to them. This was

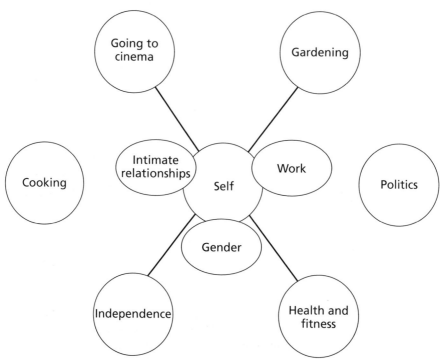

Figure 9.2 A hypothetical part of a self-schema, showing self-defining aspects (overlap with self), important aspects (connected by a line) and things occurring in daily life but not seen as important to the person (unconnected circles) (adapted from Markus and Smith, 1981)

demonstrated in a classic study by Markus (1977).

Markus (1977) investigated the dimension of independence–dependence. It was hypothesised that people who saw themselves as independent would process words related to independence more quickly than words related to dependence, and vice versa for dependent people and independent words. Prior to conducting the experiment, Markus classified people as possessing either a strong independence schema, a strong dependence schema, or as having neither schema (called aschematics). In the experiment participants were presented with 15 adjectives related to independence (for example, 'outspoken', 'individualistic') and 15 adjectives related to dependence (for example, 'submissive', 'conformist'). When each word was shown the participant had to press one of two buttons, labelled either 'ME' or 'NOT ME'. Markus recorded how quickly the three categories of participants

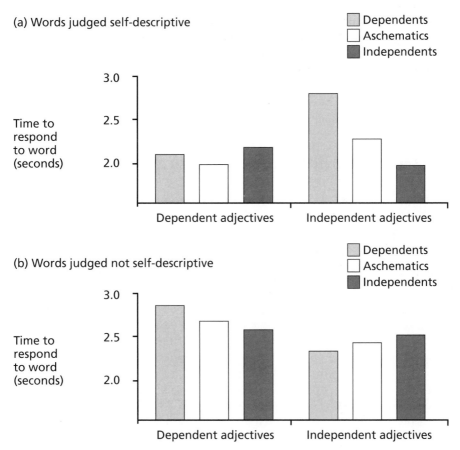

Figure 9.3 Time taken to classify dependent and independent adjectives as 'ME' and 'NOT ME' by participants with strong independence schema, strong dependence schema and aschematics (adapted from Markus, 1977)

(independence schema, dependence schema or aschematic) responded to each word. The findings are shown in Figure 9.3. As can be seen, participants with strong independence schema responded quickest to independence adjectives and much slower to dependent adjectives. In contrast, those with a strong dependence schema responded much faster to dependence adjectives and slower to independence adjectives. Notice that aschematics showed similar response times to both types of adjective. This classic experiment of Markus (1977) has been replicated using many different schemas, and has consistently shown rapid processing for information that is schema-relevant to an individual (Klein *et al.* 1989).

Self-schemas differ in three major ways from other types of schema (Rogers *et al.* 1977). First, self-schemas are larger and more complex than other schemas. Second, self-schemas are used daily or many times a day for those that centrally define the person. This daily/frequent usage of self-schemas is likely to be one main reason why they are more complex than other schemas. Daily usage means that they constantly evolve and grow. Third, self-schemas have a strong emotional component which, depending on specific circumstances and the particular self-schema of the individual may make the person feel positive or negative about themselves. We will look at this a little more in the section on discrepant selves (Section 9.3.5).

9.3.3 Individual differences in self-schemas

Research by Linville (1987) has shown that individuals differ in the extent to which self-schemas are complex. Whilst the self-schema of each person is complex relative to other types of schemas, Linville (1987) distinguishes between people with high and low self-complexity. People high in self-complexity develop and maintain many different self-aspects in their self-schema, which are relatively independent or distinct from each other. People low in self-complexity, whilst having different self-aspects in their self-schema, do not show them to be independent but are more interconnected with each other. This personality dimension of self-complexity has consequences for how different people respond to good and bad things that happen to them. People low on self-complexity allow the bad things that happen to them (for example, having a row with your best friend or not getting promotion at work) to affect all aspects of the self and consequently their entire self-schema. By contrast, people high on self-complexity manage to contain a bad event or experience to the particular self-aspect it is related to. Hence, such people are not so widely affected by the bad things that happen to them in their lives. However, the same happens for good things and it is here that people low in self-complexity allow a good thing (for example, getting promotion at work or being praised by a good friend) to affect them more generally than people high in self-complexity.

Nashby (1985) has suggested that people who think about themselves a lot are more likely to develop high self-complexity in their self-schema. People who are less self-reflective do not develop high levels of self-complexity, but may develop more complex schema about other people. This may affect how a person manages their relationship with other people – it may be that those high in self-complexity are less responsive to the needs of different people, whilst those low in self-complexity may have more developed schemas about others and, as a consequence, be more responsive and hence more rewarding to be with.

9.3.4 Possible selves

Represented within a person's schema is the past, present and future. Aspects of the self-schema that are to do with the future have been called 'possible selves' (Cantor *et al.* 1986; Markus and Nurius, 1986). Possible selves are mental representations of how we might become in the future, and can be both positive and negative. Positive possible selves may be to do with career aspirations, performance at a sport or activity, or to do with relationships with other people, for example. Negative possible selves are to do with how we fear we may become. For example, you may fear becoming old and lonely, or old and suffering major ill-health. Markus and Nurius (1986) characterise possible selves as 'the cognitive components of hopes, fears, goals and threats, and they give the specific self-form, meaning, organisation and direction to these dynamics' (1986: 954).

Possible selves are seen to serve three main functions. First, they provide incentives or motives for behaviour in order to achieve positive goals and to avoid, or try to avoid, negative ones. Second, they allow for meaning to be given to what we do in our lives and evidence strong emotional reactions to information relevant to the possible self. Third, they provide a means by which we evaluate our achievements and failures or disappointments in life. Possible selves allow evaluation of how a person is doing in achieving a positive goal and, if they are not doing well, may result in dramatic action and life changes to get back on course. Alternatively, the possible self could be abandoned and replaced by another one if it is clear that it is not likely to be achieved or is unrealistic. People who have unrealistic or unachievable possible selves may experience mental distress, depression or poor relationships with other people. Cognitive therapy may be needed to make possible selves more realistic and achievable for the person.

9.3.5 Discrepant selves

Higgins (1987) developed **self-discrepancy theory** from the idea of self-schemas, and as a way of understanding and offering psychological treatment to people suffering from feelings of dejection and agitation. Higgins (1987) conceptualised self-knowledge in three major ways and as deriving from two sources. The three ways of conceptualising self-knowledge are in terms of the *actual* self, the *ideal* self and the *ought* self. The actual self is to do with how you see yourself – this can derive from two sources: yourself and how you think another person sees you. The ideal self is how you would like to be, or how you believe another person would like you to be. The ought self is how you feel you ought to be or how you think another person thinks you ought to be. Self-discrepancy theory suggests that when there are discrepancies between the self or another as a source then problems may arise for the individual. Potentially, there are six ways in which self-knowledge can be represented, and numerous sources of discrepancy. This is illustrated in Figure 9.4.

A discrepancy is where there is a difference between two knowledge of self types or between the two sources of a particular type. For example, you may see your 'actual own self' as successful, friendly and positive to be with. In contrast, you may perceive another person – your best friend, say – as seeing you as not particularly successful, unfriendly and negative. Such a discrepancy would need to be resolved in one direction or another. For example, you could break the relationship with your best friend so as to remove the perception you believe he or she has of you and hence remove the discrepancy.

Higgins (1987; 1997) has identified two major types of discrepancy

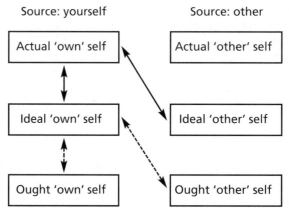

Figure 9.4 Three types of self-knowledge with 'own' and 'other' sources; there are many possible types of discrepancy; the solid lines represent one major type of discrepancy (dejected) and the broken line another type (agitated)

important to the emotional and mental well-being of a person. First, are discrepancies between the actual own self and either the ideal own self or ideal other self (or both in some cases). The negative emotional consequences of when the perceived actual own self does not live up to the person's ideal own self or the ideal other self, Higgins (1987) has labelled 'dejection-related emotions'. These include emotions such as shame, disappointment, sadness and depression. The negative emotional consequences of when the perceived actual own self does not live up to the person's ought own self or ought other self lead to 'agitation-related emotions'. These include fear, anxiety and guilt.

Higgins (1997) has called the ideal selves and ought selves self-guides, in that they offer goals and standards that a person may aspire to, and by which the person can evaluate present achievements. Higgins (1997) regards the two ideal selves (own and other) as having a promotion focus in that they guide a person towards positive outcomes. The two ought selves (own and other) are regarded as having a prevention focus in that they help a person avoid negative outcomes.

Higgins's self-discrepancy theory provides an analysis and specific reasons to help understand why a person may be depressed (actual-ideal discrepancy) or highly anxious (actual-ought discrepancy). This allows a cognitive approach to psychotherapy to be made that attempts to change the person's self-knowledge, or how the person perceives his or her self, or how the person believes another individual perceives him or her.

9.3.6 Evaluation

The cognitive approach to personality through the concept of self-schemas is a more recent development in personality psychology. The idea of a schema is well established and accepted in both cognitive psychology and cognitive development, and dates back to the early work of child psychologists such as Jean Piaget (1952). A strength of the self-schema approach to personality is that it is strongly embedded in the scientific tradition through extensive use of experiments. The self-schema also takes the concept of traits or personality differences into looking at cognitive structures or mental representations. This aids understanding the relationship between personality and behaviour through an appreciation of the mental processes causing the behaviour.

The shortcomings of the self-schema approach are that the concepts are not sufficiently well defined and are too vague. Also, it is difficult to know exactly when a self-schema is being used by a person, or, if being used, what particular aspect is operating. Since only behaviour can be observed, the concept of a self-schema remains a hypothetical construct that does not really exist. Nevertheless self-schemas offer a rich interpretation of mental processes that relate to personality.

9.4 PERSONOLOGY: THE STUDY OF LIVES

Henry Murray (1938; 1968) developed a theory of personality and an approach to the study of an individual that attempted to reflect the complexity of the person. Murray (1938) regarded the idea of personality as a hypothetical construct, as the following quotation demonstrates: 'An individual's personality is an abstraction formulated by the theorist and not merely a description of the individual's behaviour. An individual's personality refers to a series of events that ideally span the person's lifetime' (Hall and Lindzey, 1978).

Murray's definition of personality attempts to combine the past, present, and future aspirations of a person, and acknowledges that mental processes occur at both conscious and unconscious levels. Murray's theory of personality also represents a combination of a psychoanalytic, mainly Freudian (see Chapter 3), and humanistic (see Chapter 8) approaches. Murray also believed that the study of an individual's personality was not the sole province of psychology. Other disciplines and perspectives such as biology, sociology and anthropology Murray regarded as essential to providing a full understanding of personality.

Murray coined the term personology to represent the study of individual 'human lives and factors that influence their course' (1938). Murray studied, over a period of time, a small number of people's lives in great depth from a multidisciplinary perspective.

9.4.1 Analysis of behaviour

Murray (1951) devised an elaborate system for analysing human behaviour, which attempted to reflect his idea that people are located in a time that reflects past, present and future. Murray studied people who were generally well adjusted to society rather than people who suffered mental disorders or displayed atypical behaviour. Murray's system for analysing human behaviour started with a meaningful unit located in time which he called a 'proceeding'. A proceeding is a short sequence of behaviour that is meaningful, and has a beginning and an end. For example, a telephone conversation, an interaction with a salesperson in a shop when buying something, writing a letter or sending a text message, mowing the lawn. Proceedings may be interactions between one or more other people, or interactions with an object in the environment. Proceedings may also be imaginary (internal or inside a person's head) or real (external with other people or objects). A person may be engaged in two proceedings at once – for example, shuffling a pack of cards whilst talking to another person.

Analysis of behaviour	Description	Example
Proceedings	Short, time-limited sequence of behaviour, which is meaningful, and has a beginning and an end.	Telephone conversation, sending a text message, eating lunch.
Serials	Numerous proceedings that are related in some way and occur over a long period of time.	Marriage, being a parent, friendship, work.
Serial programmes	A planned series of behaviours aimed at achieving a goal or aspiration.	Career aspirations, being a high-class sportsperson, being happy in life.

Table 9.1 Murray's (1951) system for analysing meaningful aspects of human behaviour

Proceedings that are related in some way and operate over a relatively long period of time (months or years) Murray called a 'serial'. Long-term relationships, such as friendship or marriage, would be represented by a serial. If an individual planned a series of behaviours in order to reach a goal – such as wanting to become a surgeon or chief executive of an organisation – this Murray called a 'serial programme'. A person may display a number of serial programmes at any one time in their life; these may be to do with work and career aspirations, marriage, being a parent, and leisure interests. Serial programmes also interact with one another: too much effort and attention directed at achieving career aspirations may affect a person's marriage, social life etc. Table 9.1 summarises Murray's analysis of behaviour in terms of proceedings, serials and serial programmes. This classification system was Murray's attempt to analyse meaningful episodes, short or over a long period of time, of human behaviour and the motives behind the behaviour.

9.4.2 Dynamics of personality: needs and 'press'

Perhaps Murray's most enduring contribution to understanding motivation for behaviour is his study and research into human needs. Murray made an extensive and detailed study of different human needs, which partly reflects a Freudian approach in terms of unconscious needs. Murray (1938) identified 20 human needs, and these are shown in Table 9.2 This list of needs is still regarded in contemporary psychology as an accurate portrayal of human needs (McAdams, 2001; Robinson, 1992). Murray distinguished between primary needs (needs for achievement, recognition, autonomy, dominance, etc.), and also between overt and covert needs. Overt needs are those that are acceptable to the individual, others and society to express in behavioural form. In contrast, covert needs cannot freely be expressed in behaviour without upsetting other people or going against 'rules' of society. The expression of covert needs for the individual is usually reflected in their conscious fantasy life or dreams. For example, a novelist may be able to express covert needs in what he or she writes.

Murray regarded everyone as having needs, and thought that each need varies in strength between different people, and within the same person, but at different times in their lives. Needs may also come into conflict, and when this happens the most important need will be attended to first. If the conflict is between a primary and secondary need, the primary need will dominate. If the conflict is between a relatively strong and relatively weak need, the strong need will take precedence.

Murray (1938), in his more holistic approach to personality, recognised that motivations of human behaviour driven by needs were only part of the story. The environment also exerts a strong influence on human behaviour, and may at times over-ride the needs of a person. To acknowledge the importance of environmental influences (people or objects) Murray introduced the concept of 'press'. The concept of press represents forces in the environment, other people or objects, which may help or frustrate a person in reaching their goals or aspirations in life. Examples of press that may hinder a

Need	Description
Abasement	To submit passively to external force
Achievement	To accomplish something difficult
Affiliation	To form and maintain meaningful relationships
Aggression	To overcome opposition forcefully
Autonomy	To be independent and resist coercion
Counteraction	To master or make up for a failure, or overcome fear
Defendance	To defend the self against assault, criticism, blame
Deference	To admire and support or emulate a superior
Dominance	To control one's human environment
Exhibition	To make an impression; to be seen and heard
Harm avoidance	To avoid pain, physical injury and illness
Infavoidance	To avoid humiliation/embarrassment
Nurturance	To feed, help, console, support, protect, comfort
Order	To put things in order
Play	To seek enjoyable relaxation; to act for fun
Rejection	To exclude, abandon or reject another
Sentience	To seek and enjoy sensual impressions
Sex	To form and further an erotic relationship
Succurance	To have a supporter, to have needs gratified
Understanding	To ask or answer general questions

Table 9.2 Murray's (1938) list of 20 human needs (adapted from Murray, 1938)

person are poverty, unemployment, loss of security and marital discord. Examples of press that may facilitate a person to achieve their goals in life include friendships, positive rewards and encouragement from other people, and satisfying intimate relationships. For Murray it is the person's subjective interpretation or perception of the environment that matters in terms of press on the individual.

In summary, the dynamics of personality are represented by the needs of the person and the individual's perception of the press in their environment. These two dynamics come together to determine human behaviour, in consequence needs interact with press to produce behaviour patterns that are characteristic of an individual. Some people are dominated in their lives by a needs/press interaction; this Murray called a 'unity-thema'. This provides meaning to a major part of a person's life. For example, a deeply religious person would display a unity-thema in their behaviour, as would a world-class athlete or someone at the top of a particular career. All the time Murray, in this relatively complex analysis of personality dynamics, is trying to provide an approach that reflects the meaning of a person's life to that person.

9.4.3 Personality assessment

Working within a psychoanalytic tradition, Murray developed a number of techniques for personality assessment. The most widely known, and one that is used today, is a projective personality test (see Chapter 2) called the Thematic Apperception Test (Murray, 1943).

You are referred back to Chapter 2, Section 2.3.9, for an explanation of projective techniques such as the Thematic Apperception Test (TAT) and the Rorschach inkblot test. The TAT consists of 30 cards, each showing one or more people in an ambiguous situation (see Figure 2.6). The story a person makes up about a card will, for Murray, reflect needs of the person, and how the person perceives forces (press) in the environment to be operating on him or her. The story usually also reflects how the person relates to other people, and what their goals, and aspirations in life may be. A story about a TAT card may also reveal conflict between needs, and possible resolutions may be suggested by the psychologist to the person undertaking the TAT.

Murray's theory of human motivation and his identification of 20 human needs influenced McClelland to focus on the need for achievement (McClelland et al. 1953). McClelland modified Murray's Thematic Apperception Test to produce a projective test to investigate a person's need for achievement (called NAch by McClelland). With this McClelland identified people who were high and low in need for achievement (NAch). This allowed him to develop psychological treatments to foster need for achievement in children and adults initially presenting as low in need for achievement (McClelland, 1961).

9.4.4 The study of lives

Murray's interdisciplinary approach to the in-depth study of the individual led him to conduct an intensive study of 52 male undergraduates over a six-month period. This was conducted at Harvard University by a team of 28 researchers representing a wide range of specialisms in psychology and different disciplines. Data on each of the 52 individual lives of these undergraduates were accumulated through interviews, questionnaires, observations and a range of life history methods. Murray ensured that at least two researchers were looking at the same aspect of people's lives in an attempt to reduce error and individual bias in measurement and assessment of personality. Murray created what he called a 'diagnostic council' which brought together all the findings and assessments of the 28 researchers to form a detailed analysis of a single person's life. The analysis reflected Murray's theory and ideas, looked at earlier in this chapter, and brought together all the different points of view and perspectives of the 28 researchers. This detailed, multiperspective study of a single person produced a life story integrating past, present and future (McAdams, 1992).

Murray's approach to personality and the study of a person was unique at the time, and represented a sustained attempt to study a person in their everyday life over a significant period of time. In many ways Murray's approach can be seen as a reaction to behaviourism (see Chapter 7) and the study of rats in cages in an attempt to produce laws of human behaviour). For Murray each person is unique and occupies a unique place in time, society and culture.

9.4.5 Evaluation of Murray's personology

Murray attempted to integrate a range of themes and ideas that were around at the time. Murray's personology attempts to bring together psychoanalysis and humanistic psychology. At the same time both conscious and unconscious motivations (needs) are recognised as operating within the person. The behaviourists focused on environmental forces (rewards and punishments), Murray attempted to bring together needs and environmental forces (press) to understand a person and his or her behaviour. The most enduring and empirically researched aspects of Murray's work are to do with his thorough analysis of human needs and the projective technique of the Thematic Apperception Test.

More generally, Murray promoted wide interest in psychoanalysis in the United States of America in the 1940s and 1950s, and gained acceptance for psychoanalysis in many quarters of psychology.

Criticisms of Murray's personology are that the theory is too complex and that many aspects of personology have not resulted in empirical research. However, White (1948; 1987) used personology to study and analyse the individual lives of adults over significant periods of time. Beyond this, little research in the mainstream of personality psychology has been based on Murray's theory and concepts. Nevertheless, Murray is regarded as an important influence in the development of personality psychology. This influence is at a more general level and to do with putting the person at the centre of psychology.

9.5 PSYCHOBIOGRAPHY

How do you talk about and understand your own life and the lives of other people? In everyday conversation and interaction with people a story or narrative is often used. A story or tale about a particular incident in a person's life may be told or, in the case of a written biography or autobiography, the complete life, from birth to death, of the person may be attempted. Whether in everyday conversation or through written accounts of a person's life, biography is a common, well-regarded and accepted method for understanding a person's life. In what follows we shall look at attempts made by psychologists to bring a degree of rigour and psychological framework to **psychobiography** (Elms, 1994; McAdams, 1999).

9.5.1 Definition and theoretical frameworks

The study of individual lives by psychologists goes back over a hundred years to Freud's famous case studies (see Chapter 3). His most well known and most frequently written about are the case studies of Dora, Little Hans, the Rat Man and the Wolf Man. In each of these Freud attempted to highlight his theoretical concepts to show the complex, unconscious workings of the mind and how mental disturbances, such as neurosis, resulted from internal conflict. However, there are many criticisms that can be made of case studies, and Freud has been criticised for recalling only the data from his sessions with his patients that confirmed or was consistent with his theory.

Psychobiography differs from the case study approach of Freud in that it attempts to be more systematic and comprehensive, and may employ more than one theoretical framework to understand the life of the target person (McAdams, 1988). A definition of psychobiography is offered by McAdams as follows: 'the systematic use of psychological (especially personality) theory to transform a life into a coherent and illuminating story' (1988: 2).

Psychobiography differs from biography in that it attempts to use psychological theory in a systematic and consistent way to understand the complexity and totality of a person's life. Notice also from the above definition that psychobiography also attempts to produce a coherent story that provides psychological insight into a person's life. This insight will allow explanations and understanding of why the person behaves in certain ways, how their mind works and the nature of their personality. In contrast to biographies, the focus is almost entirely on psychological aspects of thought and behaviour.

The first psychobiography is considered to be Freud's study of Leonardo da Vinci (1916). Here Freud did not look at the whole life of Leonardo but a particular childhood fantasy, in order to understand Leonardo as an adult. The childhood fantasy that Leonardo had was as follows: 'when I was still in my cradle, a vulture came down to me, opened my mouth with his tail and struck me many times with his tail against my lips' (Freud, 1916). Freud interpreted this fantasy as representing themes of homosexuality and infantile dependency in Leonardo. For Freud, the symbolic interpretation of the fantasy was twofold. First, the vulture's tail was seen as a phallic symbol and, second, the bird represents the mother figure. Freud then claimed that when Leonardo painted the Mona Lisa, in his early fifties, he found this to be a substitute for the love of his mother, which he had craved throughout his life. Freud's psychological study of Leonardo da Vinci, as you can see, is made within Freud's theoretical framework and Freudian symbolism. Whilst this study may be regarded as psychobiography, it is limited because it only deals with one particular aspect of Leonardo's life, and may be criticised because the childhood fantasy may be open to numerous different and non-Freudian interpretations. A further shortcoming is that Leonardo da Vinci was dead, and so no attempt could be made to see how the individual regarded this interpretation.

Over the past 20 years there has been growing interest in and an increasing number of publications analysing people's lives from a psychobiographical perspective (Runyan, 1990; McAdams, 1999). Whilst there was been a tendency for psychobiographies to work from a psychoanalytic or 'depth psychology' perspective, this is not exclusively the case. Depth psychology perspectives have drawn on the theories of Freud, Jung and Erikson, and on object relations approaches. Erikson's ego psychology approach (see Chapter 4) was applied to individuals through Erikson's psychohistory method (Erikson, 1975; 1958). However, psychobiographies have also been written from the perspectives of learning theory, the humanistic approach and McClelland's theory of motives. Some psychobiographies will draw on a number of different theoretical perspectives in their psychobiography, as is the case with Edel's (1985) study of the American novelist Henry James.

9.5.2 Guidelines for psychobiography

Alexander (1988) has produced a set of nine guidelines to help psychobiographies in relation to which aspects of a person's life may be most valuable and psychologically important to study. These are summarised in Table 9.3.

Guideline	Description of guideline
Primacy	Importance of early childhood experiences or, more generally, what comes first
Frequency	Frequently occurring psychological events or behaviours are important
Uniqueness	Events, behaviours, etc., which stand out or are unusual
Negation	Where a person strongly denies what seems true to others, or turns reaction into opposite
Emphasis	Where an event, behaviour or thought is overemphasised or exaggerated
Omission	Where there is a gap or lack of knowledge about a period or particular aspect of a persons life
Error or distortion	Where some aspect of a life story does not appear coherent or logical
Isolation	Where some aspect of a person's life does not fit in with the rest or stands out as separate
Incompletion	Where an event, behaviour or thought is not, or does not seem, complete

Table 9.3 Guidelines for psychobiography when interpreting and analysing a person's life (adapted from Alexander, 1988)

- The primacy guideline recognises the importance of childhood experiences, a fundamental tenet of developmental psychologists for understanding the adult personality.
- The frequency guideline suggests that frequently occurring events, behaviours or mental states in a person's life are worth focusing on. For example, for a person who experiences panic attacks on occasions over a number of years, there may be a link to traumatic events in their life (death of a relation, breakdown of marriage, etc.).
- At the other extreme is the guideline of uniqueness – events, behaviours and thoughts that stand out in a person's life may provide psychological

insight. This is what Freud did when analysing and interpreting the 'vulture fantasy' of Leonardo da Vinci, which we considered earlier.

- The negation guideline does reflect a psychodynamic principle that strong denial of something by a person may be because what is being denied is meaningful. In a similar way, negation may also be turning something into its opposite – for example, excessive laughter instead of crying.
- In contrast to negation, the guideline of emphasis is where a person emphasises or exaggerates, often something that seems normal or routine for other people.
- Omission suggests that a gap or lack of knowledge about an aspect or a period in a person's life may be psychologically interesting. The omission might also be a failure to remember an event that other people might remember clearly and with strong emotional significance. This guideline of omission may be seen to have similarities with Freud's concept of repression.
- The guideline of error or distortion is where some aspect of a person's life story does not seem coherent or logical. Equally, a person may make a distortion that cannot be true – for example, saying we lived in a mansion when it was in reality a small terraced house. The psychobiographer would want to understand the significance of the distortion and whether for the person in terms of their present conditions a terraced house may seem like a mansion if the person is homeless.
- The next guideline is that of isolation; this is where some aspect of a person's life, or thoughts, does not fit and stands out as separate or isolated from the context of what is being said or a person's behaviour. For example, suppose you are walking along a shopping street and you suddenly do a handstand. The handstand would be an isolated behaviour, an odd behaviour to perform in that context and in need of psychological explanation.
- The ninth and final guideline is that of incompletion; this is when an event, behaviour or thought does not seem finished or completed. For example, a person could say that they had spent three years studying law with a view to becoming a lawyer. Next the person says that a couple of years after completing their law studies they worked as a secondhand-car salesperson. There seems to be something missing and the story does not seem complete in relation to what you had expected.

Alexander's (1988) guidelines may help the psychobiographer in terms of which aspects of a person's life to pay particular attention to. What these guidelines do not do is help with knowing which theoretical perspective or perspectives to adopt, and how to resolve conflicting interpretations of a person's behaviour or thoughts.

9.5.3 The problem of competing explanations

Runyan (1981) selects a particularly dramatic event in a person's life to highlight the problem of competing explanations and difficulties with deciding which explanation or explanations may be right. The event Runyan (1981) focuses on is to do with the famous painter, Vincent Van Gogh, who when 35 years old, cut off the lower part of his left ear and took it to a prostitute in a brothel where he asked her to look after it. Runyan (1981) looked at different psychobiographical accounts of Van Gogh's behaviour and came up with more than 12 different explanations. To give you a flavour of the different explanations, three are given below.

- Van Gogh experienced conflict over his homosexual feelings for another artist, Paul Gauguin, and regarded his ear as a phallic symbol. Cutting off the ear symbolised self-castration.
- Van Gogh was experiencing psychotic hallucinations and cut off his ear in an attempt to stop hearing sounds and voices that he found disturbing.
- Van Gogh's brother, Theo, was about to get married and Van Gogh feared he would lose financial support from his brother as a consequence. Cutting off his ear was a response to feelings of rejection by and loss of his brother.

These three explanations all derive from a psychodynamic interpretation of Van Gogh's self-mutilating behaviour. It may be that numerous explanations are appropriate, especially since, within a psychoanalytic framework, behaviour is overdetermined. By overdetermined is meant that there is more than one cause for any human behaviour or thought/fantasy/dream.

Where there are competing explanations, two approaches may be adopted. First, each needs to be assessed against criteria such as coherence with other aspects of the person, credibility and comprehensiveness of the explanation (Runyan, 1982). If a number of explanations remain from such an assessment then it may be that all are appropriate and offer different insights into the life of the person.

9.5.4 Evaluation of psychobiography

Psychobiography is an attractive approach to the study of personality since it attempts to capture the full psychological picture of a person's life. However, it may appear quite subjective and dependent upon the theoretical perspective of the psychobiographer. As with case studies, it is difficult to see how generalisations can be made to other people, but this is not the prime objective of psychobiography.

Elms (1994) identifies a number of potential shortcomings of psychobiography; these include eventism, inadequate evidence, critical period fallacy, neglect of social and historical factors, overpathologising, and dangers of reconstruction. Eventism concerns the tendency to focus on a small number of major or traumatic events in a person's life to explain the person's whole life. The critical period fallacy is where over-emphasis is given to childhood experiences; this is often a criticism where a Freudian approach is used. Overpathologising is similar to eventism, but where the person's life is seen in terms of mental disorder or breakdown to the relative exclusion of more 'normal' states. Finally, dangers of reconstruction are where childhood experiences or memories, for example, are reconstructed from adult accounts. Perhaps the most worrying example of this is the debate over recovered memories (Mollon, 2000). Here, psychoanalysts have been accused of encouraging adults to think they were abused in childhood, by 'recovering' memories from their adult patients.

Psychobiography represents quite a different approach to the study of personality to those we have looked at in previous chapters of this book. Psychobiography does offer a structured and theoretical framework from which to make an intense psychological study of the life of a person. As such, it offers insights that are not available from other approaches to the study of personality. In consequence, psychobiography should be seen as a valuable contribution to personality psychology.

9.6 SUMMARY

- Stability of personality traits may be conceptualised as longitudinal (over time) or cross-situational. Situational factors also determine human behaviour. The present view is that both dispositions and situations interact to cause behaviour. Situations are analysed from the point of view of psychological features, with the concept of response freedom being important. Where there is a high degree of response freedom, personality traits exert a strong influence on behaviour; where response freedom is low, situational factors exert a stronger effect on behaviour. Situations may be classified according to the competency–demand hypothesis.
- A schema is a mental representation of knowledge that we have about the world; self-schemas are mental representations of knowledge that we have about ourselves. Self-schemas serve three important functions for the individual: aid in remembering information, to organise information, and to understand new situations/people. Individual differences exist along the high- and low-complexity dimension. People who think about themselves a lot are more likely to develop complex self-schemas. Aspects of the self-schema to do with the future are called possible selves. Self-discrepancy

theory concerns the actual self ideal self and ought self. When discrepancies occur between these, the individual may experience mental distress.

- Henry Murray developed personology psychology to represent human lives and factors that influence a person's life. Murray analysed human behaviour in terms of proceedings, serials and serial programmes. Murray conducted a detailed analysis of human needs, distinguishing between primary and secondary needs. Forces in the environment influencing how a person thinks and behaves Murray called 'press'. To assess personality Murray developed a widely used projective technique called the Thematic Apperception Test (TAT). He conducted a multidisciplinary in-depth study of people's lives over a six-month period using a diagnostic council.

- Psychobiography differs from a case study because it represents a more systematic and comprehensive approach; it may employ one or more theoretical frameworks to analyse and interpret the behaviour of a person. McAdams defines psychobiography as the systematic use of psychological theory to provide an insightful story about one person's life. Nine guidelines have been produced to assist psychobiography. These include primacy, frequency, uniqueness, negation, emphasis, omission, error or distortion, isolation and incompletion. Deciding between competing psychological explanations is an issue for psychobiographers; often the simplest, more coherent explanations are accurate. However, human behaviour is overdetermined and as such more than one explanation is acceptable.

9.7 FURTHER READING

Mischel, W. (1999) *Introduction to Personality* (6th edn). Fort Worth, TX: Harcourt Brace College Publishers. Mischel initiated a major debate in personality about the person and the situation. Chapter 18 of this book provides a more detailed account and evaluation of the interactionist approach that is now commonly accepted in personality psychology.

McAdams, D.P. (2001) *The Person: an integrated introduction to personality psychology*. (3rd edn). Forth Worth, TX: Harcourt College Publishers. The chapter entitled 'Social-cognitive adaptations' (Chapter 9) provides a more detailed account of the self-schema approach, together with a wider look at social-cognitive approaches to personality. Chapter 8 of this text also provides a more detailed account of Henry Murray's approach and theory of human needs. McAdams is an enthusiast of Murray, and has adopted some of his procedures and theoretical ideas in his approach to psychobiography. Chapters 11 and 12 look at approaches to the study of personality based on detailed analysis and interpretation of individual lives.

Glossary

16PF is a widely used personality questionnaire developed by Raymond Cattell. The 16PF measures sixteen source or general traits. See also **surface and source traits**. Also used to help uncover the meaning of dreams.

Anal psychosexual stage is the second stage of personality development in Freudian theory. It follows the **oral stage** and occurs in the second year of life. This stage is concerned with controlling excretion of faeces. May result in an anal personality.

Analytic psychology is the term for the theory of personality developed by Carl Jung.

Archetypes are systems or structures in the collective unconscious in Jungian theory which exert strong influences on the person. Archetypes include the magician, the hero, the wise man, and god. The archetypes of persona, anima ans animus, the shadow and the self have evolved as separate systems. See also **Collective Unconscious**.

Attachment theory was developed by John Bowlby, it is the emotional relationship or bond that develops between the child and mother. Ainsworth suggested three types of attachment: secure, anxious and avoidant.

Behavioural approach to personality is concerned with how a person acquires and learns sets of behaviour through reinforcement of stimulus-response bonds.

Behaviourist approach to personality attempts to formulate laws and principles about how behaviour results from shaping, reinforcement and punishment in relation to stimulus-response bonds.

'Big five' personality traits are those of neuroticism, extroversion, openness, agreeableness and conscientiousness. The five personality traits are regarded as the most important aspects of personality. Developed by Costa & McCrae.

Biological perspective to personality attempts to identify the extent to which personality may be determined by genetic inheritance.

Birth order was thought to be of importance to Adler for determining personality. Relates to first born, second born and last born.

Borderline personality refers to people whose personality exists at the border between neurotic and psychotic dysfunction. Such people often show dysfunction in their interpersonal relationships. Developed by Kernberg.

Case studies are used in personality research to provide an in-depth understanding of a person. A case study may be conducted over a long or short period of time. See also **idiographic approach** and **qualitative** approach to personality.

Child analysis was developed by both Anna Freud and Melanie Klein. Klein gave a child a special set of toys to play with and interpreted play in psychoanalytic terms.

Classical conditioning was developed by Ivan Pavlov, and relies on learning by association with a naturally occurring behaviour such as a reflex , for example, salivation at the sight of food when hungry.

Cognitive approach to personality considers mental processes and thought as important to understand how and why a person behaves in certain ways.

Collective unconscious or transpersonal unconscious is a term in Jungian theory referring to the idea that certain thoughts and predispositions are the product of evolution and passed on from generation to generation. The collective unconscious contains **Archetypes.**

Collectivism is a term used in cross-cultural psychology to describe cultures that place value on group achievement and group values. Contrasts with **individualism.**

Conditional positive regard is a more common form of interaction between people. It is where positive regard is given upon condition that a person behaves in a way another wishes. A key concept in Rogers' humanistic psychology. See also **unconditional positive regard.**

Confounding variables in an experiment are variables not controlled by the experimenter and ones which may cast doubt on the validity of the findings of an experiment.

Correlational research is where psychologists seek to establish relationships between two or more variables. Negative and positive correlations may be found.

Countertransference in psychoanalytic therapy is the feeling the psychoanalyst has to the client. These are analysed with another psychoanalyst.

Cross-situational consistency is the idea that people behave consistently, and in line with their personality traits, across a range of situations. For example, an extrovert will behave in an extrovert way in many different situations.

Cross-situational consistency is the idea that people behave in similar ways in different situations and that behaviour reflects a person's personality.

Death or aggressive instinct in psychoanalytic theory is one of two fundamental instincts that drive thought and behaviour. See also **libido or sex instinct.**

Debriefing is where each participant in personality research is informed about all aspects of the research immediately after taking part.

Deception should be avoided in personality research. Deception is where the participant is misled about the experiment or not informed about what the experiment will involve.

Defence mechanisms are devices employed by the ego in psychoanalytic theory to protect a person's personality. Defence mechanisms fall into three general categories: those that deny, those that falsify and those that distort reality.

Dependent variable in an experiment is the measure taken by the psychologist. See also the **independent variable.**

Depressive position is a developmental position in Klein's Object Relations theory of personality. It occurs between 3 and 6 months. It is characterised by the child fearing loss of the mother. The task of the ego is to see the mother as a whole person or object.

Determinism is the idea that personality is determined, either biologically or psychologically, and hence predictable in principle. Contrasts with **freewill.**

Discrepant selves is a concept in self-discrepancy theory. It is the idea that a person may show discrepancy between their actual, ideal and ought selves. Discrepancy may lead to mental suffering. See also **self-discrepancy theory.**

Dispositional approach or trait approach to personality looks at single traits that make up the personality of an individual. Dispositions are relatively stable over time and across situations.

Dispositional approach to personality is based on the idea that people have relatively stable characteristics or traits which influence how they think and behave.

Dreams in psychoanalytic and Freudian theory have a manifest content, this is what is actually recalled, and a latent content, this is the hidden and unconscious meaning of the dream.

Ecological validity is the extent to which an experiment in psychology can be generalised to reflect real life. Some experiments conducted in psychology laboratories are artificial and do not reflect everyday life. In such cases it is difficult to generalise findings beyond the laboratory.

Ego in Freudian theory develops out of the id. The ego is responsible for the survival and continuation of the individual and operates according to the reality principle. The ego contains defence mechanisms and manages the competing demands of the id and the superego.

Ego psychology was primarily developed by Erik Erikson. Erikson focussed on the development of the ego throughout the lifespan.

Electra complex is the female version of the Oedipus complex.

Encounter groups were developed by Carl Rogers to allow people to explore their own thoughts and feelings in a group setting.

Environmental perspective to personality attempts to identify the environmental forces and influences on personality.

Erogenous zones in Freudian theory are of key importance in a child's psychosexual development and include the mouth, anus and genital areas.

Existential philosophy is concerned with questions such as the meaning of life and the nature of human experience. Existential philosophy informed the development of **humanistic psychology.**

Extroversion is a general trait regarded by Hans Eysenck as centrally important in personality. Extroversion is the tendency to like the company of people, and to be outgoing. See also **introversion.**

Five factor model of personality developed by Costa & McCrae. It uses the 'big five' personality traits to suggest that behaviour is consistent with the combination of traits in any one person. See also **'Big five' personality traits.**

Fixation at a Freudian psychosexual development stage occurs when the sexual instinct fixates on a particular erogenous zone, for example the mouth and an oral fixation.

Free association is a technique developed by Freud in which the person is asked to repeat all that comes to mind. It is used to try to understand the unconscious – repressions, dream, Freudian slips, etc.

Freewill is the idea that people are able to chose how to think and behave, and are free to change their personality. The opposite view is that of **determinism.**

Fully functioning person is a person who is fully in touch with the here and now and open to the constant flow of experience. Related to the humanistic approach of Carl Rogers.

Fundamental attribution error is the tendency people show to overestimate the importance of personality traits and underestimate the importance of situational forces in determining behaviour.

Hierarchy of needs is to do with Abraham Maslow's humanistic psychology. Maslow characterises human needs to be of five types: physiological, safety, belonging and love, self-esteem and self-actualisation needs. Needs lower in the hierarchy have to be satisfied before moving on to higher needs.

Humanistic approach to personality places emphasis on the person's conscious, subjective experiences and how a person may reach his or her full potential.

Id in Freudian theory is the original and oldest part of the personality, and contains the basic instincts such as sex, death, hunger and thirst. The id is the source of all mental energy and operates according to the pleasure principle.

Identity was investigated by Erikson in relation to his psychosocial stages of development. The stage is characterised by an identity crisis which the individual should establish. The ego strength of fidelity should be achieved.

Idiographic approach to personality focuses on the person in an attempt to understand and describe the unique personality of any one individual. Contrasts with the **nomothetic** approach.

Implicit personality theories is a term used to reflect the fact that people hold their own ideas and informal theories about their own and other people's personality.

Implicit self-judgement is to do with learned helplessness and concerns how people judge abilities such as intelligence as fixed or changeable. See also **learned helplessness.**

Incongruence in Rogers' humanistic psychology is where there is a difference between a person's self-concept and ideal self or between ideal self and organismic self. See also **organismic self.**

Independent variable in an experiment is the variable which is manipulated by the experimenter. See also the **dependent variable.**

Individual psychology is the term for the theory of personality developed by Alfred Adler.

Individualism is a term used in cross-cultural psychology to describe cultures that place value on individual autonomy and achievement. Contrasts with **collectivism.**

Inferiority is a basic feeling that Adler says all people have and strive to overcome. Feelings of inferiority develop in early childhood due the young infant being helpless and dependent on its carers. In extreme situation an inferiority complex may develop.

Informed consent is an ethical requirement of psychological research where participants should be given full details about the research before agreeing to take part as a participant.

Instincts in Freudian theory are fundamental causes of thought and behaviour that operate at an unconscious level and are biologically given. Instincts have a source, aim, object and impetus.

Internal-external control of reinforcement measures a person's locus of control. Internals perceive a strong relationship between what they do and what happens to them. Externals see little relationship and see outcomes as chance or luck.

Interpersonal trust was developed by Rotter, a social learning theorist, and concerns whether or not a person trusts other people. Rotter regarded interpersonal trust as a basic requirement of society.

Introjection is a defence mechanism in psychoanalytic theory where the child takes in or introjects aspects of an external object or another person.

Introversion is a general trait, opposite to extroversion, denoting a person who is reserved, less sociable and stimulated by ideas rather than other people. See also **extroversion.**

Learned helplessness was developed by Seligman, originally to explain how people suffering from depression think. Learned helplessness is where a person believes he or she has no or little control over reinforcement and rewards in their lives.

Libido or sex instinct in Freudian theory is one of two fundamental instincts driving thought and behaviour at an unconscious level. See also **death or aggressive instinct.**

Locus of control was developed by the social learning theorist Julian Rotter. It refers to a dimension of personality and to do with whether or not a person perceives their behaviour to be related to outcomes such as rewards and punishments. See also **internal- external control of reinforcement.**

Myers-Briggs Type Indicator is a questionnaire developed to measure the psychological type of a person, which derives from Jung's theory of personality.

Narcissism is self-love and is characteristic of the young child. Adults show varying degrees of narcissism, and teenagers high levels that decrease as they mature.

Narcissistic personality was described by Kohut, a psychoanalyst, to represent a person who has an exaggerated sense of self-importance and self-involvement. Such a person often has a fragile sense of self-worth and low self-esteem. See also **Self-psychology.**

Nature/nurture debate in personality concerns the extent to which personality may be due to genetics or environmental influences. Generally agreed that personality results from an interaction to biology and environment.

Nomothetic approach to personality is one in which scientific methods are employed in an attempt to establish general laws about human thought and behaviour. Contrasts with the **idiographic** approach.

Object relations theory is a psychoanalytic approach to understanding the relationships, between people and objects, that a child develops. Melanie Klein developed the object relations approach and was interested in the unconscious aspects of a child's relationships with others.

Observational learning is an important principle in the social learning approach. Bandura states that much of what we learn comes about form observing the behaviour of other people and the consequences of the behaviour.

Observational techniques in personality research include both systematic and unsystematic approaches. Observations may take place in naturalistic settings as well as the psychology laboratory.

Oedipus complex occurs during the phallic stage of psychosexual development. In males the boy desires his mother and wishes to remove his father. This results in castration anxiety. This conflict is resolved by the boy identifying with his father and giving up desires for his mother. In girls there is penis envy and feelings of shame with the female sex and desire of baby by the father. The girl identifies with the mother and takes on a female gender role to resolve the conflict.

Operant conditioning was developed by Skinner and involves learning through the consequences of behaviour. A new behaviour is learned or conditioned through shaping and reinforcement.

Oral psychosexual stage is the first stage of personality development in Freudian theory. It starts immediately after birth with the mouth being the first erogenous zone for the infant.

Organismic self is a concept in Rogers' humanistic psychology and concerns all aspects of ourself that we both are and are not aware of. It includes feelings, desires or wishes that a person has but may ignore or deny. See also **incongruence**.

Paranoid-schizoid position is a developmental position in Klein's Object relations theory of personality. It occurs in the first three months of life and the ego has to overcome fears of disintegration.

Peak experiences are rare experiences in life which include feelings of intense achievement, satisfaction and wonder in life. Relate to the humanistic approach to personality.

Personal construct theory was developed by George Kelly and is concerned with how people think about and structure their world in relation to themselves, other people and inanimate objects.

Personal constructs are the cognitive structures that George Kelly claimed that people develop in order to predict, control and adjust to the world in which they live. Each person is said to have a unique set of personal constructs.

Personal growth is a humanistic concept to do with a person growing, changing and adjusting to change throughout their life. Includes concepts such as **self-actualisation** and **fully functioning individual.**

Personal Orientation Inventory is a questionnaire that attempts to measure the humanistic concept of self-actualisation. See also **self-actualisers.**

Personal responsibility concerns a person being responsible for their actions and behaviour, what a person says and does.

Personal unconscious is a term in Jung's theory of personality. The personal unconscious contains the thoughts, perceptions and feelings that have been suppressed or ignored. The contents can be brought to conscious awareness.

Person-centred approach was developed by the humanistic psychologist Carl Rogers. This approach to counselling focuses on the person and deals with present problems the person is facing. See also **unconditional positive regard.**

Personology was developed by Henry Murray to study the individual; life in detail and over time. It uses a multidisciplinary approach and analyses a person in a structured way.

Person-situation debate amongst personality psychologists is the debate about the relative influences of forces in the situation and personality in determining behaviour. Now thought not to be an either or matter but an interaction. See also **Person-situation interaction.**

Person-situation interaction is the way in which the personality of a person and situational forces interact to produce behaviour.

Phallic stage of psychosexual development follows the anal sage in Freudian theory and occurs around the age of 4 to 5 years. The genitals become the prime erogenous zone. The most important aspect of the phallic stage is the **Oedipus complex.**

Possible selves are a part of a person's self schema and refer to how a person thinks of him or herself in the future. This may be how a person wishes to be in the future or how a person thinks they might become – either positive or negative.

Preconscious in Freudian theory refers to thoughts and memories that a person can bring to consciousness but is not presently aware of.

Projection is a defence mechanism in psychoanalytic theory where anxiety and destructive impulses are projected or attributed to external objects and people by the young child.

Projective identification is a defence mechanism in psychoanalytic theory where the ego first splits off aspects of the object which are good and bad, and then identifies with the good aspects.

Projective techniques indirectly assess personality by giving a person and ambiguous figure or picture to interpret. Examples of projective techniques include the Rorschach Inkblot Test and the Thematic Apperception Test.

Psychoanalytic approach to personality, developed by Sigmund Freud, is based on the assumption that unconscious mental processes and unconscious instinctual forces determine thought and behaviour.

Psychobiography is a systematic, comprehensive and multi-theoretical approach to study the life and personality of an individual in great depth and over a period of time. It uses psychological theory or theories to understand the complexity of a person.

Psychohistory was pioneered by Erikson and is a technique that allows for an in-depth intensive study of a person from a psychoanalytic and psychosocial perspective.

Psychological features of situations is a concept used in an attempt to understand the aspects of situations which may be powerful determinants of behaviour. Used to inform the person-situation debate.

Psychological type in Jung's theory of personality is the balance in a person between four functions – thinking, feeling, sensing, and intuiting. Also related to the general attitude of a person – introvert or extrovert.

Psychosocial stages of development were proposed by Erikson as covering the lifespan of the person. Erikson proposed eight stages, with five occurring in childhood and teenage years.

Punishment in the behaviourist approach reduces the likelihood that a behaviour will be repeated in future or extinguishes the behaviour altogether.

Q-sort technique is a method to study Rogers' ideas of self-concept and ideal self and identify causes of incongruence between them. See also **incongruence.**

Qualitative approach to personality uses methods of data collection such as case studies and in-depth interviews. Data is analysed using qualitative methods such as content analysis.

Quantitative approach to personality uses methods of data collection which can be analysed using descriptive and inferential statistics. Usually associated with the **nomothetic** approach.

Radical behaviourism takes the view that all behaviour comes from experience and can be understood in terms of behaviourist principles of conditioning.

Regression in psychoanalysis is where the adult when under stress or trauma returns to one of the psychosexual stages of development. Regression may awaken **fixations** made when originally going through the psychosexual stages.

Reinforcement is an important principle in the behaviourist approach to personality. A reinforcer, which may be positive or negative, increases the probability that a behaviour will be repeated in future.

Reliability is concerned with the extent to which a personality test produces similar results at different times. Sometimes referred to as test-retest reliability. Another type of reliability is internal consistency of a personality test. See also **validity.**

Repertory grid is a diagrammatic depiction of an individual's personal constructs and the relation between personal constructs. To do with George Kelly's Personal Construct Theory. See also **personal constructs.**

Repression is a central and important defence mechanism in Freudian theory. Repression may be described as unconscious and motivated forgetting. Traumatic and disturbing memories are repressed into the unconscious by the ego.

Repressive coping style is one where the person attempts to avoid feelings of anxiety by avoiding negative experiences that may raise levels of anxiety in the person.

Response sets are patterns of responding to a questionnaire that are consistent to a person. An example of a response set is that of **social desirability.**

Role construct Repertory Test or the **Rep Test** provides an account of how a person construct his or her world. Reflects Personal constructs as in George Kelly's theory. See also **personal construct theory.** See also **Collective Unconscious.**

Self-actualisation is where a person seeks and realises happiness, personal satisfaction and fufilment. See also **peak experiences** and **personal growth.**

Self-actualisers are people who fulfil themselves and achieve the best that they are capable of. Concerned with self-actualisation and the humanistic approach of Abraham Maslow.

Self-complexity is to do with the extent to which a person has a simple or complex self-schema. See also **self-schema.**

Self-discrepancy theory was developed form self-schemas and is to do with discrepancies that may exist between a person's actual, ideal and ought selves. See also **discrepant selves.**

Self-efficacy is a concept developed by Bandura, a social learning theorist, and is to do with whether or not a person believes he or she is able to perform certain behaviours. Measured on a scale from high to low.

Self-psychology is a psychoanalytic approach to personality developed by Kohut. It emphasises the central role that relationships with other people play in developing a sense of self for the individual.

Self-schema is a term developed by Markus to conceptualise how a person organises and represents knowledge about themselves. Self-schemas are cognitive structures and each person has their own, unique self-schema.

Self-worth is how a person evaluates themselves and is strongly influenced by what other people think of the person. Related to the humanistic approach of Carl Rogers.

Single person research represents a combination of the experimental method and qualitative methods such as case studies. Both quantitative and qualitative anslysis of data may be carried out.

Social desirability is a bias that may be present in responses to a personality questionnaire caused by an individual answering questions in ways that put them in a more favourable light than they actually are.

Social learning theory was developed by psychologists such as Bandura and Rotter. In contrast to radical behaviourism, social learning theorists take the view that cognitions or internal thought processes must be taken into account to explain how people learn.

Splitting is a defence mechanism that Melanie Klein said infants in their first year of life used. Objects and part-objects are split into good and bad elements.

Style of life In Adler's theory of personality is how a person approaches life and interacts with others. Adler proposed four styles of life: ruling type, getting type, avoiding type and socially useful type.

Sublimation is a defence mechanism in psychoanalytic theory where threatening unconscious impulses derived from the id are redirected in socially acceptable behaviour such as work, artistic creation and writing.

Superego in Freudian theory is made up of two components: the person's ego ideal and sense of conscience and feelings of guilt. The superego is influenced by parental and societal values.

Superiority in Adler's theory of personality is when the individual attempts to overcome feelings of inferiority. May result in a superiority complex.

Surface and source traits were suggested by Raymond Cattell. Source traits are general traits which cannot be observed; surface traits relate directly to behaviour and cluster together to form source traits.

Temperaments are general and complex aspects of personality such as sociability, emotionality and general activity level.

Thematic Apperception Test or **TAT** is a projective personality test in which a person is shown a picture of one or more persons in an ambiguous situation. The idea is for the person to create or 'project' a story into the ambiguous picture.

Traits are hypothetical constructs which have both cognitive and emotional components. Traits make up the personality of an individual and relate to how a person behaves. Allport distinguished between cardinal, central and secondary traits, cardinal traits influence behaviour in a wide range of situations.

Transference in psychoanalytic therapy is the feelings that the client or patient has or ' transfers' to the analyst. The psychoanalyst analyses the transference to understand child-parent relationships of the client in early life.

Twin studies are used in personality psychology to help understand the contribution of nature and nurture to personality. Monozygotic or identical twins and dyzygotic or fraternal twins are both studied.

Unconditional positive regard is where a person is valued and respected for what they are. This is an important concept in Rogers' humanistic approach to personality. See also **conditional positive regard.**

Unconscious is a level of thought which occurs outside of a person's conscious awareness. In Freudian theory the greatest part of the mind is unconscious and contains instincts and drives that determine conscious thought.

Validity is concerned with how well a personality test actually measures what it claims to be measuring. Types of validity include content validity, criterion validity and construct validity. See also **response sets.**

Vicarious reinforcement is to do with social learning theory and observational learning. Here the observer watches another person being rewarded for behaving in a certain way and then believes that if he or she behaves in the same way reward will also follow. See also **social learning theory** and **observational learning.**

Bibliography

Abraham, K. (1927) The influence of oral eroticism on character formation. In K. Abraham (ed.) *Selected Papers on Psychoanalysis*. London: Hogarth.

Abramson, L.Y., Seligman, M.E.P. and Teasdale, J.D. (1978) Learned helplessness in humans: critique and reformulation, *Journal of Abnormal Psychology* 87, 49–74.

Adler, A. (1927) *The Practice and Theory of Individual Psychology*. New York: Harcourt, Brace & World.

Adler, A. (1931) *What Life Should Mean to You*. New York: Plenium Press.

Adler, A. (1932) *What Life Should Mean to You*. New York: Putnam.

Adler, A. (1933) The meaning of life. In H.L. Ansbacher and R.R. Ansbacher (eds) *The Individual Psychology of Alfred Adler*. New York: Harper (1956).

Adler, A. (1935) The fundamental views of individual psychology. In H.L. Ansbacher and R.R. Ansbacher (eds) *The Individual Psychology of Alfred Adler*. New York: Harper, 1956.

Adler, A. (1956) *The Individual Psychology of Alfred Adler: A systematic presentation in selections from his writings* (eds H.L. Ansbacher and R.R. Ansbacher). New York: Basic Books.

Adler, A. (1964) *Social Interest: a challenge to mankind*. New York: Putnam.

Adler, A. (1973) *Superiority and Social Interest: A Collection of Later Writings* (eds H.L. Ansbacher and R.R. Ansbacher). New York: Viking Compass.

Ainsworth, M.D.S. (1989) Attachments beyond infancy, *American Psychologist* 44, 709–16.

Ainsworth, M.D.S., Bell, S.M. and Stayton, D.J (1971) *Individual Differences in Strange Situation Behaviour of One-year-olds*. In H.R. Schaffer (ed.) *The Origins of Human Social Relations*. London: Academic Press.

Ainsworth, M.D.S., Blehar, M., Waters, E. and Wall, S. (1978) *Patterns of Attachment*. Hillsdale, NJ: Erlbaum.

Alexander, I.E. (1988) Personality, psychological assessment and psychobiography, *Journal of Personality* 56, 265–94.

Allport, G.W. (1937) *Personality: a psychological interpretation*. New York: Holt.

Allport, G.W. (1942) *The Use of Personal Documents in Psychological Science*. New York: Social Science Research Council.

Allport, G.W. (1954) *The Nature of Prejudice*. Boston: Beacon Press.

Allport, G.W. (1955) *Becoming: basic considerations for a psychology*. Newhaven, CT: Yale University Press.

Allport, G.W. (1960) *Personality and Social Encounter: selected essays*. Boston: Beacon Press.

Allport, G.W. (1961) *Pattern and Growth in Personality*. New York: Holt, Rinehart & Winston.

Allport, G.W. (1967) An autobiography. In E.G. Boring and G. Linzey (eds), *A History of Psychology in Autobiography*, Volume 5. New York: Appleton-Century-Crofts.

Allport, G.W. (1969) Autobiography. In E.G. Boring & G. Lindzey (eds), *A History of Psychology in Autobiography*, Volume 5. New York: Appleton.

Allport, G.W. and Odbert, H.S. (1936) Trait names: a psycho-lexical study, *Psychological Monographs* **47**, 1–171.

American Psychological Association (1990) Ethical principles of psychologists (Amended June 1990), *American Psychologist* **45**, 390–5.

Badcock, C. (1994) *Psycho-Darwinism: a new synthesis of Darwin and Freud*. Glasgow: HarperCollins.

Bandura, A. (1971) *Social Learning Theory*, (2nd edn). Morristum, NJ: General Learning Press.

Bandura, A. (1977a) *Self-efficacy: the exercise of control*. New York: Freeman.

Bandura, A. (1977b) *Social Learning Theory*. Englewood Cliffs, NJ: Prentice Hall.

Bandura, A. (1977c) Behaviour theory and models of man, *American Psychologist* **29**, 859–09

Bandura, A. (1978) The self-system in reciprocal determinism, *American Psychologist* **33**, 344–58.

Bandura, A. (1986) *Social Foundations of Thought and Action: a social-cognitive theory*. Englewood Cliffs, NJ: Prentice Hall.

Bandura, A. (1989) Human agency in social cognitive theory, *American Psychologist* **44**, 1175–84.

Bandura, A. (1991) Social cognitive theory of moral thought and action. In W.M. Kurtivness & J.L. Guentz (eds) *Handbook of Moral Behaviour and Development*. Volume 1: Theory. Hillsdale, NJ: Erlbaum.

Bandura, A. (1997) *Self-efficacy: The Exercise of Control*. New York: Freeman.

Bandura, A. and Walters, R.H. (1903*) Social Learning and Personality Development*. New York: Holt, Rinehart & Winston.

Bandura, A., Ross, D. and Ross, S.A. (1961) Transmission of aggression through institution of aggressive models, *Journal of Abnormal and Social Psychology* **63**, 575–82.

Bandura, A., Ross, D. and Ross, S.A. (1963) Imitation of film-mediated aggressive models, *Journal of Abnormal and Social Psychology* **66**, 3–11.

Bannister, D. (1977) *New Perspectives in Personal Construct Theory*. New York: Academic Press.

Bannister, D. and Fransella, F. (1971) *Inquiring Man: the theory of personal constructs*. Harmondsworth: Penguin Books.

Bannister, D. and Salmon, P. (1966) Schizophrenic thought disorder: specific or diffuse? *British Journal of Medical Psychology* **39**, 215–19.

Barrick, M.R. and Mount, M.K. (1991) The big five personality dimensions and job performance: a meta-analysis, *Personnel Psychology* **44**, 1–26.

Bartholomew, K. and Horowitz, L.M. (1991) Attachment styles among young adults: a test of a four category model, *Journal of Personality and Social Psychology* **54**, 656–62.

Baumeister, R.F. (ed.) (1993) *Self-esteem: the puzzle of law self-regard*. New York: Plenium Press.

Bell, M.D., Billington, R. and Becker, B. (1986) A scale for the assessment of object relationships: reliability, validity and factorial invariance, *Journal of Clinical Psychology* **42**, 733–41.

Bell, M.D., Billington, R., Cicchetti, D. and Gibbons, J. (1988) Do object relations deficits distinguish BPO from other diagnostic groups? *Journal of Clinical Psychology* **44**, 511–76.

Belmont, L. and Marolla, F.A. (1973) Birth order, family size and intelligence, *Science* **182**, 1096–101.

Bernal, M.E., Knight, G.P., Garza, C.A., Ocampo, K.A. (1990) The development of ethnic identity in Mexican-American children, *Hispanic Journal of Behavioural Sciences* **12**(1), 3–24.

Berrenberg, J.L. (1987) A measure of God-mediated and exaggerated control, *Journal of Personality Assessment* **51**, 194–206.

Billig, M. (1999) *Freudian Repression: conversation creating the unconscious*. Cambridge: Cambridge University Press.

Blum, G.S. (1968) Assessment of psychodynamic variables by the Blackie pictures. In P. McReynolds (ed.) *Advances in Psychological Assessment*, Volume 1. Palo Alto, CA: Science and Behaviour Books.

Bond, M.P., Perry, C.J, Gautier, M. and Goldenberg, M. (1989) Validating the self-report of defense styles. *Journal of Personality Disorders* **3**, 101-12

Bowlby, J. (1969*) Attachment and Loss*, Volume 1: Attachment. New York: Basic Books.

Bowlby, J. (1973) *Attachment and Loss*, Volume 2: Separation, anxiety and anger. New York: Basic Books.

Bowlby, J. (1980) *Attachment and Loss*, Volume 3: Sadness and depression. New York: Basic Books.

Bowlby, J. (1988) *A Secure Base*. New York: Basic Books.

Breakwell, G.M., Hammond, S. and Fife-Shaw, C. (eds) (2000) *Research Methods in Psychology* (2nd edn). London: Sage.

Breger, L. (2000) *Freud: Darkness in the Midst of Vision*. New York: John Wiley & Sons.

Brennan, K.A. and Shaver, P.R. (1995) Dimensions of adult attachment, affect regulation and romantic relationship functioning, *Personality and Social Psychology Bulletin* **21**, 267–83.

British Psychological Society (1998) *Code of Conduct, Ethical Principles and Guidelines*. Leicester: British Psychological Society.

Bruner, J.S. and Postman, L. (1947) On the perception of incongruity, *Journal of Personality* **18**, 203–33.

Buss, A.H. and Plomin, R. (1984) *Temperament: early developing personality traits*. New York: Wiley.

Buss, A.H., Plomin, R. and Willerman, L. (1973) The inheritance of temperaments, *Journal of Personality* **41**, 513–24.

Buss, D.M. (1991) Evolutionary personality psychology, *Annual Review of Psychology* **42**, 459–91.

Cain, D.J. (1990) Celebration, reflection and renewal: 50 years of client-centred therapy and beyond. *Person-centered Review* **5**(4), 357–63.

Cantor, N. and Mischel, W. (1979) Prototypes in person perception. In L. Berkouritz (ed.), *Advances in Experimental Social Psychology*, Volume 12. New York: Academic Press.

Cantor, N., Markus, H.H., Niendenthal, P. and Nurius, P. (1986) On motivation and the self-concept. In R.M. Sorrentino and E.T. Higgins (eds) *Handbook of Motivation and Cognition*. New York: Guildford.

Carlson, E.A. and Sroufe, L.A. (1995) Contribution of attachment theory to developmental psychopathology. In D. Cicchetti and D.J. Conen (eds), *Developmental Psychopathology*, Volume 1: Theory and methods. New York: Wiley.

Caspi, A., Elder, G.H., and Bem, D.J. (1988) Moving away from the world: life-course patterns of shy children, *Developmental Psychology* **24**, 824–31.

Cattell, R.B. (1950) *Personality: a systematic, theoretical and factual study*. New York: McGraw-Hill.

Cattell, R.B. (1965) *The Scientific Analysis of Personality*. Chicago: Aldine.

Cattell, R.B. (1973) A check on the 29-factor Clinical Analysis Questionnaire structure on normal and pathological subjects, *Journal of Multivariate Experimental Personality and Clinical Psychology* **1**, 3–12.

Cattell, R.B. (1974) Raymond B. Cattell. In G. Lindzey (ed.) *A History of Psychology in Autobiography*, Volume 6, 61–100. Englewood Cliffs, NJ: Prentice Hall.

Cattell, R.B. (1979) *Personality and Learning Theory*, Volume 1. New York: Springer.

Cattell, R.B. (1983) *Structured Personality-Learning Theory: a holistic multivariate research approach*. New York: Praeger.

Cheung, F.M., Leung, K. and Zhang, J.X. (1998) Indigenous Chinese personality constructs, *Journal of Cross-Cultural Psychology* **29**.

Church, A.T. (1987) Personality research in a non-western culture: the Philippines. *Psychological Bulletin* **102**, 272–92.

Ciccethi, D. and Barnet, D. (1991) Attachment organisation in maltreated preschoolers, *Development and Psychopathology* **3**, 397–411.

Cohen, J. (1992) Spouse type similarity and prediction accuracy: testing a theory of mate selection, *Journal of Psychological Type* **24**, 45–53.

Comstock, G. and Strasburger, V. (1990) Receptive appearances: television violence and aggressive behaviour, *Journal of Adolescent Health Care* **11**(1), 31–44.

Coolican, H. (1999) *Research Methods and Statistics in Psychology* (3rd edn). London: Hodder.

Cooper, H., Okamara, L.R. and McNeil, Pl. (1995) Situation and personality correlates of psychological well-being, social activity and personal control, *Journal of Research in Personality* **29**, 397–417.

Costa, P.T. and McCrae, R.R. (1985) *The NEO Personality Inventory*. Odessa, FL: Psychological Assessment Resources.

Costa, P.T. and McCrae, R.R. (1992) *The NEO-PI-R: professional manual*. Odessa, FL: Psychological Assessment Resources.

Costa, P.T. and McCrae, R.R. (1994) Stability and change in personality from adolescence through adulthood. In C.F. Halveson, G.A. Kohnstamm, C. Roy, P. Martin (Eds.) *The Developing Structure of Temperament and Personality from Infancy to Adulthood*. Hillsdale NJ: Erlbaum.

Craik, K.H. (1986) Personality research methods: an historical perspective, *Journal of Personality* **54**, 18–21.

Cranner, P. (1991) *The Development of Defense Mechanisms: Theory, research and assessment*. New York: Springer-Verlag.

Crockett, W.H. (1982) The organisation of construct systems: the organisation corrollary. In J.C. Mancuso and R. Adams-Webber (eds), *The Construing Person*. New York: Praeger.

Csikszentmihalyi, M. (1990) *Flow: the psychology of optimal experience*. New York: Harper Perennial.

Das, A.K. (1989) Beyond self-actualisation, *International Journal for the Advancement of Counselling* **12**, 13–27.

Decarvalho, R.J. (1992) The humanistic ethics of Rollo May. *Journal of Humanistice Psychology* **32**, 7–18.

DeMann, A., Ledue, C. and Labreche-Gauthier, L. (1992) Parental control in childrearing and multidimensional locus of control, *Psychological Reports* **70**, 320–2.

DeMoya, C.A. (1997) Scores on locus of control and aggression for drug addicts, users and controls, *Psychological Reports* **80**, 40–42.

Derakshan, N. and Eysenck, M.W. (1997) Interpretative biases for one's own behaviour in high anxious individuals and repressors, *Journal of Personality and Social Psychology*.

Digman, J.M. (1990) Personality structure: emergence of the five factor model. In M.R. Rozenweig and L.W. Porter (eds), *Annual Review of Psychology*, Volume 41, 417–40. Palo Alto, CA: Annual Reviews Inc.

Dion, K.L. and Dion, K.K. (1973) Correlates of romantic love, *Journal of Consulting and Clinical Psychology* 41, 51–6.

Diveck, C.S. (1975) The role of expectations and attributions in the alleviation of learned helplessness, *Journal of Personality and Social Psychology* 31, 674–85.

Diveck, C.S. (1991) Self-theories and goals: their role in motivation, personality and development. In R.A. Deinstbier (ed.), *Nebraska Symposium on Motivation*, Volume 38. Lincoln: University of Nebraska Press.

Diveck, C.S. (1996) Capturing the dynamic nature of personality, *Journal of Research in Personality* 30, 348–62.

Diveck, C.S. and Leggett, E.L. (1988) A social-cognitive approach to personality and motivation, *Psychological Review* 95, 256–73.

Domino, G. and Alfonso, D.D. (1990) The personality measure of Erikson's life stages: the Inventory of Social Balance, *Journal of Personality Assessment* 54, 576–88.

Duck, S.W. and Allison, D. (1978) I liked you but I can't live with you: a study of lapsed friendships, *Social Behaviour and Personality* 8, 43–7.

Dulaney, D.E. (1962) The place of hypothesis and intentions: an analysis of verbal control in verbal conditioning. In C.W. Eriksen (ed.), *Behaviour and Awareness*. Durham, NC: Duke University Press.

Edel, L. (1985) *Henry James: a life*. New York: Harper & Row.

Ellenberger, H.F. (1970) *The Discovery of the Unconscious*. London: Allen Lane; New York: Basic Books.

Elms, A.C. (1988) Freud as Leonardo: why the first psychobiography went wrong, *Journal of Personality* 56, 19–40.

Elms, A.C. (1994) *Uncovering Lives: the uneasy alliance of psychobiography and psychology*. New York: Oxford University Press.

Endler, N.S. (1989) The temperamental nature of personality, *European Journal of Personality* 3, 151–65.

Erikson, E.H. (1950) *Childhood and Society* (2nd edn). New York: Norton.

Erikson, E.H. (1958) *Young Man Luther: a study in psychoanalysis and history*. New York: Norton.

Erikson, E.H. (1963) *Childhood and Society* (2nd edn). New York. Norton.

Erikson, E.H. (1964) *Insight and Responsibility*. New York: Norton.

Erikson, E.H. (1968) *Identity, Youth and Crisis*. New York: Norton.

Erikson, E.H. (1969) *Gandhi's Truth: On the Origins of Military Non-violence*. New York: Norton.

Erikson, E.H. (1974) *Dimensions of a New Identity*, Jefferson Lectures, 1973. New York: Norton.

Erikson, E.H. (1975) *Life History and the Historical Moment*. New York: Norton.

Erikson, E.H. (1980) *Identity and the Life Cycle*. New York: Norton.

Ernst, C. and Angst, J. (1983) *Birth Order: its influence on personality*. New York: Springer.

Exner, J.E. (1986) *The Rorschach: a comprehensive system*, Volume 1. New York: Riley.

Eysenck, E.J. (1973) *Eysenck on Extroversion*. New York: John Wiley & Sons.

Eysenck, H.J. (1947) *Dimensions of Personality*. London: Routledge & Kegan Paul.

Eysenck, H.J. (1952) The effects of psychotherapy: an evaluation, *Journal of Consulting Psychology* **16**, 319–24.

Eysenck, H.J. (1967) *The Biological Basis of Personality*. Springfield, IL: Charles C. Thomas.

Eysenck, H.J. (1985a) Incubation theory of fear/anxiety. In S. Reiss and R.R. Bostsui (Eds.) *Theoretical Issues in Behaviour Therapy*. Orlando, FL: Academic Press.

Eysenck, H.J. (1985b) *The Decline and Fall of the Freudian Empire*. Harmondsworth: Penguin.

Eysenck, H.J. and Eysenck, M.W. (1985) *Personality and Individual Differences: a natural science approach*. New York: Plenium Press.

Eysenck, H.J and Rachman, S (1965) *The Causes and Cures of Neurosis*. London: Routledge & Kegan Paul.

Farber, I.E. (1963) The things people say to themselves, *American Psychologist* **18**, 185–97.

Fargas, J.P. and Bond, M.H. (1985) Cultural influences on the perception of interaction episodes, *Personality and Social Psychology Bulletin* **11**, 75–88.

Feist, J. and Feist, G.J. (1998) *Theories of Personality*. (4th edn), Chapter 5. McGraw-Hill.

Fiske, S.T. and Taylor, S.E. (1984) *Social Cognition*. Reading, MA: Addison-Wesley.

Fordham, F. (1973) *An Introduction to Jung's Psychology*. Harmandsworth: Penguin Books.

Frankl, V.E. (1955) *The Doctor and the Soul*. New York: Knopf.

Frankl, V.E. (1958) On logotherapy and existential analysis, *American Journal of Psychoanalysis* **18**, 28–37.

Fransella, F. and Thomas, L. (Eds.) (1988) *Experimenting with Personal Constructs Psychology*. New York: Routledge & Kegan Paul.

Freud, A. (1936) *The Ego and the Mechanisms of Defence*. London: Hogarth Press.

Freud, A. (1945) Indications for child analysis. In Volume 4 of *The Writings of Anna Freud*. New York: International Universities Press (1968).

Freud, A. (1962) Assessment of pathology in childhood. In Volume 5 of *The Writings of Anna Freud*. New York: International Universities Press (1969).

Freud, A. (1965) Normality and pathology in childhood. In Volume 6 *of The Writings of Anna Freud*. New York: International Universities Press (1965).

Freud, A. (ed.) (1986) *The Essentials of Psychoanalysis: the definitive collection of Sigmund Freud's writing.*

Freud, S. (1900/1976) *The Interpretation of Dreams*. Pelican Freud Library, Volume 5. Harmondsworth: Penguin.

Freud, S. (1901/1976) *The Psychopathology of Everyday Life*. Pelican Freud Library, Volume 5. Harmondsworth: Penguin.

Freud, S. (1905/1977) *Three Essays on the Theory of Sexuality*. Pelican Freud Library, Volume 7. Harmondsworth: Penguin.

Freud, S. (1916) Leonardo da Vinci: a study in psychosexuality. In the Standard Edition of *The Complete Psychological Works of Sigmund Freud*, Volume XX. London: Hogarth Press.

Freud, S (1920/1984) *Beyond the Pleasure Principle*. Pelican Freud Library, Volume 11. Harmondsworth: Penguin.

Freud, S. (1923/1984) *The Ego and the Id*. Pelican Freud Library, Volume 11. Harmondsworth: Penguin.

Freud, S. (1926) Inhibitions, symptoms and anxiety. In the Standard Edition of *The Complete Psychological Works of Sigmund Freud*, Volume XX. London: Hogarth Press.

Freud, S. (1927/1985) *The Future of an Illusion*. Pelican Freud Library, Volume 12. Harmondsworth: Penguin.

Freud, S. (1930/1985) *Civilization and its Discontents*. Pelican Freud Library, Volume 12. Harmondsworth: Penguin.

Freud, S. (1933) *New Introductory Lectures on Psychoanalysis*. New York: Norton.

Freud, S. and Breuer, J. (1895) *Studies in Hysteria*. Pelican Freud Library, Volume 3. Harmondsworth: Penguin.

Funder, D. and Sneed, C. (1993) Behavioural manifestations of personality: an ecological approach to judgemental accuracy, *Journal of Personality and Social Psychology* **64**, 479–90.

Furnham, A. (1988*) Lay Theories of Behaviour: everyday understanding of problems in the social sciences*. New York: Pergamon Press.

Furnham, A. and Bradley, A. (1997) Music while you work: the differential distraction of background music on the cognitive test performance of introverts and extraverts, *Applied Cognitive Psychology* **11**, 445–55.

Galton, F. (1869) *Hereditary Genius*. London: Macmillan.

Galton, F. (1884) Measurement of character, *Fortnightly Review* **42**, 179–85.

Garcia, J. and Koelling, R.A. (1966) Relation of one to consequence in avoidance learning, *Psycholonomic Science* **4**, 123–24.

Gay, P. (1988) *Freud: a life for our time*. London: Dent & Sons.

Geller, L. (1982) The failure of self-actualisation theory, *Journal of Humanistic Psychology* **22**, 56–73.

Goldberg, L.R. (1981) Language and individual differences: the search for universals of personality in lexicons. In L. Wheeler (ed.), *Review of Personality and Social Psychology*, Volume 2. Beverley Hills, CA: Sage.

Goldwert, M. (1992) *The Wounded Healers: creative illness in the pioneers of depth psychology.* Lantham, MD: University Press of America.

Gottesman, I.J. (1963) *Heritability of Personality.* Psychological Monographs 77, 1–21.

Grosskurth, P. (1986) *Melanie Klein: her world and her work.* New York: Knopf.

Hall, C.S. and Lindzey, G. (1978) *Theories of Personality* (3rd edn). New York: Wiley.

Hall, C.S. and van de Castle, R.L. (1963) An empirical investigation of the castration complex in dreams, *Journal of Personality* 33, 20–9.

Hall, R.V., Lund, D. and Jackson, D. (1968) Effects of teacher attention on study behaviour, *Journal of Applied Behaviour Analysis* 1, 1–12.

Hammond, W.A. and Romney, D.M. (1995) Cognitive factors contributing to adolescent depression, *Journal of Youth and Adolescence* 24, 667–83.

Hartmann, H. (1964) *Papers on Psychoanalytic Psychology: psychological issues.* (Monograph No.14). New York: International Universities Press.

Hazan, C. and Shaver, P. (1987) Romantic love conceptualised as an attachment process, *Journal of Personality and Social Psychology* 52, 511–24.

Hempel, C.G. (1966) *Philosophy of Natural Sciences.* Englewood Cliffs, NJ: Prentice Hall.

Henderson, V. and Diveck, C.S. (1990) Adolescence and achievement. In S. Feldman and G. Elliot (Eds.), *At the Threshold: adolescent development.* Cambridge, MA: Harvard University Press.

Higgins, E.T. (1987) Self-discrepancy: a theory relating self and effect, *Psychological Review* 94, 319–40.

Higgins, E.T. (1997) Beyond pleasure and pain, *American Psychologist* 52, 1280–1300.

Hoffman, E. (1994) *The Drive for Self: Alfred Adler and the founding of individual psychology.* Reading, MA: Addison-Wesley.

Hofstede, G. (1980) *Culture's Consequences: international differences in work-related values.* Beverly Hills, CA: Sage.

Hogan, R. and Hogan, J. (1995) *Human Personality Inventory Manual.* (2nd edn). Tulsa, OK: Hogan Assessment Systems.

Ihelivich, D. and Gleser, G. C. (1971) Relationships of defense mechanisms to field dependence–independence. *Journal of Abnormal Psychology* 77, 296–302.

John, O.P. (1990) The 'big five' factor taxonomy: dimensions of personality in the natural language and questionnaires. In L.A. Pervin (ed.) *Handbook of Personality: theory and research.* New York: Guildford.

Jones, A. and Crandall, R. (1986) Validation of a short index of self-actualisation, *Personality and Social Psychology Bulletin* 12, 63–73.

Jones, E. (1953) *Sigmund Freud: life and works*, Volume 1: The Young Freud, 1865–1900. London: Tavistock.

Jones, E. (1955) *Sigmund Freud: life and works*, Volume 2: Years of Maturity, 1901–1919. London: Tavistock.

Jones, E. (1957) *Sigmund Freud: life and works*, Volume 3: The Last Phase, 1919–1939, London: Tavistock.

Jung, C.G. (1960) *Synchronicity: an acausal connecting principle*. In *Complete Works of Carl Jung*, Volume 8. Princeton: Princeton University Press.

Jung, C.G. (1961) *Memories, Dreams and Reflections*. New York: Random House.

Jung, C.G. (1964) *Man and His Symbols*. Garden City, NY: Doubleday.

Jung, C.G. (1936) The archetypes and the collective unconscious. In H. Read, M. Fordham and G. Adler (eds) *Collected Works*, Volume 9. Princeton: Princeton University Press.

Jung, C.G. (1954) Psychological aspects of the mother complex. In H. Read, M. Fordham and G. Adler (eds) *Collected Works*, Volume 9. Princeton: Princeton University Press.

Kahn, S., Zimmerman, G., Csikszentmihalyi, M. and Getzels, J.W. (1985) Relations between identity in young adulthood and intimacy at midlife, *Journal of Personality and Social Psychology* **49**, 1316–22.

Kalechstein, A.D. and Nowicki, S. (1977) A meta-analytic examination of the relationship between control expectancies and academic achievement: a 11-year follow-up to Findley and Cooper, *Genetic, General and Social Psychology Monographs* **123**, 29–56.

Kapalka, G.M. and Lachenmerger, J.R. (1988) Sex-role flexibility, locus of control and occupational status, *Sex Roles* **19**, 417–27.

Kelly, G.A. (1955) *The Psychology of Personal Constructs*. New York: Norton.

Kelly, G.A. (1969) *Clinical Psychology and Personality: The selected papers of George Kelly*. New York: Wiley.

Kelly, G.A. (1970) A brief introduction to personal construct theory. In D. Bannister (ed.). *Perspectives in Personal Construct Theory*. London: Academic Press.

Kemp, S. (1988) Personality in Ancient Astrology. *New Ideas in Psychology* **6**, 267–72.

Kernberg, O.F. (1975) *Borderline Conditions and Pathological Narcissism*. New York: Aronson.

Kernberg, O.F. (1976) *Object Relations Theory and Clinical Psychoanalysis*. New York: Aronson.

Kernberg, O.F. (1992) *Aggression in Personality Disorders and Perversions*. New Haven: Yale University Press.

Kernberg, O.F. (1995) *Love Relations: Normality and Pathology*, New Haven, CT: Yale University Press.

Kernberg, O.F., Selzer, M.A., Koenigsberg, H.W., Carr, A.C. and Applebaum, A.H. (1989) *Psychodynamic Psychotherapy of Borderline Patients*. New York: Basic Books.

Klein, M. (1932) *The Psychoanalysis of Children*. London: Hogarth Press.

Klein, M. (1935) *A Contribution to the Psychogenesis of Manic-depressive States*. London: Hogarth Press.

Klein, M. (1946) Notes on some schizoid mechanisms. In M. Klein (1975) *Envy and Gratitude, and Other Works*. New York: Delta Books.

Klein, M. (1952) *Envy and Gratitude*. London: Tavistock.

Klein, M. (1955) The psychoanalytic play technique: its history and significance. In J. Mitchell (ed.) *The Selected Melanie Klein*. New York: Free Press (1986).

Klein, M. (1964) *Contributions to Psychoanalysis, 1921–1945*. New York: McGraw-Hill.

Klein, S.B., Loftus, J. and Burton, H.A. (1989) Two self-reference effects: the importance of distinguishing between self-descriptiveness judgements and autobiographical retrieval in self-referent encoding, *Journal of Personality and Social Psychology* 56, 853–65.

Kline, P. (1972) *Fact and Fantasy in Freudian Theory*. London: Methuen.

Klopfer, B. and Davidson, H.H. (1962) *The Rorschach Technique: an introductory manual*. New York: Harcourt, Brace & World.

Kohut, H. (1971) *The Analysis of the Self*. New York: International Universities Press.

Kohut, H. (1977) *The Restoration of the Self*. New York: International Universities Press.

Kuhn, T. (1970) *The Structure of Scientific Revolutions* (2nd edn). Chicago: University of Chicago Press.

Lefcourt, H. (1976) *Hours of Control: current feuds in theory and research*. Hillsdale, NJ: Erlbaum.

Lewin, K. (1938) *The Conceptual Representation and Measurement of Psychological Forces*. Durham, NC: Duke University Press.

Lewin, K. (1951) *Field Theory in Social Science: selected theoretical papers* (ed. D. Cartwright). New York: Harper & Row.

Linville, P.W. (1987) Self-complexity as a cognitive buffer against stress-related illness and depression, *Journal of Personality and Social Psychology* 52, 663–76.

Loehlin, J.C. and Nichols, R.C. (1976) *Heredity, Environment and Personality*. Austin: University of Texas Press.

McAdams, D.P. (1988) Biography, narrative and lives: an introduction, *Journal of Personality* 56, 1–18.

McAdams, D.P. (1992) Unity and purpose in human lives: the emergence of identity as a life story. In R.A. Zucker, A.I. Rubin and S.J. Franks (eds) *Personality Structure in the Life Course: essays on personology in the Murray tradition*. New York: Springer.

McAdams, D.P. (1994) A psychology of the stranger, *Psychological Inquiry* **5**, 145–8.

McAdams, D.P. (1997) Three voices of Erik Erikson, *Contemporary Psychology* **42**, 575–8.

McAdams, D.P. (1999) Personal narratives and the life story. In L. Perrin and O. John (eds) *Handbook of Personality Theory and Research* (2nd edn). New York: Guildford Press.

McAdams, D.P. (2001) *The Person: an integrated introduction to personality* (3rd edn). Fort Worth, TX: Harcourt College Publishers.

McClelland, D.C. (1961) *The Achieving Society*, New York: Free Press.

McClelland, D.C., Atkinson, J.W., Clark, R.A. and Lowell, E.L. (1953) *The Achievement Motive*. New York: Appleton-Century Crofts.

McCrae, R.R. and Costa, P.T. (1989) The structure of interpersonal traits: Wiggins' circumflex and the five factor model, *Journal of Personality and Social Psychology* **56**, 586–95.

McCrae, R.R. and Costa, P.T. (1990) *Personality in Adulthood*. New York: Guildford Press.

McCrae, R.R. and Costa, P.T. (1997) Personality trait structure as a human universal, *American Psychologist* **52**, 509–16.

Manaster, C.J. and Perryman, T.B. (1979) Manaster-Perryman manifest content early recollection scoring manual. In H. Olson (ed.) *Early Recollections: their use in diagnosis and psychotherapy*. Springfield, IL: Charles C. Thomas.

Marcia, J.E. (1966) Development and validation of ego-identity status, *Journal of Personality and Social Psychology* **49**, 156–69.

Marcia, J.E. (1980) Identity in adolescence. In J. Adelson (ed.) *Handbook of Adolescent Psychology*. New York: Wiley.

Marcia, J.E. (1994) The empirical study of ego identify. In H.A. Bosma, T.L.G. Graafsma and D.J. de Levita (eds) *Identify and Development: an interdisciplinary approach*. Thousands Oaks, CA: Sage.

Marin, P. (1975) The new narcissism. *Harper's Magazine* (Oct.), 45–6.

Markstrom-Adams, C. (1992) A consideration of intervening factors in adolescent identity formation. In G.R. Adams, T.P. Gullotta and R. Montemayor (eds) *Adolescent Identity Formation: advances in adolescent development*. Newbury Park, CA: Sage.

Markus, H. (1977) Self-schemata and processing information about the self, *Journal of Personality and Social Psychology* **35**, 63–78.

Markus, H.R. and Kitayama, S. (1991) Culture and the self: implications for cognition, emotion and motivation, *Psychological Review* **98**, 224–53.

Markus, H.R. and Kitayama, S. (1994) A collective fear of the collective: implications for selves and theories of selves, *Personality and Social Psychology Bulletin* **20**, 568–79.

Markus, H.H. and Nurius, P. (1986) Possible selves, *American Psychologist* **41**, 954–69.

Markus, H. and Smith, J. (1981) The influence of self-schema on the perception of others. In N. Cantor and J.F. Kihlstrom (eds) *Personality, Cognition and Social Interaction.* Hillsdale, NJ: Lawrence Erlbaum.

Maslow, A. (1970) *Motivation and personality* (2nd edn). New York: Harper & Row.

Maslow, A.H. (1971) *The Further Reaches of Human Nature.* New York: Viking.

May, R. (1953) *Man's Search for Himself.* New York: Norton.

May, R. (1969) *Love and Will.* New York: Norton.

Mirels, H. (1970) Dimensions of internal and external control, *Journal of Consultancy and Clinical Psychology* **34**, 226–28.

Mischel, W. (1968) *Personality and Assessment.* New York: Wiley.

Mischel, W. (1979). On the interface of cognition and personality: beyond the person–situation debate, *American Psychologist* **34**, 740–54.

Mischel, W. (1991) *Finding Personality Coherence in the Pattern of Variability.* Eastern Psychological Association Distinguished Lecture. New York.

Mischel, W. (1999) *Introduction to Personality* (6th edn). Fort Worth, TX: Harcourt Brace.

Mischel, W. and Shoda, Y. (1998) Reconciling process dynamics and personality dispositions, *Annual Review of Psychology* **49**, 229–58.

Mitchell, J. (1974) *Psychoanalysis and Feminism.* Harmondsworth: Penguin Books.

Mollon, P. (2000) *Freud and False Memory Syndrome*, Cambridge: Icon Books.

Monte, C.F. (1999) *Beneath the Mask: an introduction to theories of personality* (6th edn). London: Harcourt Brace College Publishers.

Mooney, S.P., Sheman, M.F. and LoPresto, C.T. (1991) Academic locus of control, self-esteem and perceived distance from home as prediction of college adjustment, *Journal of Consulting and Development* **69**, 445–48.

Murray, E.J. and Jacobson, L.I. (1978) Cognition and learning in traditional and behavioural psychotherapy. In S. Garfield and A.E. Bergin (eds) *Handbook of Psychotherapy and Behaviour Change* (2nd edn). New York: Wiley.

Murray, H.A. (1938) *Explorations in Personality.* New York: Oxford University Press.

Murray, H.A. (1943) *The Thematic Apperception Test Manual.* Cambridge, MA: Harvard University Press.

Murray, H.A. (1951) Toward a classification of interaction. In T. Parsons and E.A. Shils (eds) *Towards a General Theory of Action.* Cambridge: Harvard University Press.

Murray, H.A. (1962) *Explorations in Personality.* New York: Science Editions.

Murray, H.A. (1968) A conversation with Mary Harrington Hall, *Psychology Today* **2**, 56–63.

Myers, D.G. (1992) *The Pursuit of Happiness. Who is Happy – and Why.* New York: Morrow.

Myers, I.B. (1972) *The Myers-Briggs Type Indicator*. Palo Alto, CA: Consulting Psychologists Press.

Myers, L.B. (2000) Deceiving others or deceiving themselves?, *The Psychologist* **13**(8), 400–3.

Nashby, W. (1985) Private self-consciousness, articulation of the self-schema, and the recognition memory of trait adjectives, *Journal of Personality and Social Psychology* **49**, 704–9.

Neimeger, G.J. and Hall, A.G. (1988) Personal identity in disturbed marital relationships. In F. Fransella and L. Thomas (eds). *Experimenting with Personal Construct Psychology*. London: Routledge & Kegan Paul.

Newman, J. and Taylor, A. (1994) Family training for political leadership: birth order of United States state governors and Australian prime ministers, *Political Psychology* **15** 435–42.

Ochse, R. and Plug, C. (1986) Cross-cultural investigation of the validity of Erikson's theory of personality development, *Journal of Personality and Social Psychology* **50**, 1240–52.

Pennington, D.C. (2000) *Social Cognition*. London: Routledge.

Perls, F.S. (1969) *Gestalt Therapy Verbatim*. La Fagette, CA: Real People Press.

Pervin, L.A. (1994) A critical analysis of current trait theory, *Psychological Inquiry* **5**, 103–13.

Peterson, C. (1993) Helpless behaviour, *Behaviour Research Therapy* **31**, 289–95.

Phares, E.J. (1978) Locus of control. In H. London and J.E. Exner (eds). *Dimensions of Personality*. New York: John Wiley & Sons.

Piaget, J. (1952) *The Origins of Intelligence in Children*. New York: International Universities Press.

Plomin, R., Chipauer, H.M. and Loehlin, J.C. (1990) Behavioural genetics and personality. In L.A. Pervin (ed.), *Handbook of Personality: theory and research*. New York: Guildford.

Plomin, R. (1994) *Genetics and Experience: the interplay between nature and nurture*. Newbury Park, CA: Sage.

Plomin, R. and Daniels, D. (1987) Why are children in the same family so different from one another?, *Behaviour and Brain Sciences* **10**, 1–60.

Plomin, R., Chipner, H.M. and Loehlin, J.C. (1990) Behaviour genetics and personality. In L.A. Pervin (ed.) *Handbook of Personality: theory and research*. New York: Guildford Press.

Popper, K. (1963) *Conjectures and Refutations: the growth of scientific knowledge*. New York: Harper & Row.

Raskin, R.N. and Hall, C.J. (1979) A narcissistic personality inventory. *Psychological Reports* **45**, 590.

Raskin, R.N. and Hall, C.J. (1981) The narcissistic personality Inventory: alternate form reliability and further evidence of construct validity, *Journal of Personality Assessment* **45**, 145–62.

Raskin, R.N. and Shaw, R. (1988) Narcissism and the use of personal pronouns, *Journal of Personality* **56**, 393–404.

Reid, D.W. and Zeigler, M. (1981) The desired control measure and adjustment among the elderly. In H.F. Lefcourt (ed.) *Research with the Locus of Control Construct,* Volume 1: Assessment Methods. New York: Academic Press.

Rescorla, R.A. (1988) Pavlovian conditioning: it's not what you think it is, *American Psychologist* **43**, 151–60.

Richard, R.L. and Jex, S.M. (1991) Further evidence for the validity of the Short Index of Self-actualisation, *Journal of Social Behaviour and Personality* **6**, 331–8.

Roazen, P. (1971) *Freud and his Followers.* New York: Meridian Books.

Roazen, P. (1976) *Erik H. Erikson: the power and the limits of vision.* New York: Free Press.

Robinson, F.G. (1992) *Love's Story Told: a life of Henry A. Murray.* Cambridge, MA: Harvard University Press.

Rogers, C.R. (1969) *Freedom to Learn.* Columbus, OH: Charles E. Merrill.

Rogers, C.R. (1951) *Client-Centred Therapy: its current practice, implications and theory.* Boston: Houghton-Mifflin.

Rogers, C.R. (1959) A theory of therapy, personality and interpersonal relationships, as developed in the client-centred frameworks. In S. Koch. (ed.) *Psychology: A study of science,* Volume 3. New York: McGraw-Hill.

Rogers, C.R. (1961) *On Becoming a Person.* Boston: Houghton-Mifflin.

Rogers, C.R. (1970) *Carl Rogers on Encounter Groups.* New York: Harper & Row.

Rogers, C.R. (1982) A psychologist looks at nuclear war: its threat, its possible prevention, *Journal of Humanistic Psychology* **22**, 9–20.

Rogers, C.R. and Skinner, B.F. (1956) Some issues concerning the control of human behaviour, *Science* **124**, 1057–66.

Rogers, T.B., Kuiper, N.A. and Kirker, W.S. (1977) Self-reference and the encoding of personal information, *Journal of Personality and Social Psychology* **35**, 677–88.

Rorschach, H. (1921) Psychodiagnostik. Bern and Leipzig: Ernst Bercher Verlag.

Rose, R.J., Koskenvuo, M., Kaprio, J., Sarna, S. and Lauginvainio, H. (1988) Shared genes, shared experiences, and similarity of personality, *Journal of Personality and Social Psychology* **54**, 161–71.

Ross, L.D. (1977) The intuitive psychologist and his shortcomings: distortions in the attribution process. In L. Berkowitz (ed.) *Advances in Social Psychology,* Volume 10. New York: Academic Press.

Rotter, J.B. (1954) *Social Learning and Clinical Psychology.* Englewood Cliffs, NJ: Prentice Hall.

Rotter, J.B. (1966) Generalised expectancies for internal versus external control of reinforcement, *Psychological Monographs* 80, 1–28.

Rotter, J.B. (1980) Interpersonal trust, trustworthiness and gullibility, *American Psychologist* 35, 1–7.

Rotter, J.B. (1982) *The Development and Applications of Social Learning Theory: selected papers.* New York: Praege.

Rotter, J.B. and Hochreich, D.J. (1975) *Personality.* Glenview, IL: Scott Foresman.

Rotter, J.B., Chame, J.E. and Phares, E.J. (1972) *Applications of a Social Learning Theory of Personality.* New York: Holt, Rhinehart & Winston.

Rowan, D.G., Compton, W.C. and Rust, J.O. (1995) Self-actualisation and empathy as predictors of marital satisfaction, *Psychological Reports* 77, 1011–16.

Rowe, D.C. (1987) Resolving the person-situation debate: invitation to an interdisciplinary dialogue, *American Psychologist* 42, 218–27.

Royce, J.R. and Powell, A. (1983) *Theory of Personality and Individual Differences: factors, systems and processes.* Englewood Cliffs, NJ: Prentice Hall.

Runco, M.A., Ebersole, P. and Mraz, W. (1991) Creativity and self-actualisation, *Journal of Social Behaviour and Personality* 6, 161–7.

Runyan, W.M. (1981) Why did Van Gogh cut off his ear? The problem of alternative explanations in psychobiography, *Journal of Personality and Social Psychology* 40, 1070–7.

Runyan, W.M. (1982) *Life Histories and Psychobiography: explorations in theory and method.* New York: Oxford University Press.

Runyan, W.M. (1990) Individual lives and the structure of personality psychology. In A.I. Rabin, R.A. Zucker and R.A. Emmons (eds) *Studying Personality and Lives.* New York: Springer.

Rushton, J.P. (1990) Sir Francis Galton, epigenetic rules, genetic similarity theory, and human life history analysis, *Journal of Personality* 58, 117–40.

Rushton, J.P., Fulker, D.W., Neale, M.C., Nias, D.K.B., and Eysenck, H.J. (1986) Altruism and aggression: the heritability of individual differences, *Journal of Personality and Social Psychology* 50, 1192–8.

Russell, G. (1992) Response of the macho male to viewing a combatant sport, *Journal of Social Behaviour and Personality* 7(4), 631–8.

Rykman, R.M. (2000) *Theories of Personality* (7th edn). United Kingdom: Wadsworth Learning.

Sanford, N. (1963) Personality: its place in psychology. In S. Koch (ed.) *Psychology: a study of science*, Volume 5. New York: McGraw-Hill.

Schacht, A.J. and Howe, H.E. (1989) Psychologists' theoretical orientation and MBTI personality type, *Journal of Psychological Type* 18, 39–42.

Segal, J. (1992) *Melanie Klein.* London: Sage.

Seligman, M.E.P. (1975) *Helplessness.* San Francisco: W.H. Freeman.

Seligman, M.E.P. (1992) Wednesday's children, *Psychology Today* 25, 61.

Seligman, M.E.P., Abramson, L.Y., Semmel, A.R. and Van Baeyer, C. (1979) Depressive attributional style. *Journal of Abnormal Psychology* **88**, 242–7.

Shaver, P.R. and Clark, C.L. (1994) The psychodynamics of adult romantic attachment. In J.M. Masling and R.F. Bornstein (eds). *Empirical Perspectives on Object Relations Theory*. Washington, DC American Psychological Association.

Sheffield, M., Carey, J., Patenaude, W. and Lambert, M.J. (1995) An exploration of the relationship between interpersonal problems and psychological health, *Psychological Reports* **76**, 947–56.

Shoda, Y., Mischel, W. and Wright, J.C. (1993) The role of situational demands and cognitive competencies in behaviour organisation and personality coherence, *Journal of Personality and Social Psychology* **56**, 41–53.

Shostrum, E.L. (1963) *Personal Orientation Inventory*. San Diego, CA: EdITS/Education and Industrial Testing Service.

Shostrum, E.L. (1974) *Manual for the Personal Orientation Inventory*. San Diego, CA: Educational and Industrial Testing Service.

Skinner, B.F. (1938) *The Behaviour of Organisms*. New York: Appleton-Century-Crofts.

Skinner, B.F. (1974) *About Behaviourism*. New York: Knopf.

Skinner, B.F. (1988) The operant side of behaviour, *Journal of Behaviour Therapy and Experimental Psychiatry* **19**, 171–9.

Smith, M.L. and Glass, G.V. (1977) Meta-analysis of psychotherapeutic outcome studies, *American Psychologist* **32**, 752–60.

Smith, P.B. and Harris Bond, M. (1998) *Social Psychology Across Cultures* (2nd edn). London: Prentice Hall.

Steiner, R. (1985) Some thoughts about tradition and change arising from an examination of the British Psychoanalytic Society's controversial discussions (1943–1944), *International Review of Psycho-analysis* **12**, 27–71.

Stephenson, W. (1953) *The Study of Behaviour*. Chicago: University of Chicago Press.

Sulloway, F.J. (1996) *Born to Rebel: birth order, family dynamics and creative lives*. New York: Pantheon Books.

Thorndike, E.L. (1911) *Animal Intelligence: experimental studies*. New York: Macmillan.

Tokar, D.M. and Subrick, L.M. (1997) Relative contributions of congruence and personality dimensions to job satisfaction, *Journal of Vocational Behaviour* **50**, 482–91.

Triandis, H.C. (1997) Cross-cultural perspectives on personality. In R. Hogan, J. Johnson and S. Briggs (eds), *Handbook of Personality Psychology*. San Diego, CA: Academic Press.

Trill, J.J. and Sher, K.J. (1994) Relationship between the five factor model of personality and Axis I disorders in a non-clinical sample, *Journal of Abnormal Psychology* **103**, 350–60.

Wallston, K.A. and Wallston, B.S. (1981) Health locus of control scales. In H.M. Lefourt (ed.) *Research with the Locus of Control Construct*, Volume 1: Assessment Methods. New York: Academic Press.

Wang, P.T.P. and Sproule, C.F. (1984) An attributional analysis of the locus of control construct and the Trent Attribution Profile. In H.M. Lefcourt (ed.) *Research with the Locus of Control Construct*, Volume 3: Extensions and limitations. New York: Academic Press.

Ward, I. and Zarate, O. (2000) *Introducing Psychoanalysis*. Cambridge: Icon Books Ltd.

Ware, A.P. and John, O.P. (1995) *Punctuality Revisited: personality, situations and consistency*, 103rd Annual Meeting of American Psychological Association. New York (August).

Watkins, C.E. (1992) Birth order research and Adler's theory: a critical review, *Individual Psychology* 48, 357–68.

Watkins, C.E. (1994) Measuring social interest, *Individual Psychology* 50, 69–96.

Watson, J.B. (1925) *Behaviourism*. New York: Norton.

Watson, J.B. and Raynor, R. (1920) Conditioned emotional reactions, *Journal of Experimental Psychology* 3, 1–14.

Weinberger, D.A. (1990) *The construct validity of the repressive coping style*. In J.L. Singer (ed.) *Repression and Dissociation*. Chicago: University of Chicago Press.

Westen, D. (1990) Psychoanalytic approaches to personality. In L.A. Pervin (ed.) *Handbook of Personality Theory and Research*. New York: Guildford Press.

Whitbourne, S.K., Zuslag, M.K., Elliott, L.B. and Waterman, A.S. (1992) Psychosocial development in adulthood: a 22-year-old sequential study. *Journal of Personality and Social Psychology* 63, 260-71.

White, R.W. (1948) *The Abnormal Personality*. New York: Ronald Press.

White, R.W. (1987) *Seeking the Shape of Personality: a memoir*. Marlborough, NH: Homestead Press.

Whyte, L.L. (1978) *The Unconscious before Freud*. London: Julian Friedmann Publishers.

Wink, P. (1992) Three types of narcissism in women from college to midlife, *Journal of Personality* 60, 7–30.

Winnicott, D.W. (1969) The mother-infant experience of mutuality. In C. Winnicott, R. Shepherd and M. Davis (Eds.) (1984) *Psychoanalytic Explorations*. Cambridge, MA: Harvard University Press.

Winnicott, D.W. (1986) *Home is Where we Start From. Essays by a psychoanalyst*. New York: Norton.

Wright, J.C. and Mischel, W. (1987) A conditional approach to dispositional constructs: the local predictability of social behaviour, *Journal of Personality and Social Psychology* 53, 1159–77.

Wright, J.C. and Mischel, W. (1988) Conditions of hedges and the intuitive psychology of traits, *Journal of Personality and Social Psychology* 55, 454–69.

Young-Bruehl, E. (1988) *Anna Freud: a biography*. New York: Summit Books.

Zajonc, R.B. and Mullaby, (1997) Birth order: reconciling conflicting effects, *Psychological Review* 82, 74–88.

Zimbardo, P.G., Haney, C., Banks, W.C. and Jaffe, D. (1982) The psychology of imprisonment. In J.C. Brigham and L. Wrightsmann (eds), *Contemporary Issues in Social Psychology* (4th edn). Monterey, CA: Brooks/Cole.

Index